The Story Of The Great Upheaval

by Joseph A. Maillet

The Acadian and francophone community of Nova Scotia

Acadian symbols

The Acadian flag

The Acadian flag was chosen in Miscouche, PEI in 1884 at the second national Acadian Convention. The flag was designed and suggested by Father Marcel François Richard, and was sewn by Marie Babineau. The first flag is now preserved in the Acadian museum at Université de Moncton.

To honour the French heritage of Acadians, the Acadian flag is based on the blue, white and red flag of France. The blue band represents the harmony between sea and sky, the white represents purity of the spirit and peace in the present, while the red symbolizes the pain and suffering of the past.

The yellow star, symbol of the Virgin Mary, was added to the upper left corner of the blue band to represent the Catholic faith. This star of the sea, Stella Maris, provides Mary's light and protection to guide mariners through storms and around shoals, toward the future.

Evangeline

The story of Evangeline, written by Henry Wadsworth Longfellow in 1847 as a poem of 1,400 lines, tells about the tragic events of the Acadian Deportation through the fictional narrative of two lovers.

Evangeline Bellefontaine and her fiancé, Gabriel Lajeunesse, are suddenly separated in 1755 when the British decide to expel the Acadians from Nova Scotia. The story takes place in the village of Grand-Pré. Evangeline promises Gabriel that their love will protect them from harm. Despite the pain and suffering, she never loses hope of finding her lover again one day. After years of wandering, she finally traces Gabriel to a hospital in Philadelphia. She comes to his side and Gabriel dies in her arms. A short time later, she dies as well, of a broken heart.

A wonderful bronze statue of Evangeline, designed by Louis-Philippe and Henri Hébert, was unveiled in 1920 at what is now the national historic site of Grand Pré. This statue symbolises the loyalty and courage of the Acadian people.

The Deportation Cross

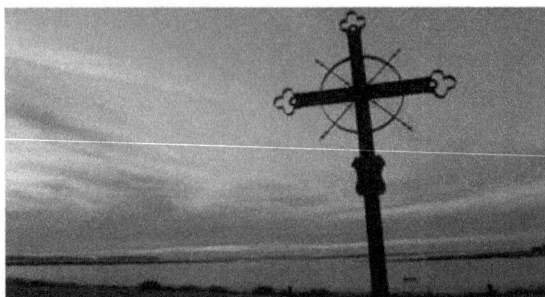

In 1924, the Deportation Cross was erected near the railway about one mile from the memorial church at the national historic site of Grand-Pré. It was erected in memory of the Acadians deported in 1755. In 2005, the cross was moved to Horton Landing, where hundreds of Acadians waited in the fall of 1755 to be transported to the ships anchored in Minas Basin. They were deported to the British American colonies on the Atlantic coast. Acadians living in the other communities along the Bay of Fundy were deported in the same way. During the fall of 1755, more than 6,000 Acadians were deported from Nova Scotia.

Acadian Monument

On 2 December 2003, the Government of Canada adopted the content of the Royal Proclamation by Queen Elizabeth II, recognizing the historic facts of the Deportation of the Acadian people and the suffering they endured. At the same time, the Government of Canada officially declared 28 July of each year as the Day of Commemoration of the Great Upheaval, the name commonly used to describe the period of the Deportation, which began in 1755 and continued until 1763.

On 28 July 2005, to mark the 250th anniversary of the Deportation, a replica of the Deportation Cross was unveiled at the Halifax water front. This commemorative monument faces Georges Island in the port of Halifax, where hundreds of Acadians were imprisoned during the Great Upheaval from 1755 to 1763.

The Story Of The Great Upheaval

Acadian Tragedy

Joseph A. Maillet

Hammonton, New Jersey

The Story Of The Great Upheaval

Acadian Tragedy

By Joseph A. Maillet

Printed in the United States of America

9 780738 830926   0 1 4 9 5

To order additional copies of this book, contact:
Joseph A. Maillet
362 S. Third St.
Hammonton, New Jersey 08037
Phone 609 561 1947

Email: jamaillet@comcast.net

This book is dedicated to the memory of

Charles Maillet

who gave his life for his beloved Canada
during the expulsion period in 1756.

Still stands the forest primeval; but under
the shade of its branches
Dwells another race, with other customs and
language .
Only along the shore of the mournful and misty
Atlantic
Linger a few Acadian peasants, whose fathers
from exile
Wandered back to their native land to die in
its bosom.

Henry Wadsworth Longfellow

from Evangeline

Author's notes.

O Canada
Our home and native land!

The opening line to the Canadian National Anthem. The music was composed by Calixa Lavallée, and the original words were penned by Judge Adolphe-Basile Routhier, for the celebration of the "Congrès national des Canadiens-Francais" in 1880. In 1908 Robert Stanley Weir wrote the English version that is commonly used today. This song is loved by all Canadians.

My father was especially proud of that song. He was born and reared in Cap Lumiere, New Brunswick, Canada. It was there, at Cap Lumiere, that the descendants of the Maillet family returned following the peace treaty between France and England that ended the deportation proceedings.

At the beautiful church in nearby Richibuctou Village can still be found documents dating back to the mid 1700s detailing the lives of the early settlers, and the Maillet family. It was at this church that I was inspired to write this book, after I stopped by to inquire about my family tree.

My father, and many other Canadians, were motivated to immigrate to the United States in the early 1900s to seek employment in the prosperous mills opening up throughout the North East United States. He never forgot where he came from, and always "O Canada" was in his heart. He met, and wed my mother, Rose Gallant, in Fitchburg, Massachusetts in 1927. I was born in 1930.

During the trying times of the depression years in the 1930s, we spent what time we could in Canada. My most precious memories are of our visits to Canada.

Many years later, in my sixties, after the passing of my parents, I still longed to visit the place that meant so much to me in my youth. I had especially wanted to visit my elderly uncle, Edmund Maillet; the last remaining patriarch of the Maillet family, still living at Cap Lumiere. He had many wonderful stories to tell about the history of Cap Lumiere and the nearby MicMac natives. He took me to an Indian reservation a few miles away where I met some of the local First Nation people.

Between Uncle Edmund, the MicMacs, and the Catholic Church at Richibuctou Village, the idea of researching and documenting this story was born. My research brought me in contact with Professor Steven White of the University of Moncton, in Moncton, New Brunswick, Canada.

I would like to express my deepest appreciation to Professor White for his assistance in providing me with information dealing with "The Expulsion of the Acadians." He was also able to trace my lineage back to 1675, to my early ancestors in Paris, France.

I am also grateful to Mr. Gilbert Sewell, a member of the First Nation from Bathurst, New Brunswick, Canada, for allowing me to utilize information gleamed from his CD, "Exploring An Ancient North American Indian Civilization."

I hope and pray I have kept sacred the tenets and beliefs of these wonderful and noble people.

Finally, I would like to thank my lovely wife, Theresa, for her patience and for standing by me and enduring our many travels throughout the world seeking knowledge related to the writing of this book. It has been a long and hard struggle. Without her, this would not have been possible.

CHAPTER ONE

The Orphanage

His name was Jacques. He was born in Paris, France in 1695; and this is his true story. For the sake of spontaneity I have written this in fiction form, but the historical events actually occurred.

Life in France during the early part of the eighteenth century was anything but enjoyable. Wars were raging throughout the region, and to add to the misery, crops were failing. On top of all this, the weather in winter was so severe even the estuaries that normally stayed ice free were freezing over. When the starving people rose to revolt, they were met with the militia and hanged. Finally, disease stepped in to alleviate the population of its suffering.

By the time Jacques was nine years old, both his parents had succumbed. He went to live with his aunt, Sarah. She had her share of misfortune also. Both her husband and son had perished.

Aunt Sarah tried the best she could to care for herself and Jacques, but there simply was not enough to go around. Rather than see the lad become another statistic, she pleaded with her parish priest for assistance. The only recourse was to place him in St. Joseph's Orphanage in Paris. Arrangements were made and it was decided that Father Gould would arrive early Monday morning to transport him to the orphanage and arrange his admission.

And so, the saga begins.

Monday morning, as they awaited the arrival of Father Gould, Aunt Sarah dressed the boy as best she could. She packed his meager clothing in a cloth sack.

He was tall for his age, but hard times and the scarcity of food left him gaunt and gangly, still he managed to display a warm personality. He had his mother's blond hair, and his father's bright blue eyes.

With tears rolling down her cheek, she held him close to her and said, "As soon as things get better, I will come for you."

"Don't worry, Aunt Sarah," he replied. "I'll be all right." Somehow, he knew he would not be seeing her again for a long time.

Father Gould arrived and was admitted into their humble home. His presence made them feel as if an angel of God had arrived and the Lord's hands were outstretched to them, to comfort them. As Father Gould made the sign of the cross, Aunt Sarah and Jacques knelt to receive his blessing.

"Pax et benedictio Dei omnipotentis, Patris, et Filli, et Spiritus Santci, descendat super te, et maneat semper." Intoned the priest.

Aunt Sarah made the sign of the cross and replied, "Amen."

Upon arising, she gave Jacques a final hug and a kiss.

"Be a good boy, now." She walked him to the waiting carriage. Father Gould helped Jacques into the seat.

As they rode off, Jacques turned back, smiled, and waved to her. She gave a forced smile, waved, and with tears in her eyes, ran back into the house.

It was a bright sunny day, with naught a cloud in the sky. The weather was very warm, not a good day for a buggy ride.

Along the way, Father Gould felt he should make some small talk to get the boy's mind off his worries. The only sound, until then, had been the horse's hoofs on the hard ground.

"It sure is hot, isn't it, Jacques," said Father Gould. He ran his finger around his tight fitting collar.

"Yes, Father," he replied. He was in no mood to chat.

The boy was dressed in an old tattered shirt, way to big for him, evidently once worn by his deceased uncle. His pantaloons were also too big, being held at the waist by an old piece of rope. The only items of clothing of his that were any good were the sabots he wore of his feet. His blond, tattered hair kept getting into his eyes when the wind blew. He just sat there motionless, weeping silently.

As they passed an old ram shackled cottage, an elderly couple was tending to their sparse garden. The man removed his hat and bowed reverently at the priest. The woman said, "Good afternoon, Father." Father Gould nodded, mumbled something, and kept going.

"There goes another one," said the elderly man to his wife.

"Poor lad," she replied.

Nearing the orphanage, Jacques saw the building for the first time. It was a huge building, with a very high fence enclosing the grounds.

"Here we are, Jacques," said Father Gould, as he stopped at the main entrance.

The horse snorted, as if to indicate that he was glad they had arrived. He looked about.

Father Gould helped the boy disembark and led him to the front gate. He yanked on a lanyard dangling above the door, ringing the bell inside. In a few minutes, the door opened and a nun, completely dressed in black, peered out. She said, "Good afternoon, Father," when she recognized the priest.

"Good afternoon, Sister."

She bade them enter, closing the door behind them. She led the way to the Mother Superior's office. As they entered the long hallway, laughter could be heard coming from one of the classrooms. She knocked on the Superior's door. A soft voice from within was heard, "Please, enter."

The sister opened the door and announced Father Gould was visiting with a youngster. The Mother Superior rose to greet the visitors as they entered.

She was a little on the tall side, with the most pleasant smile. Her face seemed to be that of a young woman, although she was up in age.

After the pleasantries, Father Gould told the Mother Superior that the poor lad had no place to go, his parents passed on and his aunt could not afford to care for him.

"His name is Jacques. I'm afraid you will have to take another one," said Father Gould.

"We will manage, Father."

Father Gould blessed the boy and admonished him to be a good boy. He then took his leave.

As he stood there, alone, Jacques had some apprehensions about being here.

"Well now," said the Mother Superior, "so, your name is Jacques?"

"Yes, Mother," he replied, still standing and holding his sack of clothing.

"That is a wonderful name."

"Is that all you have, Jacques?" asked the Mother Superior, pointing to the sack slung over his shoulders.

"Yes, Mother."

"Well, bring it along, and I will show you where you can stay."

She led the way down the hall and opened a door to one of the dormitories. There were twenty-four small beds in the room, twelve on either side. Each had a small wooden box at the foot of the bed.

"This one will be yours, Jacques," said the Mother Superior, pointing to one of the beds in the middle of the room. "You may put your things in the trunk." She opened the lid and helped Jacques neatly put his meager clothing away. She then led him down the hall to another room. She knocked on the door which was opened by another nun. The Mother Superior entered and invited Jacques to follow her.

"Good morning, class," said the Mother Superior. All the children replied, "Good morning, Mother Superior." The classroom was filled with young boys, all neatly dressed, and aged between eleven and sixteen years of age.

"Class, this is Jacques. He will be staying with us. Please make him feel welcome." She turned to the sister teaching the class.

"Sister Theresa, can you assign Jacques a seat in your classroom?"

Sister Theresa replied she would take good care of Jacques, and placed him in one of the empty seats in the back of the classroom.

And so began Jacques stay at the orphanage where he would learn his basic lessons in reading, writing, math, and so on. Back in the dormitory he met with the other boys assigned to that room. The boy next to him in the dorm was a tall boy who seemed to be sort of the leader of the group. He was the oldest boy in the room at sixteen years of age.

Jacques stood by his assigned cot, not knowing what to do next. He looked all around trying to access the situation. All eyes were on him. The boy next to him said, "What's your name?"

"Jacques."

"Name's André," replied his new friend, as he extended his hand.

The boys gathered around the newcomer for a better look.

"What kind of place is this?" asked Jacques.

"This is Saint Joseph's...you'll like it here."

"How long have you been here, André?"

"Four years!"

Jacques looked over his newly made friend. He was anxious to learn as much as he could about the place. He had a thousand questions. André introduced all the other boys to the newcomer.

André assured him he would like it here. He would be given clean clothes and plenty to eat every day.

Jacques looked around his new home trying to assimilate the outcome of his future. There were twenty-four wooden beds, with small mattresses. Each had a neat pillow and blankets. There were other rooms upstairs also. A large outhouse was located behind the main building for all to use. The nuns lived across the street in a large stately building.

Jacques was surprised to find that there was ample food for all the boys. Each new boy had to have his hair sheared down to the scalp upon entering the orphanage. That was a bit unnerving to him. It also marked him as the new kid.

Of course, the first night for Jacques was the hardest. As he lay there, his thoughts were of his beloved parents that sacrificed so much for him that he might survive while they lingered in misery and sickness. If only he could join them. He vowed to himself that someday, he would find peace someplace on earth.

That was Jacques's world for the next few years.

Father Gould was a regular visitor. Every Friday was confession day, so the boys went to the sanctuary to pray and have Father Gould hear their confessions. This was Jacques's favorite place. He loved the solitude. He also enjoyed the Sunday masses.

It was on one of Father Gould's visits, that day in July of 1708, four years after entering the orphanage, that Jacques's life was to change.

On that day Father Gould entered the classroom and said he had an important announcement to make. The Mother Superior was with him. She held her hands together, as if in prayer and bowed her head.

'Something is up,' thought Jacques.

"Boys," said the Father, "the reason I am here is because a government official called on me yesterday and asked for my help. It seems the army needs volunteers to go to Acadie because it is feared that the British are planning an attack on one of the French forts.

"The regular soldiers are needed here since we are still at odds with the British. The Governor of Nova Scotia has placed an urgent call for more soldiers to help defend the fort at Port Royal, should the English attack. The King does not think this attack will take place therefore if volunteers go, probably nothing will happen."

All the boys looked at each other in amazement.

"How many of you are willing to volunteer to go to Canada?" asked the Father. Without hesitation, all the boys raised their hands.

"Good, thank you," said Father Gould. "I will notify the authorities. It looks like we have about fifty boys willing to go. There will be boys from other regions joining also."

Jacques could not believe what he was hearing. His heart raced with anticipation. He longed to see what was outside. He had, so to speak, been cooped up for years, protected from the evils of the outer world.

Back in the dormitory there was joy and happiness for the older boys, but sadness for the younger boys. The younger ones wanted to go also, but that would not be possible.

A few days later the Mother Superior entered the dormitory and announced that the volunteers were to leave right away. With her were two French soldiers. One of them had large stripes on his sleeve. She introduced Sergeant LeBlanc.

"Good morning, men," said Sergeant LeBlanc. "My name is Sergeant LeBlanc. This is Private LeClair. We hate to ask you to leave this wonderful place, but our government is looking for volunteers for duty in Acadie. We will take you to our training base in Paris, and once trained you will board ships for Port Royal. We don't think anything will happen, but just to play it safe, and to show the English we have the manpower, you will be stationed there."

Jacques was eager to enlist and travel; to see the world.

The boys were led outside, and as they exited the orphanage, the nuns stood by tearfully watching their charges. "God be with you, boys," said the Mother Superior."

Outside, four more regular army soldiers awaited them. The boys were lined up four abreast and the march began. They all turned and waved to the nuns they had come to know and love throughout the years.

Upon arriving at the training base, the boys were given a cursory physical exam by a physician. Sadly, some of the boys were returned to the orphanage.

Then it was off to the quartermaster's building for uniforms. The Army had a hard time outfitting such small bodies, but they managed. Finally, they were led into the dining hall and fed. It was a feast fit for a king! Codfish stew, and fresh bread, all you could eat. "I like it!" said Jacques.

The boys were marched to their new dormitory. The bunks were made of tough canvas tied to a wooden frame, two tiers high. After sleeping on small beds for so long this was like heaven. André and Jacques found bunks next to each other so they can chat like they used to.

That first evening, as Jacques lay in his wonderful soft bed, with a full belly, new clothing, his mind still couldn't believe that this was really happening. He lay awake for the longest time telling himself over and over that he was finally going to see some of the world.

The next few weeks were spent training the new recruits.

"I have never seen better behaved soldiers," remarked a drill instructor to Sergeant LeBlanc.

"Its no wonder," he replied, "you should have seen how good they were treated."

The boys were taught the rudiments of military life; how to march, how to load and fire weapons, etc. The smallest boy in the group was singled out to be a drummer. He was giving lessons and taught how to keep cadence. Another small boy was singled out to be the standard bearer. They would lead the regiment in all their marches.

By August, that happy day in 1708, the regiment was prepared for departure. They were marched to the quay along the Seine River to board barges for the trip downriver to the port city of LeHarve, twenty men to each barge. Jacques and André managed to board the first. Army Captain Francois Chalbert, Sergeant LeBlanc, and a few army regulars were also on board. The barge captain helped the men stow their equipment. This would be their home for the next four days. The barge captain and his wife lived on the barge year round. She hung her laundry on the roof of the cabin, so the lads were not permitted to climb up there.

After ridding themselves of their equipment, they went topside. From that vantage point, they could see the other barges waiting to be loaded. In the distance was the Cathedral of Notre Dame, a most imposing structure.

Horses on either bank of the canal were harnessed and ropes passed from the barge to the horse handlers. The horses would tow the barges all the way. When all was ready, the rope holding the barge to the pier was untied, and she was ready to go. As the barge drifted slowly away, the lads on board waved to their compatriots waiting their turn.

Looking back, soon all that could be seen of the great city was the steeple of the Cathedral of Notre Dame. André looked at Jacques and said, "Well, this may be the last view we will ever see of Paris."

"I will miss Paris," replied Jacques.

The barge sat low in the water. She was fully loaded with goods for Port Royal. There was not much room for the soldiers, but they managed. The barge trip provided a leisurely view of the countryside as it floated along. The sun played on a large vineyard valley that contained the remains of a medieval village. Jacques could not get over the breath-taking scenery.

"This sure is something different, isn't it?" said Jacques.
"It sure is," replied André.
As the sun set, the barge arrived at a small village.

"We camp here for the night, boys," said the captain.

The horses were released, and the barge made fast to a pier. One of the barge crewmen climbed the top of the cabin and cast a fishing line into the river. Some of the soldiers went topside to see if he would catch anything. Soon, he got a strike and reeled in his line. They saw him pull something in.

"What is that?" they asked.
"An eel, dammit!" he replied.
"Is that good to eat?"
"Yeah, but I wanted something else." The eel was taken aboard and cooked.

The warm summer evening was filled with the sounds of crickets and frogs chirping and croaking in the distance --- the smell of hyacinths in the air. The barge captain lit lanterns, and the lads prepared their sleeping places. They all sat around chatting.

"What do you think it will be like in Canada?" asked Philippe. They all had their own answers.

"Well, I heard," said André...the boys leaned forward to hear what he had to say, he was the oldest so they assumed he was the wisest. "I heard they have wild savages there!" The answer sent shivers in some of the boys.

"Yeah, well, if they mess with me," said young Joachim. "I'll blow them away with my musket!" That reply made some of the boys break out with laughter.

The captain, holding a large kettle, came in. "Would you lads care for some tea?"

"Yes, sir," they replied. He filled their cups, and they enjoyed the refreshing drink.

Early the following morning, the horses were again hitched. Large wooden barrels full of fresh water were loaded, along with some rations, and the journey continued. The four-day trip ended at the port city of LeHavre. Upon arrival the lads gathered topside to catch a glimpse of the great city. The horse on the right was unhitched, leaving the other horse to tow the barge to a nearby pier where she was made fast.

LeHavre was an exciting place for the young lads. The port was bristling with activity as merchants hawked their wares. The waterfront was congested with shops of every description. Anchored nearby in the bay were numerous ships.

"Jacques, can you smell the salt air?" asked André.
"Yes, isn't it great?"
"Look at all the sailors all over the place."

CHAPTER TWO

Crossing the Atlantic

Among the many vessels anchored at the port of LeHavre, two stood out. They were huge tri-masted ships, towering over everything nearby.

"Those two big ships must be ours," said André, as they stood on the deck of the barge. He pointed to Le Venus and Le Loire. There was an air of excitement being in a strange city. The sights and sounds were something they had never seen before.

Sergeant LeBlanc informed the boys that they could go ashore, "Be back before sundown!" he ordered.

"Let's go ashore and look around, Jacques," said André, excitedly.
"Sounds good to me."
All the lads had the same idea and left the barge in one large group. While walking around, they encountered the other lads from the orphanage, also ashore to stretch their legs. The people of LeHavre were surprised to see the young soldiers wandering around.

"Are they Boy Scouts?" asked one old timer to another.
"They're wearing army uniforms," said the other.
"Where are you fellows going?" inquired a shopkeeper.
"Acadie," replied the lads.
"My word. Can you believe that"? he exclaimed.
At sunset, the lads reported to their respective barges. Oil lamps were lit and preparations made to bed down.

"Would you lads be caring for some hot tea?" Asked the captain of the barge, making his usual evening rounds.

"Yes, Sir," replied the young troopers, scrambling to retrieve their mess kits.

"Here ye go, lads," said the captain, as he poured the tea, each boy eagerly holding his own tin cup.

"Thank you, Captain," echoed throughout the barge. The boys chatted away frantically, finally causing Sergeant LeBlanc to break up the banter.

"Turn in. We have a full day ahead of us tomorrow," he ordered.

"Yes, sir," they replied.

Early the next morning the boys were up, eager to see what would happen next. They could see some activity aboard Le Venus, the ship closest to them. They watched as a large boat was lowered, manned by eight oarsmen and a coxswain. The boat made for their barge. As the boat neared, a line was passed from the barge to the rowboat. Once the tow line was secured, the barge was untied from the pier and the order was given by the coxswain to 'man oars.' The oarsmen, all in unison, positioned their oars, and with great effort soon had the barge drifting towards the ship. As they neared the ship, lines were lowered and the barge made fast.

Army Captain Francois Chalbert, Sergeant LeBlanc, and the regular army soldiers were the first to board. The lads then boarded the ship. As they came aboard, they were directed to stand to one side.

Standing at the quarterdeck to greet them was Captain Don Charette with his first-officer, Lawrence Babineau, and midshipman, André Boudreau. Army Captain Chalbert, the first to board, explained to the captain that this was the regiment assigned to Port Royal. Captain Charette was aghast when he saw young boys boarding his ship.

"These are young boys!" he exclaimed to the army captain.

"Yes, Sir," he replied. "This is what the army feels will be sufficient to deter any planned attacks by the British against Port Royal." The captain shook his head in disbelief.

"Mister Babineau, show the officers to their quarters," said Captain Charette.

The first-officer led the army officers below to their special quarters, then the captain turned to the midshipman and said, "Mister Boudreau, show the soldiers to their quarters.

The midshipman led the solders below to a large room. They had to stoop to walk about. The ceiling was only five feet high. As they entered, they saw strange looking canvas sacks neatly tied up to the overhead. At the far end of the room was a long table. Mister Boudreau showed them where to stow their equipment. They were to tie their 'sea bags' to a long wooden rail. He removed his naval hat, while they gathered around him. He was wearing a bright blue tunic and black trousers. His brown hair was neatly pulled back and tied. He stood over six feet tall and was well developed, a rather handsome individual. He had a hard time in the room since he was so tall.

"My name is Midshipman Boudreau...you will address me as 'Mister Boudreau.' "You will address the captain as 'Captain Charette,' not as 'Mister Charette.' Our crossing will take two months; therefore, it is important that you learn your way around and what we will expect from you. The most important thing for you to learn right now is not to waste fresh water. You will all receive one container of water per day. The Master-At-Arms will dole out the water. Anyone caught stealing water will be severely punished. You will wash your clothes in seawater. We want no fighting, and no thievery. When you hear the boson's pipe and the word being passed, 'All hands on deck' you will drop what you are doing and get your asses topside immediately. I will be watching, and anyone getting there late will be one sorry individual.

"When you get up in the morning, you will trice up your hammock to make room to move about." He then took them on a tour of the ship. Up on deck he pointed out the various duties they would be performing.

"This is the port side, or larboard side," he said, pointing to the left as they went forward. "This is the starboard side," pointing to the right.

"When you want to go forward, use the starboard side, and when you want to go aft, use the port side. That way you don't bump into the crew members as they go about their duties."

While at the helm, Mister Boudreau pointed out the compass and binnacle. As the captain walked by, the soldiers come to attention.

"Relax, men," said Captain Charette; an ordinary looking man of average height, he could pass as one of the crew. His clothing was not much different from any other sailor on board. His hair was graying a bit at the temples. He wore an ordinary seaman's cap. His face was well tanned, and his beard neatly trimmed. He had a pleasant smile and piercing brown eyes. His long black jacket clashed with his baggy trousers. A gust of wind hit the side of the ship causing it to lean a bit to one side.

"Looks like the wind is picking up a bit," said the captain.

"Aye, Sir," replied the midshipman.

"Well, take care of our brave soldiers, Mister Boudreau," said the captain as he walked away.

"Aye, Sir."

Mister Boudreau led his charges back to their quarters. "You men will be assigned duties and I don't want any goldbricks here."

In a few days, all fifty of the soldiers and equipment were aboard. The other ship would transport another fifty soldiers to Port Royal.

Early, on the day of departure, the boson's pipe blared and they heard the words ring out, 'All hands on deck.' Frantically, they clambered out of their hammocks and dashed to their assigned place topside, not wanting to be the last one. Mister Boudreau, it seemed was the last person to arrive. The captain and first-officer arrived and made their way to the poop deck overlooking the crew.

"Men," said the captain,   "the ship is fully provisioned, the wind is in our favor, and now we humbly ask the Great Navigator, Our Lord and Savior, to see us safely across, we pray in His name, Amen."

"Amen," echoed the crew.

Captain Charette turned to his first-officer and said, "Mister Babineau, make ready for sailing."

"Aye, Sir," he replied. Then in a loud and booming voice, shouted, "Make ready for sailing. All hands turn to."

A flag was raised to the topmast indicating to all present at sea that the ship was about to raise anchor.

Like a finely tuned watch, the crew members prepared the great ship to get underway. Some manned the anchor capstan, some the helm, some climbed the rope ladders leading to the yardarms to unfurl the sails. Orders were shouted to the men aloft to let loose the top mainsail while the men on the capstan took in the anchor. Other sails were unfurled.

The boy soldiers were in awe at the spectacle before them. After the main sail was lowered, it soon caught the wind and billowed, forcing the ship to lean heavily to one side. As more sails were lowered, the ship seemed to creak and groan as the wind tried to topple the masts. Like a giant awakening from a deep slumber, stretching his muscles, the ship leaned with the wind and started to move.

"We're moving," said André, excitedly, trying to maintain his balance.

"Steer west, Mister Babineau," said the captain.

"Steer west, Aye, Aye, Sir," replied the first-officer.

The helmsman deftly steered the ship out to sea in a westerly direction as ordered. They would try to follow the 45th parallel across the Atlantic to Acadie.

As she picked up speed, the sea sprayed the deck with salt water. Jacques, standing in the front, got a taste of it. He grinned from ear to ear. The midshipman dismissed the soldiers from their station. Free to roam, they gathered aft to view the port of LeHavre. Seagulls gathered around the ship, circling and squawking, looking for a handout. As they put out to sea, the shoreline seemed to dwindle. Soon, only the tops of the highest buildings could be seen.

"There goes the last view of our homeland," said Philippe, sadly. No one said anything.

All fifty boys stood at the far end of the ship, looking toward the fading shoreline.

Midshipman Boudreau would keep the boys busy during the crossing. They would all be assigned certain duties. They would assist the sail maker, carpenter, cook, and in general keep the ship clean. Mister Boudreau assigned some of the boys to lookout duty for four-hour periods.

"How will we know when our four hours are up?" asked Antoine.

"The quartermasters keep track of time. They strike a bell every half hour. When you first go on duty, they will ring eight bells. After the first half hour, the bell will ring once. This means you have been on duty one half hour. On the second half hour of your watch, the bell will ring two. Every half hour, the count will be increased until it rings eight times. When it rings eight bells you know you have been on duty for four hours, and the count starts all over again."

Later, chores done for the day, Jacques and André meandered aft. The ship, now under full sail, glided majestically onward. At the helm, they saw the tall figure of André Doucet.

"Well, how do you like being sailors?" asked Mister Doucet.

"I like it just fine, Sir," replied Jacques.

"Me too," said André.

"That's good…looks like we will be having good weather tomorrow," said Mister Doucet.

"How can you tell, Sir?" asked Jacques.

"See the color of the clouds in the West?"

As they beheld the sky looking west, the spectacular view before them was awesome. Never had they seen a sunset over water. The crimson colored clouds displaying nature's beauty was breathtaking.

"Sailors have a saying," said Mister Doucet. "Red sky at night, sailor's delight. Red sky in the morning, sailor take warning."

"So, if the sky is red at night, that means we will have good weather the following day?" asked Jacques.

"That's right, lad," replied the helmsman.

"Sir," asked André, "how do you know where you are going?"

"We steer by the ship's compass," he replied. Then he pointed out the compass. "The needle always points north, so we always know which direction we are going."

A few minutes after sunset, the ship's lanterns were made ready and put in position. A lantern was lit high up above the crow's nest and another well astern. Any ship at sea at night would be able to see those lights. As night fell, the rest of the boys gathered topside and aft before retiring. They beheld another of nature's wonders. The sea fluoresced eerily in the wake of the ship.

Later, below decks, the hammocks were untied and the lads tried their hands at the art of climbing into the sack. There was much laughter as they attempted the task of hoisting themselves up and in. Eventually, all settled in. It was dark in the room. Lanterns were not permitted for fear of fire, and only one port was open.

As Jacques lay in his hammock, he could feel it swinging from side to side. At peace with the world, and the gentle swaying of the ship, he felt a sort of euphoria. Could it be there was a lingering memory of the joy he felt as a baby when his mother rocked him in his cradle.

The following day did indeed turn out to be beautiful as predicted by Mister Doucet. The ship's course was corrected to clear the English Channel and make for the Atlantic.

A few weeks later, rising early and going topside, Jacques was aware that the sky was reddish towards the rising sun. I had better tell the others, he thought.

" André," said Jacques, "the eastern sky is bright red!"

"Oh, I guess that means there will be bad weather," he replied. André was quick to pass this information on to his fellow soldiers to impress them with his knowledge of seamanship. They scoffed at his prediction. The following day the sky was overcast, with ominous looking dark clouds and the wind seemed to be picking up.

"Maybe André was right," said Joachim, as he scanned the horizon later.

"I hope not," replied Joseph. "I don't like it when it gets rough."

As night approached, the wind was stronger than ever, and the rain started. The creaking and groaning of the masts reverberated inside the hull and the great ship was leaning increasingly.

"Take in sails, Mister Babineau," ordered the captain.

Le Venus strained against the wind to keep herself upright. The lifeline, a rope extending fore and aft, was hooked up. Two men were assigned to man the helm. The hatches were made fast and the young soldiers were confined to their quarters. Huge waves pounded against the sides of the ship.

The soldiers took to their hammocks for relief. Since the hammock swings opposite the sway of the ship, more or less maintaining an even keel, it was the only place they could find relief. Still, it was more than some of the lads could take. The scourge of seafarers took over, the unending mal-de-mer.

From his hammock, Jacques turned to André and said, "Remember when Mister Doucet, the helmsman, asked us how we like being sailors…and I said, 'I like it', well, I changed my mind."

André did not respond, he just lay there staring at the overhead, and then he jumped out and grabbed a nearby bucket. There were buckets all over the lower decks, usually filled with sand. These were to be used to fight fires.

Mercifully, the storm only lasted a few days, and calm returned.

" André was right," said Philippe. "He said we would be having bad weather."

"Hey, André," said Joachim, "let us know when the next storm is coming, so we can get ready for it."

"Don't feel so bad," said Joseph, "even Sergeant LeBlanc and the regular soldiers stayed in their hammocks!"

Six weeks out of LeHavre, on a very warm September day, the boson's pipe blared, 'All hands on deck."

"Wonder what's going on," asked Jacques to the others as they fell in.

"Mister Babineau," said the captain, standing on the poop deck, overlooking the crew. "Take in all sails."

"If they take in all sails," said André, "won't the ship stop?"

When all sails were taken in, the ship did indeed stop.

"Lower boats," Mister Babineau, ordered the captain. Boats were lowered on the port side, and manned. The sailors in the boats were heavily armed. They rowed out a few yards from the ship, and waited.

"Lower rope ladders," Mister Babineau, said the captain. Rope ladders were slung over the port side of the ship. Looking up at the yardarms, they saw armed crew members on lookout. There was bewilderment amongst the youngsters.

The next order from the captain was one they never expected.

"Swim call!"

Mister Boudreau, the midshipman, dismissed the soldiers. "You men can go in for a swim if you wish." He explained that the armed sailors were there to ward off sharks. The lookouts would give the first warnings.

There seemed to be mad mayhem as the crew dashed for the gunwales and jumped into the briny deep. Scantily clothed bodies were all over the place, laughing and frolicking. The boy soldiers enjoyed the spectacle before them as they watched the sailors enjoying the ocean water. None of the soldiers went for a swim.

"I can't swim," said Jacques.

"Neither can I," said André.

"Hey, Sergeant LeBlanc," said Dominique, "why aren't you going in?"

"I can't swim, either," he replied. This brought laughter to the boys.

Later, under full sail again, in a gentle wind, Le Venus continued westward.

In early October, the lookout shouted, "Land ho."

"Where away?" asked Mister Babineau.

The lookout pointed to the north. "Two points off the starboard bow, Sir."

The first-officer went below to notify the captain. The captain arrived topside with a long-glass to determine where they were. Mister Babineau pointed in the direction given by the lookout. As the captain peered through his long-glass, he saw a few small sloops in the distance, apparently fishing. Then he recognized the distinct shape of the harbor beyond.

"Canso," said the captain, to Mister Babineau. He handed his long-glass to his first-officer so he could look.

"You are absolutely right, Captain," said the first-officer. They had arrived at Acadie.

"Steer west-sow-west, Mister Babineau," ordered the captain.

"West-sow-west, Aye, Sir," replied the first-officer. The ship's course was changed.

The word quickly spread throughout the ship; land had been sighted. Eager to get a glimpse of the new world the young soldiers were permitted to gather topside. Off in the distance could be seen the outline of Acadie. The verdant hills were spectacular. Their welcoming committee consisted of a school of dolphins playfully swimming near the prow of the ship. A little closer to land brought the sea gulls. As the mess-boys dumped garbage over the side, the gulls gathered over the jetsam.

A week or so later, Le Venus rounded Cape Sable and entered Baie Francais, better known today as the Bay of Fundy. Looking to the right one could see the long mountain ridge extending all along the bay. Soon, a narrow opening was seen in the ridge. It was the entrance to the river and it was called 'The Gut.' The ship made for the entrance. High mountains on either side towered above the sails as she entered. Once safely past the entrance, the ship made a left turn.

There before them was nature's most awesome sight, the Annapolis River! Where just moments before, they were tossed to and fro; now protected by the mountain ridge, the ship glided peacefully in the natural breakwater.

The river sparkled as the sun's rays playfully reflected from the tiny waves. The lush greenery of the mountains, the blue-sky above, and the happy mood of the sailors all added to the magic of the moment.

The river is sixteen miles long. It is six miles across at its widest point tapering towards its end in a long triangular shape until it becomes a mere half mile wide at the terminus. Looking south, one sees the land gradually sloping upward. This southern ridge provides many of the delicious wild fruits found in the area; apples and cherries.

As the ship glided eastward for two miles, it encountered an island. That island is now named Goat Island. There was passage on either side, but the best way seemed to be to the north. Once clear of Goat Island, the fort could be seen six miles distant in the intervale.

The boson piped all hands on deck. The soldiers and the crew assembled.

"Make ready the gun," Mister Babineau, ordered the captain.

"Did you hear that?" said Edmund. "They are going to use the gun!"

"Maybe the captain wants to scare away the Indians," said Philipe.

Mister Boudreau, the midshipman, hearing the bantering, said, "We always fire the gun when we approach Port Royal to let them know we have arrived, and as a form of greeting."

"Ready to fire, Sir," said the gunner's mate.

"Fire!" replied the captain.

With a deafening roar, the cannon discharged. Flames shot out towards the fort. Dense smoke rose into the air. A few minutes later Port Royal returned the compliment. First the flash could be seen followed a few seconds later by the sound of their gun. Sails were taken in and the ship slowed to a crawl. When she was near the fort, the captain ordered the anchor lowered.

Captain Charette entered into the ship's log:

Arrived Port Royal, Monday October 8, 1708, six bells into second watch.

CHAPTER THREE

Port Royal

Upon arriving at Port Royal, Captain Charette, army Captain Francois Chalbert, and First Officer Lawrence Babineau paid their respects to the governor of Acadie, whose office was in the fort.

Governor Subercase greeted them warmly and led them to his study. He was impeccably attired in a blue tunic with bright white trousers that stopped just below the knees where his stockings took over. His bright black leather shoes sported bows across the tops. He was a heavy man, about five-eight, with brown hair. His large brown eyes put you at ease.

"How was your trip, Captain?" asked the jovial Governor.

"Very well, Sir," replied the captain. "May I present Captain Chalbert and my First Officer, Mister Babineau."

The Governor shook hands with Captain Chalbert and Mister Babineau, and offered them some libation.

"With all respect, and we thank you, Sir, but...could we instead have some fresh water?" asked Captain Chalbert.

"Yes..." intoned Mister Babineau, "we haven't had fresh water for weeks."

"Of course," replied the governor. "I should have known."

With all the preliminaries put aside, Captain Charette presented the ship's manifest for the Governor's inspection.

"Fine, fine, excellent..." said the Governor after looking over the report. He had requested some supplies and was grateful to receive them.

"How are the soldiers?" asked the Governor. Captain Charette looked at army Captain Chalbert, who looked back at him, raising his eyebrows. The Governor caught the motion and sensed something amiss from their behavior.

"The soldiers are fine, Governor...however, they are really not what you requested," said army Captain Chalbert

"Not what I requested?" said the Governor, as he made a face, raising his hands as if to expect a better answer.

"No, Sir," he replied. "They are all young volunteers, from twelve to sixteen years of age. Most of them came from orphanages."

"That's preposterous!" blurted the Governor. "How can this be?"

"I suppose, Sir, that the French authorities deemed this would be sufficient to deter any possible incursions by the English on Port Royal."

"I just can't believe this," stammered the Governor, shaking his head. After a long pause he said, "Well, they are here now, so we will just have to accept it. Have them report tomorrow morning with all their equipment."

The following day the soldiers disembarked. They formed ranks on the dock, with the smallest boys in front...one with a drum, and the other with their banner. Captain Chalbert took his position at the head of the regiment. When all was ready, Sergeant LeBlanc ordered, "Forward." Keeping time with the drummer, banner waving, they followed the captain to the fort. The gates were opened and the regiment crossed the bridge over the moat into the fort. Once inside, they were to line up in front of the flag pole facing the administration building.

In front of the building, all neatly lined up were the regular army soldiers, all resplendent in their French Army uniforms. The two groups faced each other. At the head of the French Army regiment was the governor himself.

They were greeted by Governor Subercase, and given a welcome speech. The Governor was impressed with the sight before him. They may be young, but by God, they look great, he thought to himself.

As Jacques and the other new arrivals looked about, they were awed with the sights before them. The beautiful formation of regular French soldiers before them was inspiring. At the forefront of their formation, they also had a boy with a drum, and another youngster was holding the flag of France.

There were horses tied in front of some of the buildings. The one thing that really caught Jacques's eye was the appearance of some of the people there. These were dressed in animal skins and stood apart from the soldiers. Their hair was pitch black, and their faces were of a reddish hue. Arms folded in front, they stood tall and proud as they surveyed the new arrivals.

" André," Jacques whispered to his friend next to him, "look at those people."

"Yes," he replied, "I was looking at them. Maybe they are Indians."

"I hope they are friendly."

As they waited, Jacques noticed smoke rising from the chimney of a nearby large building...the dining hall. The wind blowing in their direction carried from the dining hall. The aroma was something they had never experienced before.

" André," said Jacques, "what's that smell?"

"I don't know, but God, does that smell good!"

The new arrivals looked at each other in wonderment, and mumbled things back and forth.

"What seems to be the problem?" asked the Governor, as he noticed the excitement amongst the soldiers. He was inspecting the new arrivals.

"With all due respect, Sir," said Captain Chalbert, who stood in front of the troop, and also got a whiff of the aroma wafting from the dining hall. "What is that smell?"

"It's only the cook preparing our meal," replied the governor.

"You must excuse us, Excellency," said the captain. "We haven't had meat in years!"

"Did you hear that?" said Jacques to the others. "Meat!"

The soldiers were unbelieving. Royalty and rich landowners only ate meat.

"Well," replied the Governor, "lets eat!"

The first order was to store all their guns and black powder in the armory, then relieved of this burden, they were led into the large dining hall. Each was given a tin plate, and a large tankard, and made to pass by a long table where they were served. A large burly chef sliced thick slabs of beef from a roasted hindquarter; fresh potatoes and green beans rounded out the meal. At the end of the table was a large bucket holding fresh well water. Eagerly, they filled their tankards with the precious drink and gulped it down, quickly refilling again. The water supply aboard the ship had reached such a rancid state before arriving that it had to be cut with rum to make it potable.

During the meal, Jacques said to André, "The closest we ever got to eating something like this was the few times my father brought home some chicken meat."

"You were lucky," replied André, "we never even had that!"

The meal was far beyond their wildest imaginations. Later that afternoon, after being allowed to bathe in fresh water and clean their clothes, the soldiers were to meet their hosts. The local peasants would put them up in their homes according to the laws that stipulated the locals would provide billets for the soldiers. This was a common practice everywhere French soldiers went. Every family within a three-mile radius was required to come to the fort for this occasion.

The soldiers lined up on one side, and the locals on the other side. When a soldier's name was called out, the first villager in line stepped forward and greeted him. When Jacques's name was called out, he stepped forward and met

Antoine Hebert.

"My name is Antoine Hebert," said the local host, as he shook Jacques's hand. "Welcome to Acadie."

"Thank you, Sir," replied Jacques. "My name is Jacques Maillet, from Paris."

Antoine, a thirty-eight year old native who looked no more than twenty, was a large powerful man. Farming had honed his muscles rock hard. His faded cotton shirt, a pullover with a wide opening at the front, revealed a hairy chest. His trousers were cut at the knees and shredded. He wore Indian moccasins on his feet.

Antoine led the way to the river's edge.

"You can put your things in the canoe," he said. Then, he pushed the canoe into the water and instructed Jacques to wade out and get in, which he did. The water was chilling, filling his boots. Antoine did the same, wading out into the water before getting in. Jacques couldn't understand why he had to get his feet wet.

"We have to put the canoe in the water first before we get in, otherwise the rocks will tear the bottom out if we push it into the river heavily loaded."

"I guess I have a lot to learn," said Jacques. He was given an oar and instructed how to paddle. "You paddle on one side, and I'll paddle on the other," said Antoine.

Jacques didn't like the idea of traveling in a canoe. This was a clumsy craft at best, and he didn't know how to swim. He figured if he went in his knapsack would hold him up, so buoyed by that thought he proceeded to paddle.

"You are doing good, Son," said Antoine, as they paddled across the river.

As he looked around, Jacques saw the farms scattered on the far side, all close to the river. All the farm houses had thatched roofs, and all had smoke rising from their chimneys. He saw cows lazily chewing their cuds, and horses penned in large enclosures. Sheep were everywhere, chickens roamed every which way, dogs were barking, children played. The leaves had changed colors and those that were still clinging displayed a bright variety.

As they paddled across, nearing the opposite shore, Antoine pointed out the various farms, who lived here and who lived there; all French names common in France.

"This is my place," said Antoine, as he steered the canoe to shore.

Still deep in the water, he said, "You have to get out now, Jacques."

Jacques stepped into the deep water again, up to his knees, followed by Antoine. Mister Hebert pulled the lightened canoe ashore careful not to rip its bottom. Antoine's wife, Jeanne, seeing them approach went out to greet them, along with her children, who acted giddily upon seeing the stranger. They ran up to Antoine and lovingly gave him hugs, all the while looking over the soldier boy.

"Hello, Papa," they happily greeted their father.

"Hello, you little rascals," he jokingly replied.

Jeanne, holding five month old, Pierre, stepped forward to meet the new arrival.

"Jeanne," said Antoine, to his wife. "This is Jacques Maillet, from Paris."

Jacques looked into her face and saw the most beautiful woman he had ever seen, her beauty instantly captivated him. Her face was soft and radiant, with big brown eyes and a full womanly figure. Her white bonnet was striking on her long, curled, brown hair. The pink bodice, over her white shirt, laced at the front showed she was all woman. Her brown linen dress just added to the picture of loveliness. Her wooden sabots gleamed on her feet.

As Jeanne looked at Jacques, she could plainly see that he was just a youngster.

"Jacques, from Paris," she said, adding. "How old are you?"

"Thirteen, Ma'am," he replied.

"My word, how could your parents let you join the army at such a young age?"

"Both my parents are dead, Ma'am,"

"Oh, I'm sorry to hear that."

"Thank you, Ma'am."

"Well, you are here now, so I guess we will have to take care of you, won't we?"

"I won't be any trouble, Ma'am, and I will do whatever I can to help."

"Well, we certainly need your help...don't we children," she said. The girls standing there looked on in amusement.

"Jacques," said Antoine, "meet the children...this is Agnes," as he pointed out the biggest child. "She is thirteen, just like you. And this is Marie," pointing to the next biggest child, "she is eleven. This is Magdelaine, she is eight," as he pointed out the little girl with the long blond hair and bright blue eyes. The little girl smiled bashfully at the soldier. He smiled back.

"This is, Louis...he is six years old. This is, Pierre Benjamin, he is five. This is Paul," being held by Agnes, "he is only a little over a year old. And this little guy," he said as he looked at baby Pierre nestled in Jeanne's arms, "This is just plain, Pierre."

"Come inside, Jacques," said Jeanne. "We will get you settled and have supper."

As Jacques followed Jeanne into the house, he could feel his feet squishing from all the water his boots had taken in.

"I'd better empty my boots before I go in," he said. The children laughed when they saw him remove his boots and pour the water out.

"You need some moccasins, Jacques," said Antoine.

"Yes, Sir."

Antoine showed Jacques to his room. He was to share the room with Louis, and Pierre Benjamin. There were three comfortable beds all neatly made up in that room. Jeanne came in with some of Antoine's old clothes and a pair of moccasins donated by the oldest girl. Antoine then took Jacques on a tour of the farm.

"Have you ever milked a cow?" asked Antoine.

"Until today, I have never even seen a cow!" he replied.

"Well, we will teach you everything about farming. You will enjoy it."

Antoine pointed out where each crop was planted; potatoes, corn, beans, turnips, rye, and hay. He had a large tract of land.

At supper, Jacques was treated to a marvelous chicken stew, fresh bread, and apple pie for dessert. He couldn't get over the quality of foods here.

"Misses Hebert," said Jacques, after supper, "that was the best meal I have ever had in my life."

"Oh, you are too kind," she replied.

"No Ma'am. We never ate like this in France in all my life."

He went on to talk about the staple in France, mostly dark bread and potato soup. Later on, while sitting by the fireside, Antoine gave Jacques a taste of delicious spruce beer. The children all asked him questions; what was it like in the orphanage, which he would not talk about, but quickly changed the subject. He spoke openly about the ocean crossing. He asked most of the questions about life in Acadie.

He enjoyed watching Antoine milk the cows at evening time, and feed the animals. Chores done for the day, they retired very early. They would be up before sunrise.

The next day, Jacques was awakened by the sound of a rooster crowing. He had never heard that before. The sun was just rising. Another wonderful aroma made its way to his nose. As he was about to get up, Antoine entered his room.

"Jacques," said Antoine, "see if this will fit you." He gave him some garments for working around the farm. A cap, linen socks, cotton shirt, and an old pair of his trousers made from a heavy material. Jacques eagerly dressed and went downstairs to greet the early risers. The wonderful aroma turned out to be eggs frying on a pan over the fireplace. Jeanne, and the eldest girl, was preparing breakfast.

"Have a seat, Jacques," said Antoine. Jacques seated himself and was served some eggs and fresh bread. As the younger girls entered, they rushed to sit next to him. Magdelaine was first; she sat on his right, while Agnes dashed for the left hand seat. Marie sat across the table, disappointed.

Jeanne gave Jacques a tall glass of white liquid. He just stared at it for a while, then he noticed the children were all drinking the same thing, and seemed to be enjoying it. Then he tasted it. It was the most refreshing drink he had ever had. The girls laughed at him after he drank from the glass. His upper lip was covered with the white milk, and he had a wide smile.

"I have never had this before," said Jacques. The children were amazed at his statement. Milk was something as common as water in Acadie.

"I never had eggs before, either," he said.

After a hearty breakfast, Antoine took him out to the barn. The early morning air in October in Acadie was very cold. Jacques was grateful for the heavy clothes. Antoine showed him how to milk a cow. He was given a bucket and told to try his hand at it. He squeezed the teat, but nothing came out. Then Agnes entered, grabbed a bucket and proceeded to milk the cow next to his. He was amazed to see the milk flow into her bucket. He felt embarrassed. He couldn't get the hang of holding the bucket between his legs either. The bucket kept falling.

"Keep trying, Jacques," Antoine said, jokingly, "you'll get the hang of it."

Finally, he learned the proper sequence of squeezing to milk a cow. His hands were sore for a while after that. After the milking chore, he had to feed the animals. There was manure to be collected and stored for fertilizer. The horses and oxen had to be fed, along with the sheep and chickens.

The milk was kept in small noggins in such a way as to turn it thick and very sour. They delighted in eating this with bread. The leftovers were fed to the many hogs they raised.

Everyone in the family had certain chores to do. There was little idleness in Acadie. There was work to be done all day long. The girls helped inside the house with the cleaning, sewing, carting and spinning wool, cooking, knitting, etc.

Antoine needed help with cutting lumber and storing the wood for the cold days ahead. This is where Jacques came in best. His hands were to become calloused and hardened later from the heavy farm work.

Jacques wondered how Antoine was able to plow his field, plant a crop, and harvest all by himself, besides building a huge barn and adding to the farmhouse. He was to learn later that the secret was in his neighbors. Whenever someone needed help, the word was quickly spread, and the neighbors all pitched in. It was like one large family living in perfect harmony.

They did little hunting and fishing instead living off the fruits of their harvests. Most families had several horses but used oxen to plow the ground. Strangely, they had no currency, but bartered goods for the staples they desired.

Crime was unheard of, as was the birth of illegitimate children. The parish priest settled their petty quarrels. They had no physicians, yet lived to the ripe old age of eighty and even into the nineties. They were honest and happy.

Jacques had to report to the fort daily at 8 AM. He was taken across the river by Antoine and picked up later that day. At the fort, Jacques exchanged his experiences with his army friends.

"I had a delicious chicken stew for supper yesterday, and this morning I had three eggs for breakfast, with a large glass of milk!" he exclaimed to the others.

"I had lamb chops...." said another.

"I had pork..." said another.

Strangely, they all were wearing the cotton garments donated by their hosts. "I'm staying with the Heberts," said Jacques. "I'm staying with the Melansons," said André.

"I learned how to milk cows," said Jacques. And the persiflage went on.

After they had been mustered (roll call taken), the order of the day was loading the wagons at the dock with cargo from Le Venus and unloading the wagons in the fort. Some of the soldiers worked at the dock loading, while others worked inside the fort unloading.

After four grueling days of hard labor the ship was finally, empty. "Now, maybe we can take it easy," said Jacques to his friends.

The next order of business was to now load the ship with goods going back to France. The process was reversed, as they had to load huge quantities of lumber. Then they had to load tons of potatoes and apples, hundreds of pounds of dried codfish, dried beef, even furs and all manner of leather goods. Bales of wool and huge barrels of fresh water rounded out the inventory. By early November Le Venus sailed out of Acadie for France. A few days later, the sound of cannon announced the arrival of another ship. Le Loire was approaching the fort.

"You think we have to do that all over again?" Said Jacques to his friends.

"I hope not," replied André, "let the guys on board do the work."

The captain of Le Loire and the new arrivals were received at the fort in the usual display of military protocol. This time, Jacques and his friends stood with the regular French army. They smiled at the soldiers from Le Loire lined up facing them. The new arrivals were treated to a sumptuous meal just as the Le Venus crew had been.

Following their meal and dismissal, there was great camaraderie as they all got together to compare notes. The new arrivals could not believe the stories being told by the earlier soldiers. They were all billeted with locals as the earlier crew had been.

Life at the fort revolved around training and getting the fort in shape to fend off any attacks. The soldiers had to learn how to load and fire their weapons along with the cannons. The drills went on daily.

The last time this fort was attacked, in 1707, it was through clever field operations by the garrison that the fort was saved. Rather than stay in the fort and defend from within, the garrison went out to meet the foe.

That Sunday afternoon, in August of 1707, when the British ships sailed into Annapolis River and approached the fort, the garrison at that time was vastly undermanned. Governor Subercase, nevertheless, sent runners along the river to have all able-bodied men report to the fort immediately. He then sent scouts out to reconnoiter the area. They found the English advance guard approaching, and laid in ambush. They killed eight, and took two prisoners.

The prisoners informed Subercase that the English planned to advance at night, so the governor had his men line up along the river and light fires. Seeing all the fires, the English feared they would be entering a trap so they advanced no further. With the aid of the Micmacs and local militia, the soldiers were able to harass the English in the wilderness to the point of fatigue. The English retreated so fast back to their ships, that the rest of the British were dismayed and wanted no more fighting. They hoisted anchors and went home.

Since this tactic worked so well in 1707, it was Subercase's intention of honing this operation to a science. He had his men venture forth from the fort on mock drills to repel any invaders. It was of course very important for the French to know the location of their own people in the wilderness to keep from firing at each other. This was where the skill of the Micmacs came in. They were very adept at imitating the calls of animals and tracking through the wilderness surrounding the fort. A Micmac, who kept in constant communication with his fellows through animal sounds, led each detachment of soldiers. They knew exactly where all the detachments were.

It was on one of these drills that Jacques met the young Micmac Indian, Paul. Jacques was intrigued with the manner in which Paul imitated different birds, especially crows. He wanted to learn to do this. Also, his host, Antoine had told him upon his arrival at Acadie that if he wanted to survive this country he would be wise to learn the ways of the Micmacs. Jacques was determined to befriend this Indian boy and learn his secrets.

Every Sunday morning, after church services, the villagers would gather to swap stories. It was a time of great fellowship. The local Micmacs, having been evangelized by missionaries, loved to attend these services and mingle with the townspeople.

The women gathered together in a separate group, while the men met and talked in their own group. The young ladies gathered amongst themselves while the soldiers gathered together to ogle the young ladies.

The young Micmac braves met with the soldiers and discussed hunting and fishing. Jacques had never done any of this, nor had the other young soldiers. They pressed the Micmacs for details.

The Micmacs had a large camp set up along the river about four miles distant. The soldiers were invited to visit them.

Jacques asked his Micmac friend, Paul, if he would take him out fishing some day.

"Sure," replied Paul, "come anytime."

The Micmacs learned French from the many missionaries, but since they did not attend regular schools as the French children, their grasp of the French language was not as good, however, they learned enough to be able to trade and carry on a decent conversation.

"I live at the Hebert farm," said Jacques. "Do you know where that is?"

"Across river, short distance from fort?"

"Yes, that is the place."

"Sure, I find it. When you want go?"

"Saturday morning."

"I be there Saturday morning," replied Paul.

The next Saturday, Jacques was ready and eagerly awaited his friend. When Paul arrived Jacques waded out into the river and boarded the canoe. The Hebert girls were there to see him off, waving as they boys paddled away.

"Women," said Jacques, in disgust. Paul chuckled.

As they made for the middle of the river, Jacques noticed a large bird circle overhead. It had long wings and it seemed to be suspended in mid air, just lazily soaring in wide circles. He couldn't stop looking at it; he had never seen anything like it before. The bird seemed to be eyeing them, which made him feel uneasy.

"Eagle," said Paul.

Hooks baited, they sat and waited.

"How do you say fish in Micmac?" asked Jacques.

"Usgagan," he replied.

"Use-gah-gon," replied Jacques. He kept repeating it over and over, trying hard to remember. Presently, a flying insect bussed Jacques's face. He made a move to swat and kill the pesky bug.

"No kill, unless you eat!" warned Paul

Perplexed, Jacques looked at Paul. "What do you mean?" he asked.

"We not kill anything we don't eat. All things have spirit, animals, birds, insects, even trees. We communicate with spirits. Animal spirits are messengers, guides, teachers, and protectors.

"We learn many things from grandfathers; secrets of animals. We talk to spirit of animal, animal come to us. Animal spirit, man spirit, all same to creator."

Jacques was entranced. He loved what he was hearing.

The November temperature was chilly, but the boys seemed oblivious as they enjoyed being on the river. Jacque was thankful for the fine woolen garments made by the girls at the Hebert farm. They were always after him to measure him and fit him with mittens, sweaters, or socks. The cold weather in this part of the world was something that was hard to describe. The winds were the fiercest Jacques had ever seen; thank goodness for the ridge separating them from the Bay of Fundy.

Paul was dressed in warm animal skins. His trousers were made from deerskin, delicately decorated and beautifully hand sewn. He wore moccasins on his feet. Jacques eyed his attire with envy thinking to himself; someday I hope to wear something like that.

The river was very calm. The warmth of the river clashing with the chill of the air caused a light fog to rise just above the water. The mist extended to the shoreline, obscuring familiar landmarks. The sky was overcast indicating that the weather was about to change. They sat motionless as they waited for the inevitable bite.

"We leave river when weather cold. Go deep in forest," said Paul.

"Why do you want to do that?" asked Jacques

"We go forest in winter. Much warmer in forest, game closer."

Jacques was disappointed upon hearing this, he had wanted to do some more fishing later, but that would have to wait. They made a fine catch that day, and both families welcomed it.

When the snows came, farm life was limited to being shut in except for the occasional chores required such as milking and feeding the cows. Snow had to be shoveled to clear a path to the barn. There was no activity at the fort; therefore Jacques was permitted to remain with the Heberts.

Life with the Heberts during the cold winter months was the most pleasant time Jacques had ever experienced. He kept the fire going and made sure there was plenty of firewood available. Antoine showed him how to make furniture. The girls kept him busy holding their yarn in his outstretched arms while they rolled it into a ball.

The Acadians were an agrarian industrious little people, and the severe winter months found them well prepared with the summer's provision. They possessed, beside their abundant, the spontaneous gayety of the French.

The following year in the season of Lent in 1709, Jacques kept busy providing fish for the Heberts. It was a strange paradox that those people had to sacrifice going without meat every Friday during lent.

With the arrival of the warmer weather came the chore of turning the ground in preparation for planting. Jacques learned how to harness the ox and plow the ground. He turned out to be a godsend for the Heberts.

That had been the happiest year of his life.

CHAPTER FOUR

The fall of Port Royal

The summer of 1709 was a busy time for Jacques. He was either at the fort or on the farm. There was plenty to do at either place. His first year in Acadie had made a tremendous change in his physique. He could now keep up with the beefy Antoine in all aspects of farm work. The hot summer evenings were spent leisurely bathing in the Annapolis River. He was happy to learn how to swim, and relieved when the fear of crossing the river by canoe left him.

He enjoyed going on scouting forays with his friend, Paul. He learned the art of communicating with other patrols hidden in the woods by imitating the sound of birds or animals. All the patrols knew where each other were at all times. This was the secret to their success when the English attacked in 1707.

In midsummer, Paul took Jacques to visit the Micmac camp down river. This was his first visit to their camp and he was anxious to go. Jacques enjoyed riding in Paul's canoe. He learned to keep cadence while paddling, one stroke every two seconds. On the way to the campsite as they paddled along the great river, Jacques began to sing. He had heard some settlers singing while they paddled, songs that had a beat similar to the pace of paddling. Paul laughed when he heard the horrible singing.

As they neared the campsite Jacques saw the many wigwams, smoke rising from their tops. Nearing the shore, Jacques stepped out into the water and held the canoe for Paul who also stepped into the shallow water. They gingerly brought the canoe ashore, careful not to hit any rocks that could puncture the craft.

Paul led the way to his wigwam. Along the way, some Indian maidens, seeing the boys arrive, ran over to get a better look. They stared at Jacques and mumbled something between them. The sight of Frenchmen visiting the camp was nothing new to the Indians, but this visit seemed to cause a little stir.

"What are they saying?" Asked Jacques.

"They say your hair color of corn," replied Paul, as he kept on going, ignoring the girls; he had no time for their foolishness. The Indians were busy with all manner of chores. Some were treating animal skins, some were stretching the skins onto racks to air dry, others were constructing bows and arrows, baskets, and all manner of leather goods. They stopped to watch one making arrows. Jacques was surprised to see that they meticulously cut the kerf for the feathers in such a way that it forces the feathers to bend rather than run straight back. This gives the arrow a spin, increasing range and accuracy.

Paul stopped in front of his wigwam and opened the front flap wide to enter. He motioned for Jacques to follow. Inside, Paul's father, Jean-Pierre, greeted Jacques.

"Me'talein," said he.

Jacques looked to Paul for a translation.

"He say, 'How are you?'"

"Fine," replied Jacques. Paul's mother, who had seen Jacques at church services many times and remembered him said, "Weltasi newul."

"She say, 'Nice to see you.'" Said Paul.

"How do you say, 'Thank you'?" asked Jacques.

"Welalin," replied Paul.

"Way La Leen," repeated Jacques to the family. They smiled at him.

Also inside the wigwam were Paul's grandfather, Efraim, and his grandmother, Scolastique, and his younger sister, Anne. They also greeted him warmly.

Jacques was amazed at the size of the wigwam. It was also very tall. It could accommodate twelve people with ease. He was surprised to find that there was proper etiquette inside each wigwam. Only the elder males were allowed to sit at the front near the entrance, the elder females in the center, and the youngsters towards the rear. If anyone wanted to be alone, so to speak, they simply went to the far end of the wigwam and no one bothered them.

At the very top of the wigwam was a wide opening to allow sunlight in, and to let the smoke out. If it rained, there was a flap hanging down on the outside that was simply pushed over the opening using a long pole. There were horizontal braces inside which held large animal bladders. Some of these bladders were used to store rendered fat used for cooking, some held fresh water. There were beautifully made leather quivers, festooned with leather braids, for their arrows hanging from the braces also. Hanging here and there were sausages made from animal intestines. The sweet smelling aroma of dried beef, and dried fish filled the interior. Large gourds (pumpkin like vegetables) hung from the braces, which were used as storage devices. Handsome baskets made of rattan were neatly placed around the lodge. Each person had a bed made of pine boughs with a large skin covering it. Another skin was rolled over the bed to be used as a blanket if the weather was cold. Everything, including the wigwam, was made to be instantly portable when it came time to move.

"We go now," said Paul. He was going to show Jacques the rest of the camp. As they walked around, Jacques was taken with the many activities going on. Jacques stopped at a place where some Indians were busy making a canoe. He wanted to see how they made it. The workmen greeted Paul and smiled at Jacques. They said something to Jacques who looked to Paul.

"They ask, 'Do you have bread'"

"Bread? No, I don't have any bread," he replied.

"They say, 'Bring bread for canoe,'"

"You mean they want to exchange bread for their goods?"

"Yes. We love bread," replied Paul.

Jacques was to learn that the Indians did indeed love fresh bread. They had no mill to grind flour, but enjoyed trading with the villagers for bread. As they went on around the camp Jacques saw women making beautiful leather goods. He had wanted clothing like Paul's in the worse way. Now, he saw a way to get what he wanted.

Back at the Heberts, he asked Jeanne Hebert, his matron host, if she would make some bread to be used for trading. Instantly, the girls all volunteered to make him some. When the time was ready he arranged for Paul to transport him back to the camp. Armed with fresh bread, and an old iron kettle Jeanne threw in for good measure, Jacques was able to trade his goods for a fine canoe.

As he paddled his canoe home for the first time, alone, he felt he was on top of the world. Now, he had real freedom. He could come and go as he pleased. The girls anxiously awaited him when he arrived home with the new canoe. They all ran to see it after he beached it at the farm.

"That is a fine canoe, Jacques," said Antoine, as he looked it over.

"I am really glad the girls helped me get it," said Jacques.

"Well, you deserve it," said Jeanne. "You work hard on the farm for us."

When the planting and reaping were over for the year, Jacques had more time to spend with Paul. On one of his visits, Paul was going to show his friend how to shoot a bow and arrow. They hiked into the woods for a short distance to a clearing.

Paul demonstrated the technique of the bow and arrow. He pointed to a large oak tree about twenty yards away.

"You can't hit that tree from here," said Jacques. "That is too far away!"

Paul drew back on the bow and let the arrow fly. It soared high and arched nicely into the oak. Jacques was amazed at the distance the arrow could go. When he tried it, he missed the oak by ten feet. It took many tries before he could even come close, but he still could not hit the tree. "You keep trying," said Paul.

In the fall of 1709 after gathering their crops the settlers put away their farm tools and prepared for the cold weather. With most of their chores done for the year, now was the time for the newlyweds. The ripening apples provided sweet cider and refreshments. The one thing the settlers enjoyed more than anything else was visiting each other.

The younger settlers would meet at the market square and hold dances. This was where the girls managed to snag the shy young men, which eventually led to a long lasting marriage. The local Micmacs enjoyed these dances but would not participate; they simply loved to listen to the music.

When the weather turned cold, Paul invited Jacques to join him on a hunt. Finishing his chores early a few days later, Jacques set out in his canoe for the camp. As he paddled along, dressed in his Indian clothing, the geese were flying overhead heading south; their loud honking brought a smile to him. Leaving us, are you, he said to himself.

At the camp, they loaded their supplies into Jacques's canoe and paddled off.

"I show you secret place," said Paul. He directed the canoe downriver to an estuary leading into the wilderness. They followed this stream for about a half mile to its end.

"We carry now," said Paul.

They carried the canoe inland following an old trail till they came to an opening. There before them was a large pond. They placed the canoe in the pond and paddled till they came to a small stream emptying into the pond at the far end.

"This the place," said Paul. It was a marvelous spot. The sand along the pond was as fine as flour. The stream was fresh water. As Jacques looked about he was taken with the beauty of his surroundings. The leaves were in the process of changing color. All around was a beautiful symphony of foliage, brightly colored leaves, some red, some orange, and some yellow. It looked as if a rainbow had dipped here and left its calling card.

"Paul, look at all the different colors. I wonder what makes them change colors like that?" said Jacques.

"Mighty hunter in heaven kill Great Bear when weather cold. Blood drip on leaves, make red. Cook bear, fat drip make yellow."

"That is amazing, Paul," said Jacques. He was interested in all facets of Indian lore. Paul pointed out that different trees have different colored leaves. The sugar maples have red leaves. The birches, hickory, poplar all have yellow leaves. The oak trees have brown leaves. The white ash has purple leaves.

"Three things need for survival," said Paul. "Clothing, shelter, and food."

"Well, we have clothing," said Jacques.

"Yes, now we need shelter."

With their hatchets, following Paul's lead, they cut down some willow trees. They were looking for long thin branches. Then they cut some bark from birch trees and soaked them in the water. Using a long willow pole, Paul shoved one end into the soft sand and bent the other end into a large semicircle and shoved that into the ground also. Taking another pole Paul shoved the ends into the ground over the first pole, crossing it. He proceeded to do this, spacing the poles over the first such that it looked like an igloo made of bent poles. Next, he took the birch bark from the water, now subtle enough to manage, and cut it into narrow strips. He showed Jacques how to dig up some roots to use as a thread. They tied the narrow strips of bark over the lower end of the frame, followed by more bark overlapping the first and continuing until the whole shelter was layered, leaving an opening at the top. On the side away from the wind, they constructed their opening.

"Now, we have shelter," said Paul.

"Paul, that is the most beautiful shelter I have ever seen. We could actually live in that all year round."

"Yes, now we need food."

Leisurely swimming on the pond were some late departing geese. "We could have gotten a goose if we had brought our muskets along," said Jacques.

"Micmac no use gun. We never use gun till Frenchmen come. We catch bird our way."

"You mean you can hit one with an arrow?"

"No use arrow. We catch bird our way," replied Paul. He went to the canoe and retrieved a large gourd. After emptying the contents into the canoe he cut two slits in the gourd and slipped it over his head. Then he walked towards Jacques testing the slits to see if he could see through it.

"Oh, I see," said Jacques, as he beheld Paul wearing the gourd. The strange sight before him brought immense laughter. He held his sides as he rolled around on the ground laughing. It was the strangest sight he had ever seen. "You are going to scare it to death!" roared Jacques.

"No scare, you idiot!"

Paul removed all his clothing except for his trousers. He proceeded to wade into the pond, walking till the water was up to his waist then he lowered his body all the way in till only the gourd was visible. He made his way towards the geese. It looked from all appearances as if the gourd was just some piece of drifting debris. The gourd did not disturb the geese. When he was within inches of the nearest goose, he grabbed its legs and held on. The goose fluttered its wings frantically, honking, trying to fly off. The commotion scared the other birds away. Triumphantly, Paul rose from the water, carrying the bird back to shore.

"Now we have food," muttered Paul from under the gourd. Jacques was entranced again. He was learning secrets passed down from generations to generations. For thousands of years the Indians had been living here, and they learned to live with nature without the tools of the white man.

"You hold bird," said Paul, as he handed the goose to Jacques to hold, and removed the gourd. From the canoe Paul got a small leather sack of tobacco. He sprinkled some wild tobacco into the wind and prayed to the spirit of the goose, thanking it for letting itself be caught so they could eat. A quick chop with the hatchet and the bird was ready for plucking.

"You pluck...save all feathers," said Paul. "I make fire now."

Paul took his bow, and with two pieces of wood proceeded to show Jacques how to build a fire. He wrapped the bowstring around a piece of wood and held that piece on another piece on the ground. He used a stone, with an indent, to hold the top of the wood while he pushed the bow back and forth in a sawing motion. The twisting wood soon had the bottom piece smoking. In short order a glowing ember appeared. Paul placed the red-hot ember over some dried leaves and twigs and blew on it. The leaves ignited and then the twigs. They had their fire going.

The boys sumptuously ate roasted goose. Jacques thought he had learned enough to be able to survive alone in the wilderness, but everyday with Paul brought new teachings.

"Why save the feathers, Paul?" asked Jacques.

"Feathers make boot warm in winter. Feathers used in arrows."

Jacques learned that by stuffing feathers and down into the Indian mukluks in the winter, the footwear could provide warmth even in subzero weather. Everything that Paul described, Jacques wanted to learn how to say in the Micmac language. His vocabulary was increasing every week.

When it came time to leave their secret place, they ceremoniously returned the remains of the goose back to the water and left. The Hebert family was again entertained by the adventures of Jacques and Paul. At the fort Jacques recounted his adventures to his friends from the orphanage. They also had many stories to tell, but no one could top Jacques.

When the weather turned colder the Micmacs left the great river for the interior. It was warmer in the wilderness than along the river, and the game was more plentiful there.

With heavy snow on the ground the Hebert girls kept Jacques busy making him hold their yarn in his outstretched arms, so they could roll it into a ball. They measured him for caps, mitts, sweaters and stockings. They were always fussing over him. He tried his best to avoid them; his thoughts were on the outdoors and his canoe.

Activity at the fort dwindled to chores of bringing in food and firewood. For the moment the garrison relaxed.

In the spring of 1710, privateers operating out of Port Royal captured some fishing vessels from the American colonies. The crews of these vessels were brought to Port Royal for interrogation. From the American fishermen it was learned that the English were planning something big against Acadie. Large sailing ships from England were arriving and more were expected. This was disturbing news.

Scouts were sent to observe the Bay of Fundy and especially the entrance to the Annapolis River. All summer long the vigil lasted. When fall approached it was thought that the impending invasion had been postponed until the following year. The French could breathe a little easier.

Early on the morning of October 5, 1710 sails were spotted in the distance in the Bay of Fundy. As the scouts watched, to their horror more sails appeared. It looked like a huge armada was approaching. Quickly the scouts reported to the fort. The news was electrifying. The alarm was given and riders sent all along the river near the fort to warn the residents to report to the fort for protection. Men, women and children were to assemble with as much food as they could carry. Jacques and other able bodied men made many river crossings in their canoes ferrying people and goods. Inside the fort, the women and children were housed in underground bunkers safe from enemy bombardment.

On September 29, 1710, thirty-six transports escorted by four men-of-war vessels from England set out from Massachusetts. Colonel Nicholson, a well-known soldier and statesman, was appointed Commander-in-Chief of the invasion force. Colonel Vetch was second in charge. Colonel Reading was in charge of the marines.

As the invading force made its way through the Gut to enter the Annapolis River, one of the vessels, the Caesar, struck a rock and broke up with a loss of twenty-six.

The alarm had been sounded so quickly and with the necessity to ferry people across the river, Jacques had no time to change from his buckskins to his French uniform. It made no difference to him, or to his commanding officer. Every man was needed at the fort.

As the invading force sailed into view, the fort was made secure. Governor Subercase took stock of the situation. He was aghast to discover that he only had three hundred men; one hundred of them were the young French orphans!

When the English attacked in 1707,and were repelled, the defensive plan had been to send out scouts who ambushed the invaders causing so many losses to the enemy that they retreated.

Governor Subercase had to rethink his strategy this time. His thought was that if he sent anyone out there, it was sure death. He would not blame them if they deserted. He opted to stand and fight. He had done everything possible to strengthen the fort even to the point of paying out of his own pocket for provisions. At one point he made the statement that he would give his last shirt if that would help.

If it had been anyone else but Subercase, prudence would dictate that, seeing the overwhelming force, surrender would be the proper move. Not so with the brave Governor. He would stand his ground and protect his beloved Acadie!

The garrison was positioned and all guns made ready at the fort. The Micmacs were at the fort in full force, ready to do battle. The Indians were eager to send out scouting parties. Governor Subercase held them at bay.

By Monday, October 6, 1710, the enemy fleet was well inside the river and the ships anchored safely away from the range of the guns at the fort. Marines were put ashore to reconnoiter. They reported back that that had made no contact with the French. With no resistance from the settlers, the English disembarked their whole army, taking up positions on either side of the river. They advanced towards the fort.

A British Man-of-War sailed closer to the fort to engage the French with their guns. The battery at the fort opened up maintaining a heavy outpouring of shot without causing any heavy casualties. The young soldiers opened up with their black powder muskets with no effect.

Jacques and Paul were next to each other preparing to exit the fort to scout the area, as they had planned many times before. But, this would be different. They had to man the parapets and defend from within. As Jacques looked around inside the fort, he saw the many French soldiers all standing tall at the gun ports. His young friends were all next to each other, as if for comfort, all bravely facing the onslaught. He was glad his friend Paul was next to him. While Jacques was trembling with fear, he noticed that Paul stood his ground with no emotions. He vowed that he would steel himself and act like his friend. The roar of the cannons and the smell of acrid smoke was too much for some of the lads who took cover and cried.

As the English advanced on foot towards the fort, some brave French settlers, resistance fighters, took up positions in their own wooded areas and ambushed the enemy, but they were driven off. When the way was cleared, Colonel Nicholson led his regiment, in full view of the fort, with banners flying and drummers keeping cadence. They advanced to about one mile of the fort and halted awaiting reinforcements. The small band of resistance fighters made their way to the fort to carry on the fight from there.

As the large enemy force again moved towards the fort other resistance fighters took up positions and opened fire from the protection of their barns and fences. This halted the advance temporarily. The English decided to entrench where they were.

British marines, meanwhile, advanced to within four hundred yards of the fort and provided protection to the large transports unloading their supplies. The enemy now had both sides of the river covered and was well in position. The fort was more or less surrounded.

Towards evening most of the activity died down. At the fort the wounded were taken care of, women and children were allowed out for a brief spell and food was distributed to the soldiers on lookout. Governor Subercase made his rounds, checking out the situation. He asked for volunteers to exit the fort and scout the enemy positions.

The Micmacs indicated they would go. When Jacques saw that Paul was going, he quickly volunteered also. Jacques's orphan friends were shocked when they saw him preparing to leave the safety of the fort.

"Jacques, you will be killed if you go out there!" said his friend, André.

"First, they will have to see me," he replied. He was dressed in his buckskins and looked every part Micmac. The front gate was opened and the scouts exited. Later came the sound of wolves howling near the fort. Every once in a while a hoot owl was heard in the distance.

"Listen to the wolves," said the young French soldiers at the fort.

"Those are not wolves," said André. He had heard Jacques tell him that the Micmacs talk to each other in the darkness using animal calls. He was hoping the scouts were safely reporting enemy positions.

"I wouldn't want to be out there," said young Philippe.

The scouts returned safely with disheartening reports. They informed Governor Subercase that the situation was hopeless. The enemy was well entrenched and even at that moment was setting up cannons to open up at first light. The enemy was all around the fort. Some of the British soldiers would not be fighting the following day. The scouts had killed many during the night. They brought back English firearms and red tunics as souvenirs. The Governor decided to keep the bad news to himself.

During the late hours, unseen by the fort, the British moved their ships closer. Smaller English ships silently sailed past the fort to position themselves below the fort.

The women and children back in their bunkers, the young soldiers having been fed, the scouting forays over, the garrison at the fort settled down for the night.

After Jacques had been relieved of his lookout duty, he sat down to get some rest. With his back against the parapet, he gazed up at the brightly twinkling stars. How peaceful and serene they looked. He had often looked at the heavens at night when he crossed the ocean aboard Le Venus. The jeweled beauty above always fascinated him. He felt the tension of the day easing up on him and he even felt a little sleepy.

Suddenly, a thunderous roar shattered the quiet of the night when an English naval gunship nearby opened fire, sending a huge cannonball crashing in the midst of the fort. The escaping flames of the cannon lit the night sky. Jacques was jolted back to reality by the blinding flash and din. He thought his heart stopped, and he could not swallow. For the longest time, he could not get his thoughts together. He just could not comprehend what was happening. When he finally composed himself and regained his senses, he saw the young lads inside the fort crying like babies. He saw André crouch down with his arms around his head. Philippe admitted later that he had wet his pants.

The shot from the ship had landed inside the fort with a sickening thud, causing no damage. The alarm was given and the men prepared for a night invasion. Unable to see in the dark, the only targets the French had were the flash from the English guns. Their return fire was ineffective.

During the night the English raided the villages on the other side of the river, across from the fort. They were preparing for a long siege.

There was very little sleep that night for the French garrison. By daybreak the French opened up with everything they had on the English who by now were well entrenched. Micmac scouts and French rangers set out to do battle outside the fort. They killed many English soldiers, but the enemy was too numerous.

Inside the fort, Governor Subercase cautioned the young lads to conserve their shot, and only fire when they could be sure of their targets. He had seen the young troopers firing randomly at imaginary enemies.

The battle raged all day long with no end in sight. From inside the bunkers where the women and children were could be heard the cries of terrified children. Once more the fading light of day brought reprieve. Lookouts were posted and the other French were allowed to rest. Ragged, hungry, tired, the weary French soldiers sat with their backs to the bulkheads and their heads drooping to their knees.

Micmac scouts again went out at night to reconnoiter. Again the sound of wolves could be heard throughout the area. The English feared the wolves, thinking they would be attacked at night by fearsome animals. They were to learn that the Micmacs were the ones to fear.

The scouts returned and reported to Subercase. The situation was worse than the previous day. The English had brought up mortars, and more cannons. The Governor decided to let his staff officers in on the situation. They pleaded with the Governor to surrender, but he would not hear of it.

At daybreak the fighting began again. The young orphans were holding their own just as good as the regular older French soldiers. They showed they had spirit and determination. Shot coming from the naval ships did little damage to the fort. The defenders felt they could withstand the bombardment.

Soon after the fighting began, on the second day, with all the men positioned at the parapets, a strange noise was heard; the whining of an incoming shell followed by a tremendous explosion inside the fort. Steel fragments were hurled in all directions injuring many. A piece of red hot metal shattered the wooden barrier just inches from Jacques's head. Paul and Jacques looked at each other and at the splintered wood between them.

"What was that?" asked Jacques.

"Don't know!" replied Paul.

As they looked around at the source of the explosion they saw many men lying down, badly wounded. Some men were just walking about aimlessly, as if in a stupor. The young soldiers looked to the older and more experienced fighting men for an explanation of what just happened. They did not know themselves. The explosion had dug a deep hole in the ground.

As they were contemplating the explosion, another whining noise was heard; immediately followed by another blast. Debris, metal fragments, and dirt were flung far and wide inside the fort. More wounded men fell.

"It must be a new type of shot," said one of the old soldiers.

It was indeed a new type of shot. Instead of the usual solid iron ball, the new shot had explosives in them that went off after a fuse had been ignited, sending iron fragments all over. That new English invention was to prove decisive.

"How can we survive something like that?" asked other soldiers.

Cries of despair could be heard all over the fort, only to be silenced by another exploding missile inside the fort, sending more fragments all over. Soldiers tried to protect themselves by covering their heads with their arms as debris fell upon them. A piece of something struck Jacques's arm causing him to wince in pain. Thankfully, his buckskin prevented more serious harm.

"Something just hit me!" said Jacques to Paul.

"I hear something close to ear pass me," replied Paul. "We get down now."

The blue fabric worn by the French soldiers offered no protection from the flying fragments; soon they were torn to shreds.

Many of the French settlers, volunteers by decree, tired, hungry, scared, and wounded decided to escape the horrors of the battle. They wanted out, leaving the fighting to the regular army. No one objected to their leaving.

The gunners at the fort kept up a steady reply to the British barrage, which must have affected the enemy. They eventually ceased the bombardment. At night when all was quiet, the fallen were buried.

The battle raged into its ninth day, leaving the fort a complete disaster. Still the valiant Governor refused to surrender, even thou it was a lost cause.

On Sunday afternoon, October 12, the enemy fire ceased. Everyone at the fort was wondering what was going on. Surely, the English could not be surrendering. After a short lull, two figures emerged from the English side carrying a white flag.

"Look, Jacques," said Paul, "they have white flag!"

"Maybe they are surrendering," said Jacques. The word quickly spread to the wounded lying about.

"Maybe they want to parley," said André. "They must know we are finished."

Seeing the white flag, the French stopped firing. Two French officers left the fort to meet with the English. After a short discussion, the French officers blindfolded the English and led them into the fort to meet with Governor Subercase. The French did not want the English to see the destruction inside the fort. The English were taken to Governor Subercase's office.

With all his staff officers present, the Governor opened discussions.

"What is the purpose of your visit?" asked the Governor.

"We have come to offer you a chance to surrender and save your people. These are our terms," said the English. They handed the Governor the surrender document.

"You will allow me to confer with my officers," said Governor Subercase.

After a long meeting with his officers, and knowing full well that he had absolutely no chance of winning, he penned his reply to the English terms.

"We will surrender under these terms:

1.   We will be allowed to leave the fort with our colors flying, drums beating, and all soldiers are to retain their arms.

2.   Ships are to be provided to transport the French soldiers back to France.

3.   The French settlers will not be molested and permitted to retain their properties.

4.   Any French settler desiring to leave will be permitted to do so.

Signed Governor Subercase.

The English officers were again blindfolded and led outside the fort. They reported back to Nicholson. The English accepted the terms of surrender.

A day later, the gates of the fort were opened. Waiting outside astride a beautiful stallion was Colonel Nicholson. Standing, at attention, on either side of the entrance were the British Grenadiers forming the guard of honor. Waiting, in the field, were the British army under the command of Colonel Vetch. All dressed in splendid uniforms.

From the fort came the brave Governor Subercase, astride his mount, who met Colonel Nicholson half way along the bridge. Behind the Governor came the remains of his army. As the two leaders met, the Governor handed Nicholson the keys to the fort.

"Hold on to these, I may be back!" said Subercase

"My General," said Nicholson, "I salute you on a valiant defense."

Colonel Nicholson then handed the keys to his next in charge, Colonel Vetch, who was to be the interim Governor. Standing aside, Colonel Nicholson made room for the French to exit. The sight that the English beheld next was so gruesome, the English had to turn away, many vomited.

Following Governor Subercase was his staff officers followed by the French colors, and young drummer boys. Behind the French emblem came the remnants of the defenders. The most heartbreaking sights were the young boys, baldy wounded, with filthy bandages, clothing covered with caked blood. Some of the boys were helping those with leg wounds hobble along. Some were leading those that were blinded and had their faces covered with bandages. Some were carrying the seriously wounded on litters. This was too much for even the hardened English soldiers.

The Micmacs helped other wounded leave the fort. They also had suffered great losses. The women and children were escorted out. When all had exited the fort the British marched in with colors flying and drums beating. They hoisted the union jack and drank to the queen's health. They renamed the area "Annapolis Royal" in honor of Queen Anne of England.

The French soldiers, surrounded by armed guards, were escorted to waiting British ships to be transported back to France according to the terms of surrender.

Jacques, still wearing buckskins was mistaken for a French settler, and allowed to pass through the English line to the waiting line of local settlers.

The settlers, standing behind the line of guards, bade the French soldiers, farewell. Jacques waved to his old orphan friends as they were escorted to the waiting ships. They waved back and saluted him.

Some of the regular French soldiers had their wives with them. They also were allowed to board the ships. There were 258 people in all that left that day. Colonel Nicholson provided sweets for the women and children on board the ships. Rum was provided for the men. Governor Subercase was also put on board the ship to be sent back. The ex Governor of Acadie thanked Colonel Nicholson for dealing gallantly with him.

The British left a force of 300 New Englanders, and 250 marines at the fort. The rest of the enemy sailed for home.

When the Heberts arrived back at their farm, they saw the destruction the English did to their home. Most of their food was gone. The cows, not having been milked in days, were in a stressful condition. As the men attempted to milk the cows, the animals kicked and trashed about in agony. The neighbors in outlying regions that were not molested by the British came to the rescue of those near the fort.

There was an uneasy peace in the small hamlet following the victory by the British. The French and Indians gave the Brits little rest for the next few weeks.

To the consternation of the Micmacs, the British treated them with disdain and contempt. They were feared by the British more than the settlers.

With the approach of the snows, the Hebert root cellar contained enough food to last the winter thanks to the assistance of their neighbors and Indians.

Jacques decided he would winter with his friends, the Micmacs. He wanted to get away and recompose himself after the harrowing experience at the fort.

CHAPTER FIVE

Living with the Micmacs

With the arrival of the cold weather in November of 1710, it was time for the Micmacs to relocate to the interior for the winter. Jacques, now without military obligations was free to move about as he wished.

"Come with us," said Paul.

Jacques discussed it with the Heberts and decided it would be a good thing to winter with his friends. The Indians usually always went back to their favorite sites, however, the newlywed Micmacs had to find their own places deeper into the wilderness. The site chosen by the elder Efraim long ago was near a large pond. They were able to fish the pond by breaking through the ice in the winter.

Jacques found that his bed, made up of pine boughs and bear skins, was very soft and comfortable. A small fire kept the inside of the wigwam quite warm during the cold months.

Rising early the first morning in the wilderness, Jacques stepped outside, stretched his arms, looked about, and went into the thick woods. The sky was a deep overcast, and the pond was covered with a fine mist. Deep in the distance the spectral sound of a loon could be heard, carrying for miles. Nearby, he heard a twig snap and the sound of something roaming around. He told himself that the next time he ventured out alone he must carry his knife. He dashed back to the wigwam, and once inside, threw some more wood on the fire.

He was now very fluent in the Micmac language, and would not speak French again till he went back to the village and the Heberts. Life with the Micmacs was the tonic he needed to get back on his feet. He had to put the memory of the horrors of war out of his mind.

The men in the wigwam enjoyed sitting around, smoking their pipes and telling stories. The women were always busy cooking and making things from animal skins. Jacques had just been fitted with a warm pair of mukluks. The Hebert girls had made him plenty of warm woolen clothing so he was set for the cold winter months ahead.

Jacques learned that the wild tobacco used by the Indians was not only for the pleasure of smoking, but also used to appease the spirits of the wilderness and animals. The Indians held that tobacco was a powerful magical medicine.

One evening as they were gathered around the fire, the elder Efraim recounted the story of the drowned Micmac.

"We were fishing in the great river one day. There were two canoes in our group. One of the canoes tipped over and the men swam to our canoe and held on, but one of the men couldn't make it. We quickly paddled over to where he was and held on to him while we made our way to shore. When we pulled him out, he wasn't breathing. We took a rope and tied it around his ankles and hoisted him up, upside down from a large oak tree so the water would flow from him. We took an empty bladder and filled it with smoke and inserted the opening into his rectum and forced the smoke into him. Doing all we could, we sat down to rest and reflect on having lost one of our dear friends. A short time later he started to moan. He came back to us. Don't tell me tobacco isn't powerful."

A few weeks after setting up camp the first really heavy snow came. The elder Efraim was jubilant. "Now, we will hunt the moose," he said.

The Indians had made Jacques a pair of snowshoes. He had never seen anything like it and didn't quite know how to use them. They explained it to him. He would have to try it out by himself to get the hang of it. They also made him some eye protection from the glare of the white snow. It was a piece of birch bark with two tiny slits.

Early the next morning, after a hearty breakfast, the men set out. Their small dog would accompany them. Jacques and Paul brought up the rear. Jacques was getting the hang of the snowshoes. They kept him from sinking into the soft snow. The snowshoes distributed his weight over a large area thereby decreasing the amount of downward pressure per square inch on the snow. The dog had a little bit of a problem trying to keep from sinking, so he more or less hopped along.

"See these tracks," said Efraim, as he pointed out the prints in the snow, "deer, heading that way."

The little dog was going crazy sniffing all over the place. Evidently he could smell the other animals; he kept trying to mark every tree he came to. Going a little further, Efraim saw something on a tree.

"Over here, look…a bear was here not too long ago." He pointed out a tuft of hair clinging to the bark of the tree. "The bear must have rubbed himself against the tree."

Trudging along, Efraim reached out and took something from the bark of a pine tree and put it in his mouth.

"Try some of this, Jacques," said Efraim, as he pointed out a glob of dried pinesap. Jacques pried the glob off the tree and put it in his mouth. It tasted a little tart but was very chewy and kept his mouth moist. He enjoyed it. It would last for hours in his mouth. Woodpeckers opened up holes in the trees causing the sap to flow out until it dried and formed a plug, this was the well-known spruce gum used by Indians.

Proceeding on, suddenly Efraim stopped short.

"Moose…heading that way," pointing westward. He took a small leather bag containing tobacco, from around his waist, and sprinkled a small amount into the wind. As the tobacco wafted away Efraim prayed. "Spirit of the moose person. It is I, Efraim. We need food, you must help us."

Jean-Pierre blew into a birch bark moose call. To Jacque's amazement, the sound of a moose could be heard nearby.

"He is over there," said Jean-Pierre, pointing westward.

"You two boys wait here," said Efraim, "we will circle around and head him this way. Paul knows what to do."

Paul showed Jacques how to hide behind a small pine tree. The plan was to ambush the animal when it came by them. They were to spear the animal with their homemade lances. Paul was on one side and Jacques on the other. They could hear Jean-Pierre's moose call every once in a while. Jacques could feel his heart pounding with anticipation. He was getting all set for the kill. The dog followed Jean-Pierre and Efraim after the moose. They could hear him barking.

"They must see the moose," said Paul. "That is when the dog barks."

It became eerily silent for a while, and then they heard the furious barking of the dog.

"Get ready," said Paul, "when the dog barks like that, he is after the moose."

The snapping of branches could be heard as the animal crashed through the thicket. The heavy snow prevented it from making good time. Efraim and Jean-Pierre, running on either side of the animal, drove it towards the waiting boys.

"Here he comes!" shouted Paul.

Just as it neared, Paul threw his lance piercing the animal's side. Jacques quickly did the same on his side. The large animal went down. It had been hit by arrows from the elder men and was already badly wounded. Right behind the moose was the little dog, frantically snapping at flailing legs. As soon as the moose went down, Paul was on it with his knife. He quickly sliced the jugular vein. In a moment all was silent. The dog sniffed at the moose, wagging his tail as if he had brought the animal down.

"Good work boys," said Efraim when he arrived. When Jean-Pierre arrived, he looked at the fallen animal and prayed, "Thank you moose person for giving up your life that we may live."

They ceremoniously prepared the animal. The men cut long poles from saplings and made a one man towing drag by tying two long poles with shorter poles, laying the short poles across the longer ones. Quartering the moose, they put as much meat on the drags as they could. They made three drags. Then they made a lean-to shelter and built a fire. The plan was for Efraim to remain behind, guarding the rest of the meat while the younger men towed the meat to the wigwam. They would return and get the rest of the meat as soon as possible.

For days after, the men told and retold the story of the great hunt, while contently puffing on their pipes. The women listened in awe. The meat would last all winter long, and then some. The skin was highly prized. Every part of the animal was used. The bladder became a watertight container, the bones for tools and ornaments. The meat was cut into thin strips and hung over a smoking fire outside. This cured meat would last all winter long with no preservatives needed. The intestines were cleaned and stuffed with meat and herbs, and also cured by smoke rising from a small fire.

The elder men would sit around the fire at night and tell stories of how they killed their first moose by themselves. It was a tradition in the Micmac tribes that no young man would get married until he had killed a moose by himself.

They needed no books or modern conveniences to amuse themselves. They loved to tell stories, and everyone loved to listen to them.

Jacques made many hunting trips with the Indians. He learned how to set traps to snare rabbits and small game. He learned how to build an emergency shelter quickly by placing a long pole between two trees and leaning other poles over the first one and covering the whole thing with pine branches, and moss. The idea was to build it so that is provided protection from the wind.

"Once, my father built one of those," said the elder Efraim. "He had it all set and built a fire in front. But, the wind blew the fire towards the shelter while my father was in it, and he almost got burned." This drew some laughter from the youngsters.

Jacques learned how to trap beaver. Now, there was an animal. Its pelt was worth more than gold. The Europeans prized beaver pelts so much they were willing to pay anything. The proper gentry in Europe wore top hats made from beaver pelts. These prized hats were very fashionable, and expensive. The Indians traded with Europeans that sailed their ships to Acadie. The beaver pelt is one of the most luxurious of skins. Its fur is remarkably soft.

The Micmacs made snares and placed them underwater, securing one end to a submerged heavy rock. They usually placed a piece of the beaver's favorite tree next to the snare. Everyday they made the rounds collecting beaver pelts. In the winter when the ice formed over the ponds, the Micmacs would break a hole in the ice and wait for the beaver to poke its head through for air, and then they would grab its paws and yank it out.

Jacques learned what plants were edible in the wilderness and how to live off the land if he had to. Even the pine needles were nutritional, and when brewed, made a fine tea. He was taught that by scooping up a bit of ash from the fireplace everyday that this would make a fine toothbrush.

He spent many hours in the wigwam making things from leather such as shirts, trousers, and sandals. His favorite past time was making a bow and arrow. Paul made a drum from a piece of untreated skin. Skin untreated was called buckskin and had a tendency to shrink after a while. It was stiff and hard to manage, but when stretched over a hoop, it tightened and became a good drum. Paul enjoyed playing his drum for his family. They sang many Indian songs together.

"Grandfather," said Paul, "tell us about Ulgimoo, the magician."

"Oh, yes," replied Efraim. "Ulgimoo."

The family gathered around the fire to listen to the elder Efraim. He was quite a storyteller. As the wind blew outside, and the temperature dropped to below freezing, they huddled together under their heavy furs, just as content at could be. Puffing on his pipe, in the flickering light of the fire, he began.

"Ulgimoo had a magic pipe, and when he ran out of tobacco, Kiunik, the otter, would go and get him some. Ulgimoo lived over a hundred years. He had instructed his people not to bury him after he died. So, after he died they did not bury him and placed his body high up in a structure, deep in the woods. He was there all winter long, and when spring came, they went out to see if he was still there. They found him wandering about.

"Ulgimoo lived for many years after that until one day he felt ill. He instructed his people to bury him after he died, and after the second day they must dig him up and he would come back and be with them. After he died, they dug a deep grave and stacked it with many stones to make sure he stayed there. He has been there ever since."

They all laughed at his story, glad that Ulgimoo did not come back.

Efraim also told of the many battles he had fought in. The Indians were territorial and any outside tribes entering one's territory was an invitation to do battle. The worst enemy was reputed to have been the Mohawks from New York. The Mohawks took great pleasure in torturing their enemies if captured and brought back. They devised all sorts of horrible things to do to the victims causing the greatest amount of pain without killing them. If the victim did not cry out during the ordeal and subsequently died, his heart was cut out and eaten. It was assumed that one could gain the courage of the victim by eating his heart.

Efraim told of the first European settlers that came here. They, of course, were the French. The settlers were not aware of the severe cold winters in Acadia and did not come prepared to live here. They ate of the meager rations they had which did not last long and did not provide the nutrients needed for survival. They tried to eat just meat, which is not good. The Micmacs showed them what vegetations in the wilderness would help them. After learning this, they were able to survive.

The seven people in the wigwam spent the blistering cold snowy months as happy as could be. They passed the time singing and telling stories. There was always laughter. Jean-Pierre kept teasing his son, Paul, that one day he would have to leave the family and raise a family of his own. First, he would have to find a suitable mate. Then, he would have to move in with her family in their wigwam before marrying her to see if they could get along. He would have to prove that he could provide for the family, and he would have to kill a moose by himself, if possible.

In March of 1711, four months after moving to the interior, the snows had not yet stopped; in fact this month brought the most snow. They had to clear a path to exit the wigwam. One afternoon, in the midst of a heavy snowstorm, while the family gathered around the fire to brew some tea, a sound was heard in the distance. The dog instantly began barking.

"What was that?" asked Anne, Paul's younger sister, as she looked around. The dog was wagging his tail in anticipation.

"I didn't hear anything," said Mary. No one else had heard anything. Anne shrugged and went back to her sewing. Then she hear it again...a soft call from far off.

"There it is again!" said Anne. Again the dog started barking and wagging its tail.

"It must be a bear," said Jean-Pierre. The dog went to the exit flap so they let it out. Soon, the dog was barking frantically.

"Wonder what he sees," asked Paul.

Another sound came from outside. This time they all heard it. Someone was out there. Jean-Pierre put his heavy parka on and went outside to investigate.

"Be careful Jean," said Mary. The boys got their bows and arrows ready. Jean-Pierre stood up outside the cleared path and shouted, "Who is out there?"

"It is I, Father Leger, and my guide, Chrisostome," came the reply. The local missionary was making his rounds. He did not want to wait for the snows to melt, fearing someone might need him; who is ill, who has not had their baby baptized, who wants to go to confession.

Jean-Pierre went back in the wigwam and announced it was only Father Leger and his guide. They were relieved. Jean-Pierre went back out to greet the visitors.

Two travelers, weary from their trek stumbled into the wigwam, Jean-Pierre right behind them. They were encrusted with so much snow they looked like white bears. The dog was barking frantically at them, unsure just what they were. The Indian guide half carried the exhausted priest inside. Father Leger's face was covered with the white powder. As the priest brushed the snow away, Jacques was surprised to see that the priest had a full beard. Indians never had beards, so this was a strange sight. The priest's eyes were so sunken in from the cold he looked terrible. His skin was as white as the snow. Quickly, the priest reached out to warm his hands over the fire.

The Indian guide, a large man, wasn't the least bit concerned about the cold. He was a jovial and most pleasant person. He greeted everyone and smiled, and then he helped the good father with his heavy clothing. Paul put some more wood on the fire.

Mary already had tea brewed so she gave a cup to the priest and his guide.

"Here you go, Father," she said. "This should take some of the cold away."

"Thank you, Mother," said Father Leger, as he crouched near the fire. He was wearing a large crucifix around his neck and it swung dangerously close to the fire. He quickly arched back and secured it in his shirt pocket.

"My, how beautiful that is," said Mary when she saw the cross. Father Leger held it up for all to see. It was an exquisite piece of work, very well polished.

The hot tea and the warm fire brought some of his color back because the priest's skin returned to a rosy pink. Mary covered the priest with a large bearskin, which he was most thankful for.

The women prepared a meal for the visitor, which was eaten with gusto by the visitors. The guide kept coming back for more. He had a tremendous appetite.

"It's a good thing we don't have to feed him all the time," said Mary. "We would have to hunt everyday." This made them all laugh, except for the guide who just shrugged and grinned.

Father Leger, now warmed and relaxed, looking about, noticed Jacques. That's strange, thought the priest. He is dressed like a Micmac, but has blond hair and blue eyes.

"Where are you from, Son," asked Father Leger to Jacques, in the Micmac language.

"I'm from Paris, France, Father," replied Jacques, also in the Micmac language.

"Oh," said Father Leger, "then you speak French?"

"Oui, mon Pere," replied Jacques.

Father Leger was delighted to hear the French language and he asked

Jacques how he ended up here. They conversed in French and Jacques explained how his parents died, the orphanage and joining the army.

After spending the night in the lodge, the priest and his guide left the following day.

In April, the weather had warmed up enough to move back to the Annapolis River. They set up camp at the same place they had the previous year. Soon, the other Indians arrived and it was a time for rejoicing and renewing fellowships.

With a large supply of meat, Jacques set out in his canoe to visit his adopted family. Antoine Hebert, working outside saw Jacques nearing the farm. He called his family to come out and greet him. After beaching his canoe, the whole family was there to greet him with hugs and kisses. Magdelaine threw her arms around him and held him the longest. Jacques was speechless when he beheld her. She had been a little scrawny thing the last time he saw her, now she was beginning to fill out. He found it hard to keep his eyes away from her. For the first time in his life he found that fishing and hunting were not so important in his life anymore.

He was now as tall as Antoine and just as strong. Magdelaine was completely captivated by him. He was starting to sport a very thin beard, which made him look older than he was. The older girls fussed over him more than ever.

In the summer of 1711 the British commander at the fort asked the local settlers for assistance in procuring wood to rebuild the fort. When word of this reached the Catholic Pastor, Reverend Father Couvier, at Annapolis Royal, he was furious. He informed his parishioners that anyone helping the British would have their homes burned to the ground by the Micmacs. The locals then informed that British commander that they feared reprisals from the Indians should they assist the British.

"We shall see about this," stormed the commander. He ordered a captain to take a force of eighty men and march downriver to capture some Indians. He wanted to make examples of them. When the force was ready and prepared to set out, the sight of the armed soldiers spread fear throughout.

Jacques, who had been at the market square near the fort, saw the soldiers marching in the direction of the Indian camp. He quickly ran to the where his canoe was beached, pushed off and paddled feverishly across the river to the Heberts. He quickly bridled a horse, and without benefit of a saddle, was mounted and lit out for the Micmac camps below the river. He was able to warn the Micmacs of the approaching British soldiers. The Indians quickly armed themselves and prepared to do battle. Taking his bow and arrows from Paul's wigwam, he joined the Indians.

They laid in wait, hiding behind trees, signaling with crow calls. Jacques and Paul again side by side. This time the battle would be fought the Indian way. The British, unaware, marched towards the waiting Indians. The trap worked perfectly. Arrows flew from all directions. The British didn't know what was happening. Jacques and Paul, both expert marksmen with their weapons, brought down several. In a few minutes, thirty British soldiers were killed; the remainders surrendered and were taken captive.

This skirmish would go down in the annals of history as the battle of

Bloody Creek, summer of 1711. The small victory gave the French settlers much joy. The British commander had previously ordered the local settlers to remain near the fort following the fall of Port Royal. Now, with impunity, some of the settlers packed and left. The garrison now feared leaving the safety of the fort to arrest anyone.

Jacques, who had at times been treated as an outsider by some of the Indians, now found himself the object of admiration. He had fought bravely with the Micmacs, standing tall in full view of the enemy, bullets flying all around, and loosening his arrows. He was even decorated by Chief Cope, an extremely high honor. He had been presented with a feather. Had the Indians been captured, it would have demoralized the rest of the Micmacs and the settlers. The British would have had cause to boast and show off their trophies.

Before this event, the English took advantage of the French settlers by offering a small fraction of what their supplies were really worth. The English garrison now found they had to pay large sums to the settlers to provide them with essential goods following the defeat at Bloody Creek.

When it came time for the Micmacs to again move into the interior with the approach of the cold weather, Paul decided he would set up his own camp in preparation for his eventual marriage. When Jacques heard of this he pleaded with Paul to go with him. The two agreed they would try to survive the cold winter by themselves. When the time came to leave the Annapolis River, Paul and Jacques set out. They hiked deep into the wilderness. Paul was looking for a pond, not only for drinking water, but also to trap beaver.

As Jacques trailed behind Paul, he wondered how Paul knew which way to go. Everything looks the same. All the trees look alike; there is no reference point to navigate by.

"Paul," said Jacques. "I think we are just walking in circles."

"No, my friend," replied Paul, "we are heading east."

"Well, how do you know which way east is?" Asked Paul. "Everything looks the same."

"Because, the sun never sets on the north side of these trees so the north side always has green stuff on it."

Jacques noticed that Paul was right. There was some kind of green vegetation only on one side of the trees. So, if the green algae were always on the north side of the trees, they could easily navigate a straight line.

"Besides," said Paul, "we follow the flow of streams, or the cast of shadows when the sun is out, or notice the flight of the geese."

The eventually found a small pond, created by beavers. They were miles from nowhere. "How's this?" asked Paul.

"Looks good to me."

The boys unloaded their packs and the first order of business was building a shelter. They cut some long poles. Jacques thought they would build an igloo shelter, but Paul said the ground was too hard to sink the poles in. They tied the ends of three long poles together. Two of the poles would be the frame, while the third pole would be the ridgepole, or top pole. They made another A frame, securing that to the ridge pole. Everything was tied together with roots. They stacked more poles leaning against the structure, eventually covering their hut. They placed horizontal poles inside the structure for added support and to hang their meats and things. Now, they had a makeshift shelter. The cracks were filled with moss, and clay. They brought all their supplies inside and built a fire. It was remarkably warm, so much so that they had to remove their heavy parkas. The smoke rose and filtered through the cracks at the top.

Hungry and tired after trekking through the forest Jacques said he was hungry.

"We will make a warm stew now," said Paul.

"In case you haven't noticed, my friend," said Jacques. "We forgot the kettle. All we have are the metal cups and spoons."

"We never used metal kettles till the Frenchmen arrived."

"So, I guess you never had warm stew then."

"Of course we did."

"Without a metal kettle?"

"Yes."

"What did you use?"

"I will show you, my friend," replied Paul. "You build a fire outside now."

While Jacques was gathering the material to build another fire outside, Paul gathered some large stones. Once the fire was going, Paul placed the stones in the fire.

"Now, we make kettle." Said Paul. He took his hatchet and proceeded to cut into a large fallen tree. He chipped away a large round opening, roughly the size of a kettle. Then he got some water from the nearby pond with a gourd and filled the 'kettle' in the log. Once the fire had been going and the stones heated, he picked up a hot stone, using two small pieces of wood, and placed it into the kettle. The water sizzled as the hot stone sank. Removing the cooled stone, he was careful not to place that back in the fire lest it explode from the trapped steam within. He took another stone from the fire and inserted that into the kettle. In short order the kettle had boiling water.

"Now we cook stew," said Paul. Taking some of their dried meat he used that as a base. He dug up some roots and placed that in the stew along with some wild vegetation, washing everything in the pond before putting it in the stew.

After their meal, Jacques said, "Paul, that was the most delicious stew I ever had." Of course it wasn't, but he wanted Paul to think it was great. In fact, it was a very good stew. Who would have thought to make a kettle out of a fallen log? Paul explained that the Indians used this technique for thousands of years. They made their own maple syrup that way. Was there no end to the secrets of the Micmacs?

Paul and Jacques wintered in the wilderness with no problems. They hunted and treated the many skins they had. The beavers were plentiful. There was always something to do. In the evening they would sit around the fire, smoking their pipes and tell each other about their dreams for the future.

Inside the shelter at night, just before dropping off to sleep, gazing into the fire, Jacques thoughts were on the little blond haired girl at the Hebert farm. She had grown so much lately. Every time they looked at each other, they both felt something was there. He was enjoying his camping trip, but secretly he longed to be with her.

When the warmer weather returned in 1712, the boys were glad to get back to the big river. Their shelter was packed with so many furs; they hardly had any room left.

They had to make many trips back and forth from their shelter to the market square to trade their pelts. English money was now the official currency so they had to trade their furs for English pounds. Paul and Jacques did very well for themselves.

CHAPTER SIX

Initiated into the Micmac tribe

Following the capture of Port Royal, the British were enthusiastic about their new prize. Nova Scotia was rich in furs, timber, minerals, and the nearby waters provided abundant fishing.

The problem the British had was with the French settlers living there. Not only did they vex the British, they also caused the local Indians to harass the garrison stationed at Annapolis Royal. To make matters worse there was the difference in religious affiliations. This difference in faiths was the main cause of conflict.

The Roman Catholic missionaries in Canada had been very successful in proselytizing the natives, so much so, that they induced them to raid the colonies telling the natives that they would be doing the work of the Great Spirit in Heaven by ridding the colonies of the Protestant British subjects.

In 1713, France and England signed a peace treaty at Utrecht. This treaty ceded all of Nova Scotia, except Cape Breton, to the British. Now that the British were in complete control of Nova Scotia, more plans were drawn to deal with the French.

The English government demanded all French settlers living in Nova Scotia to either sign an oath of allegiance to the Crown of England, or leave. This was a reasonable endeavor, after all Nova Scotia was now a British sovereign territory.

Swearing allegiance to one's government was, and still is, common among nations. This was routinely done in all the colonies, and even today, the Americans recite the Pledge of Allegiance whenever they salute the American flag. Officials, from the President of the United States of America down to all the members who serve in the Armed Forces, swear an oath of allegiance. All immigrants who become naturalized citizens swear and oath of allegiance to the United States of America. So, demanding that the French swear and oath of allegiance to the rulers of the territory they live in was justified.

The oath required by the British in Nova Scotia would bind the French to serve England. The oath also specified that the settlers would be free to practice their religion as it applies to England. The problem was that England at that time forbid the practice of the Roman Catholic faith; therefore, it was feared by the French that the oath would require them to renounce their Roman Catholic beliefs, and in the event of war to take up arms against their own countrymen.

At the Hebert farm, late one evening, as the two men sat in their comfortable chairs by the fireplace, drinking spruce beer, Jacques and Antoine discussed the situation.

"We've been here for over a hundred years. We cleared this land and made it what it is, and now they want to kick us out!" said Antoine Hebert.

"Well, they don't want to kick us out, as you say. They just want to make sure we do not turn on them. The garrison at the fort is undermanned, and it would be easy to take the fort should the French decide to attack," said Jacques.

"You can be sure the French will fight again. We have been fighting the British for years. This place has changed hands so many times lately you never know what is going to happen."

"What do you think is going to happen?" asked Jacques.

"We've been here before. They invade and win, and we come back and take it away from them. This has happened seven times already. Acadie has changed hands many times, but we always come back. We will win again."

"I hope so," replied Jacques.

"Now, they want us to sign an oath of allegiance to England!" said Antoine, disgustedly. The Hebert girls were a little upset when they saw Antoine carry on so much. He was a powerful man, capable of taking care of himself, but usually quite good-natured; still he was not a man to trifle with.

When the British learned that the French would rather leave than sign the oath of allegiance another problem cropped up. At that time, some English settlers were arriving and taking up residence in Nova Scotia. Those newly arrived English relied on the French to provide them with essential goods. The French were also instrumental in keeping the Indians away from the English. Should the French leave; the English would be at the mercy of the hated Indians. The garrison at Annapolis Royal also depended on the locals for their supplies.

The English Governor, Nicholson, persuaded the French to stay for the time being, and put off demanding the signing of the oath of allegiance. For now, there was an uneasy peace.

Jacques maintained his dual role in Nova Scotia living with the Heberts during the summer and with the Micmacs the rest of the year.

When an Indian boy reached a certain age, he was initiated and received into the world of the warrior. When Paul came of age, he was informed that he would be initiated. Hearing this, Jacques petitioned the elders to be included. The Indian council considered his case and after deliberating decided to accept him. Some argued against him, but the majority won citing certain acts that he performed; did he not warn the tribe about the planned attack against them by the British. Did he not fight with them, even exposing himself and displaying valor? Did he not fire on the enemy? His exploits at the fort earlier were cited also.

When the day came for the initiates to start their training, Paul and Jacques eagerly joined the ranks. They were led deep into the interior for indoctrination. There were many lessons to be learned, such as survival, tracking, signaling, forms of attack, etc.

At their chosen site, Chief Cope had the initiates sit in a semicircle. He proceeded to teach them traditions passed down from generation to generation.

"Life is a circle," began the great chief. "Life begins when we are born, just as the day begins when the sun rises in the east. The east represents the ages from infant to fifteen; therefore the east is the first direction we turn to pray. The sun rises in the east bringing warmth and strength for the day. It is the direction of the children, and blessings are asked from the Creator that they may be protected and safely brought to adulthood. We call upon the eagle "Gitpu," keeper of the eastern door, to provide good fortune for us.

"We pray to the sun and call him "Egjsagamaw," which means Great Chief. We thank the sun for the dawn, and ask him for protection for our families and for good hunting, many fish, and a long life.

"We know that our enemy tribes in the west fear us because they believe we have special powers because the sun decided to shine upon us first, before them. Our enemies will not look a Micmac in the eye for fear of that special power.

"For many, many moons, our elders have instructed young warriors into the mysteries of the spirits. There are many spirits, some are human and some are non-human. The animals, plants, the winds, even the earth; are all guided by their spirits. Even stone can be given a spirit if it is shaped like an object. Some spirits are good, and some are bad.

"When you go into the woods to hunt you must be aware of the spirit of Migamawesu, the spirit of the woods. Bring wild tobacco with you when you hunt and offer it to Migamawesu. He will help you. If you do not offer him his tobacco he will be angry, and may harm you. If you offer him some tobacco he will teach you the many secrets of the woods and animals. He will then look out for you and keep you from danger. As you travel in the woods, if you listen you can hear him trampling on the dry leaves as he follows you."

Excitedly, Jacques turned to Paul and said, "Paul, I have heard him many times in the woods, I always thought it was just an animal."

"No," replied Paul, "that was Migamawesu."

"Good thing we always offer our tobacco when we go into the woods."

Chief Cope went on to say, "When you hunt and kill an animal for food, always prepare a place for Migamawesu. He will arrive and eat with you, either in human form, or perhaps as a spirit.

"The south is the second direction we turn to, to pray. This is the direction of the womenfolk. This is the direction from which the spirit woman brought the pipe to the Micmac people. We pray to the south that the womenfolk walk in a good way so they may provide strength and understanding to others.

"We live in the circle of the south for another fifteen years. The south is also the direction of the thunder spirit. It is the direction that brings the warm weather, the rains, and the seasons. It is the direction from which the geese return.

"I will now tell you about the maiden's dream. Many years ago a young maiden had a dream. She dreamt that a floating island would arrive to the shores of the land of the Micmac. This floating island had tall trees and standing on the limbs of these trees were bears. One day the floating island did arrive, and we now know that the island in the maiden's dream was a French sailing vessel. It brought us many wonderful gifts, things made of iron such as pots, pans, kettles, hatchets, knives, and the long gun. We are thankful for these gifts.

"The French also introduced us to the Great Spirit in Heaven who makes His intentions known to us through His helpers, the black robes. We have learned much from these black robes.

"The west is the third direction we pray to. We arrive at the west after spending fifteen years in the south. This is the direction of our grandfathers. This is the direction of those who have journeyed to the spirit world. We pray to the west to these spirits and ask for favors. We ask for long life, and that our children may grow strong. This is the direction where the sun leaves and sleeps for the night. This is the direction that brings darkness. As the sun leaves the sky in the west, so do we after many years leave the western direction to face the north and prepare to visit our grandfathers in the spirit world.

"We pray to Kesoult and thank him for his many gifts. He has instructed us to hunt only for the food we need a day at a time. We do not kill animals for the sake of killing. We eat the animal's flesh, and use his skin as clothing for ourselves. We hunt birds for food, and use their feathers for our ornaments. Kesoult has provided us with food we can obtain even from the waters. He has provided us with many eels which we can eat either cooked or raw. He has taught us to lay tough moose meat on stones and beat it until it becomes soft, and we can enjoy it. He has taught us to place our fish in the sun for many days to dry, which we can eat during the cold days and it will still be good. He has taught us how to make fire by using the magic stones we find at the seashore and striking them together.

"Kesoult showed our women how to preserve fire by carrying it around in rotten pine wood covered with ash. Some women even have this fire after three moons. After three moons, this fire becomes sacred and we send young men out to gather all peoples around us to come and pray with us. All the men light their pipes from this fire and then they suck the smoke and keep it in their mouths and one by one puff it out in to the face of the woman who has last preserved the spark, telling her that she is worthy above all to share in the blessings of the father of light because she has so skillfully preserved his gift. Then we dance around the fire all night.

"We are taught never to give the bones of animals we eat to our dogs, but to either burn them or toss them into the water. It is best to throw them into the water where the beaver lives, so that the beaver would be with us always. All the bones of the fish we catch from the sea must be returned to the sea, so that the species will always exist."

The lessons went on all day long, breaking from time to time for food and other duties. Late into the evening, sitting around a fire, the lessons continued.

"The north is the fourth direction we pray to. This is the direction of the white bear spirit. The bear is a medicine animal. He teaches medicine and healing to the Micmac people. The north is the direction of winter; it cleanses the earth and brings renewal of life. The north is also the direction of the white wolf that is a teacher and protector. The white wolf teaches survival and leadership. When you have arrived at the north, you have traveled on the circle of life and have arrived closer to the spirit world."

At days end they retired for the night.

The following day the chief assembled his initiates again and explained the art of oration, the telling of stories and of what took place in the past. He explained that at social gatherings such as weddings, funerals, powwows, etc. they would recite the names, events, and stories of their ancestors going back many generations. He spoke about the many battles the tribe took part in.

"I will now tell you about Jepijgam, the horned snake. The horn of this snake gives special powers to those who posses it. Attached to the forehead of an enemy it can never be removed. It will grow and wrap itself around a tree forever holding the captive.

"As you become a true warrior, you must be able to kill a moose all by yourself. This will prove to your future wife's family that you are capable of caring and providing for her. When you kill a moose, you will receive a feather for your bonnet. You will receive a feather for every enemy you kill, and every act of bravery you perform."

Jacques looked about and saw the many braves with their feathered bonnets. What tales they could tell, he pondered. He beheld the bonnet worn by Chief Cope. It had so many feathers that it trailed down to the lower part of his back. The chief was dressed in beautifully adorned animal skins with designs either painted or attached with colored porcupine quills. He was an extremely tall man with a fine physique. His hair, pitch black, was pulled back and braided under his bonnet. He wore a copper bracelet on his left arm at the wrist, which caught Jacques's eye.

"Look at that shiny thing on his arm," whispered Jacques to Paul.

"Yes," said Paul. "I was looking at that. They find that metal in the ground near the bay across the mountains from the great river."

Jacques noticed the bone handled knife in the chief's scabbard. He leaned over to whisper to Paul about that when the chief spoke, bringing him back to the moment.

"We will teach you how to make moose calls from birch bark and how to imitate the moose. We will show you how to attract the moose using the bones from his shoulder blade. When you rub the shoulder blade against a tree the moose will hear that and think there is another moose nearby getting ready to do battle. He will charge from his hiding place and expose himself.

"We will teach you how to use the birch bark moose call when you are near a pond. If you fill the moose call with water and slowly pour it back in, it will sound like a cow urinating. This will surely bring the moose to you.

"The moose has very big ears. They can pinpoint your location even over long distances. They know exactly where you are. They have a very large nose and a sharp sense of smell. For those two reasons it is almost impossible to sneak up to a moose. If you hunt the moose you must learn which way the wind is blowing by throwing sand into the air and go in the direction the wind is blowing from. You have to get him curious so he will investigate.

"The female moose will often come when called. She moves in very quietly to investigate and will camouflage herself well. An untrained person can walk within a few feet of the female and never notice her.

"The moose can be like a ghost in the woods and quietly disappear in a few seconds. It is easy for them to do so because people have a poor sense of smell and forget to look beyond the obvious.

"You will never find a dead moose in the woods. When the animal grows old it goes into the sea and turns into a whale. When the whale grows old it beaches itself, and turns into a young moose. This is why both meats have a similar taste.

"When you kill a moose you must thank its spirit for providing food for you and that you will treat its bones with respect."

Finishing his teachings for the day, the young warriors were treated to a delicious meal of venison and wild turkey. As the sun set, more wood was placed on the fire until a huge blaze was going. Chief Cope summoned the drummers. The rhythmic sounds brought a chant from one of the Indians, soon followed by others. The infectious sounds stirred the emotions of all the men and they all joined in. Chief Cope began to dance around the huge blaze. The lesser chiefs joined in followed by the younger braves and the initiates.

Jacques was beside himself with joy as he danced with his friends. The smoke from the fire rose and blended itself with the velvet black of the sky above. The heavens were aglow with twinkling stars. In the far distance came the sound of the wolves mixing with the sounds of the Micmacs, two spirits uniting. The dance continued far into the night as one by one the weary warriors slipped away to sleep.

The early rising sun found them all sprawled out, too tired to rise. It was nearly noon before the group was up and about.

"Paul," said Jacques, "that was the best time I ever had."

"Yes, it is good being here," replied Paul.

Training continued, and now it was time to learn strategic maneuvers. They were taught the art of locating each other in the wilderness when attacking an enemy. During the day, they imitated crows, in the evening they would imitate wolves, at night the owls.

They were shown how to make arrows pertaining to their tribe using different materials such as flint, bone, and even antlers.   When the arrow tips were made of flint the warriors were taught how to secure the point to the shaft, such that once it had penetrated an enemy the tip would remain behind should he attempt to remove the arrow, not very pleasant but effective. Lessons were given on how to season the shafts by tying them in bundles and hanging them over a fire.

The young warriors were led into the wilderness to learn survival and the ways of the animals.

"Here is rosehip berry," said their instructor, as he pointed to a plant. "We use this to color our clothing and for food. When you crush the seed it makes a salve good for cuts and burns. It also makes a delicious tea."

"Here is raspberry. This is also used to color things. The leaves make a good tea.   The shoots provide food for survival.   This is good for stomach problems.

"Here is plantain. The leaves can be boiled and eaten. The seeds can be dried and ground into flour. The leaves can be brushed on the skin to relieve rashes or itches. When the leaves are pounded into a poultice, the mixture heals wounds, and even sprains.

"Here is red clover which makes a good tea, also good for coughs.

"Here is spruce. This tree provides us with glue for making canoes. The dried sap makes a fine chewing gum. The leaves make a tea rich in nutrients. The roots are used to make rope to sew birch bark onto our shelters or to sew a basket.

"Here is balsam. This tree will keep you from starving in the wilderness. The leaves make an excellent tea. The sap also makes very good glue for canoes and things. You can even eat the bark, and it is good for aches and pains. The inner bark can be dried and ground into flour.

"Here is cedar. The inner bark can be braided into rope. The outer bark is what we burn in ceremonies to ward off evil spirits. Cedar boughs placed under your beds will cure some sicknesses. I've often seen bears make a nest out of cedar boughs. Thin cedar strips are used for the inner lining of our birch bark canoes. We use cedar mostly for making arrows, and even pipes."

"So much to learn," said Jacques to his friend.

"Yes," replied Paul, "we've been taught these secrets ever since our people started living here."

"You know," said Jacques, "I bet I can go into the forest by myself and live pretty good."

"That is what this is all about."

Training continued until the cold weather set in and it was time to break camp. The young warriors were now considered young braves capable of defending or even attacking other tribes.

Paul's family, along with Jacques, broke camp and moved into the interior for another winter.

In January 1714, Paul's father decided to trek across Nova Scotia to the southern shore to hunt seal. This was the time of the year when the seal spawn, and can be caught on dry land. Seal flesh is very tasty, comparable to veal. The fat of the animal was rendered for its fine oil, which the Micmacs used year round. The oil was stored in large animal bladders. The trip proved very fruitful and abundant meat was secured.

In February of 1714, they went out to hunt moose, beavers, caribou, and even bear. The Great Spirit was with them. In March, they went fishing for salmon, herrings, smelts, and sturgeon. In April, they hunted for, of all things, eggs. Ducks and large waterfowl had nests scattered all over.

Of all that Jacques learned from these wonderful people the one thing that made the deepest impression was their attitude about sharing. They would provide food and clothing for anyone visiting their camps. The elder Efraim, Paul's grandfather, told Jacques about the five maidens.

"We had settled in the wilderness. One day five maidens happen to stop at our camp. They were tired and hungry. My wife and I offered them some fresh fish and even let them use our kettle so they could cook their own meal. As they were cooking the meal they heard someone approaching. Quickly, the girls grabbed the kettle and ran the other way into the woods to eat, not wanting to be obligated to the strangers. We were entertaining the strangers when the girls came back, after eating, and acted surprised at seeing strangers. We offered the girls some food, but they declined saying they were not hungry. They whispered to me where they left the kettle. They bid the strangers and us good-bye and left. My wife and I enjoyed playing out the joke with them."

In the summer of 1714 the Micmacs returned to the Annapolis River. There was jubilation at meeting old friends. Jacques was preparing to visit the Heberts when he heard some of the Indians were planning a fishing trip in the Bay of Fundy. Jacques, now nineteen years old, with a full blond beard, opted to put off his visit so he could go fishing with his friends.

"We trek over the mountains between here and the large bay, and fish at night," said one of the elders.

That sounded exciting, something Jacques had never done before. Torches were prepared and loaded into six canoes. The torches, when lit at night and held in front of the canoe, attracted fish. All they had to do was spear them in. Jacques and Paul readied their canoe and loaded their supplies. The twelve paddled across the river to the mountain range. They portaged over the mountain to the Bay of Fundy on the other side. They set up camp near the water's edge, built a fire, and settled in waiting for dark. Their fire would serve as a beacon in the night. After it got dark the group pushed out into the bay, lit their torches and began fishing. Paul and Jacques, as usual, brought up the rear. They were the last to enter the water, so they had to stay closest to shore. An hour later a large group of Kenebeks, enemies of the Micmacs, out fishing themselves, spotted the Micmac fires. The put their own fires out and silently made for the Micmacs. The Kenebeks surrounded the Micmacs and opened fire, taking them by complete surprise. While some of the Kenebeks were slaughtering the Micmacs, other Kenebeks made for shore where the fire was; to capture any Micmacs that made it back to land.

Paul, seeing the disaster before him, had the presence of mind to quickly throw his torch into the water depriving the Kenebeks of an easy target. He turned to Jacques and shouted, "Jump!"

They abandoned their canoe and swam towards shore, unobserved. As they got close to shore, they spotted the Kenebeks waiting for survivors to arrive. Fearful of being seen, Paul saw a tree that had fallen into the water, now covered with eelgrass. He motioned for Jacques to make for the safety of the tree. Hiding under the eelgrass they were safe, for the moment. The Kenebeks were everywhere.

Terrorizing fear gripped Jacques. He had felt this fear before during the battle at the fort. His heart was pounding so much, he was sure the Kenebeks could hear it. In the dim darkness, he looked at Paul and saw Paul's lips quivering. Somehow, that made him feel better. He felt that if Paul were frightened, then he wasn't alone in feeling like that.

The wounded Micmacs not killed outright, who somehow managed to make it to shore, were captured. At the campsite, they were tortured until they died. Their cries rang out into the late night. After killing the Micmacs, the Kenebeks scalped them, and threw their bodies into the fire. As dawn neared the Kenebeks broke camp and put out to sea.

Once the coast was clear, the boys emerged and beheld the carnage before them. Horrified, the boys openly cried. They had lost ten of their best friends. They painfully made their slow way back to their own camp to relate the horrors they had witnessed.

Chief Cope was aghast when he heard their story. He ordered all braves assembled. While they waited for all the members to arrive, they had a ceremonial dance that lasted all night long. They called upon the Great Spirit to lead them and seek revenge. The dancing seemed to have imparted some sort of magical quality into each man. Word quickly spread and soon the whole Micmac nation was aroused. Hundreds of warriors, including Paul and Jacques, put out in canoes to cross the Annapolis River, then portage over the mountain range to the Bay of Fundy. They paddled across the wide Bay to a Kenebek campsite. As the Micmac force neared the shore, one of the Micmacs jumped into the water and swam madly for shore eager to do battle. He could not wait.

The Kenebeks, taken by surprise, seeing the madman coming towards them made for the safety of a building. Breaking into the building, the Micmac, hatchet in hand, proceeded to vent his anger. In short order, eight Kenebeks were killed. Chief Cope and the other Micmacs dispatched the rest of the

Kenebeks. The dead Kenebeks were scalped and their bodies tossed inside the building, which was then set ablaze.

"Now," said Chief Cope, "we will go after the chief of the Kenebeks."

The main region of the kenebeks was well known by the Micmacs. They had been battling each other for years. Traveling overland they arrived at the main Kenebek camp. They were surprised to find no resistance to their advance. As they approached, the chief of the Kenebeks came forward, arm raised as a gesture of peace.

"Chief Cope," said Kenebek Chief, Raul, "hear me."

Chief Cope halted his men. "What have you to say?" He asked.

"Chief Cope, I have heard of the evil deeds some of the Kenebeks have done to your people."

"Some of those people you speak of are all dead now," replied Chief Cope.

"Serves them right," replied Chief Raul. "I warned them not to do battle with the Micmacs, for surely they will kill us all, but they did not listen to me."

Chief Cope called for the relatives of those killed by the Kenebeks to come forward. "These are the brothers of the Micmacs your people killed. You will compensate them!"

Seeing the large number of warriors before him, knowing full well that at any moment they could all be wiped out, Chief Raul said, "Our camp and all that is in it is yours."

The angry Micmacs pillaged the camp taking everything they could carry. Paul and Jacques looted all the beaver pelts they could carry. The frightened Kenebeks stood aside and offered no resistance. The Micmacs made their way back to the Annapolis River.

After many days of mourning for the fallen Micmacs, Jacques felt he was ready to leave. He loaded his canoe with the furs and left. As he paddled along heading to the Heberts he saw a large bird circling overhead. He remembered seeing a large bird like that once before and thinking about it brought back happy memories.

He was greeted at the Heberts by their barking dog, who quickly ran over to the canoe to sniff at the load of furs. Hearing the dog, the rest of the family came out. Jacques could not believe his eyes when he beheld Magdelaine as she approached him. His heart seemed to skip a beat, and suddenly he felt light headed.

"Magdelaine," stammered Jacques. "Is that you?"

Her long flowing hair brushed her rosy cheeks when a gust of wind blew. She had not bothered to wear her bonnet. Her bodice revealed a full womanly figure and her graceful curves could be seen outlined in her long gingham gown. Her sensuous lips seemed to beckon his heart to beat faster when she smiled. Her sparkling blue eyes were dazzling. She reminded him of the first time he had seen her mother when he first arrived at the Hebert farm. She wore tiny leather moccasins, gaily decorated.

"Yes, it is," she replied. "How have you been?"

"Fine," he replied, unable to stop gazing at her. He suddenly felt warm all over.

"We've missed you," she said.

"Had I known you were so beautiful, I would have returned sooner."

Blushing, she said, "Oh, Jacques…stop that."

The rest of the family greeted him warmly. Antoine was surprised to see the beautiful furs.

"Those are beautiful furs, Jacques," said Antoine.

"Yes, they are," he replied. "I will take them to market tomorrow to trade."

After a sumptuous meal that evening the men of the house sat by the fire. Jacques recounted the events that had occurred while he was with the Micmacs.

Jacques, now six feet two inches tall, and bigger than Antoine, had a problem finding clothing to fit him after he arrived. Jeanne had to look deep to find something for him to wear after he bathed.

Jacques recounted the seal hunt and the other hunts they had gone on, but would not talk about the raid by the Kenebeks. This would remain a secret with him. The details were too gruesome. As the men sat by the fire, Antoine smoking his pipe, they discussed the British situation again.

"The English have given us one year to leave Nova Scotia," said Antoine.

"Are you going to leave?" asked Jacques.

"I don't know," he replied. "This is my home, our home. The French have been here for hundreds of years, and now they want us to abandon all that we have worked for."

"All they want is for the settlers to sign an oath of allegiance," said Jacques.

"I won't sign any oath of allegiance to the English!" retorted Antoine. "It was a dirty trick, our king giving this land to the English, after all we have done here."

"If we do not sign the oath of allegiance we will not be granted any land. All the newlyweds are leaving for New Brunswick."

"We will just have to wait and see what happens," said Antoine.

The following day, Jacques, dressed as a Micmac, set out with his furs to trade at the market square across the river. The market square was a busy place, bustling with activity as merchants hawked their wares. The settlers gathered there to trade their farm products with each other. The English were there to trade with anyone who had a commodity they were interested in. There was a general store operated by an Englishman named Mitchell, who was interested in obtaining furs to sell in Europe. French locals told Jacques that the best place to trade his furs would be with the devious Mitchell.

"Be careful when you deal with him. He will cheat you if you let him," said the Acadian farmers.

As Jacques entered the general store, the clerks stopped their sweeping and cleaning to catch a glimpse of the Micmac. This was a strange sight, a Micmac with blond hair. Usually, when a Micmac entered this store, he humbled himself and bowed courteously before doing any trading. Not so with Jacques who walked smartly up to the counter and plopped his furs there. Mitchell was taken back with the bold stance taken by Jacques.

"You buy furs? Asked Jacques, in broken French.

"Yes," replied Mitchell, as he looked the tall Indian over, still trying to figure out what gives with the blond hair. Possibly, he thought, here was a half-breed.

"How much for furs?" asked Jacques, looking down at Mitchell. The other clerks gathered for a closer look at the skins on the counter, knowing full well that Mitchell would take advantage of the ignorant Indian.

"Well now," said Mitchell, as he winked at one of his clerks and grinned, "let me see what you have here."

While Mitchell looked over the furs, Jacques walked over to where the long rifles were. He looked long at one particular rifle. Mitchell was amazed at the quality of the furs. The clerks all nodded agreement that this was a fine catch. Mitchell instantly thought of the huge sums these furs would bring in London. The beaver pelts were luxurious and would make fine hats for the upper class in Europe. The proprietor noticed Jacques eyeing the rifle and deviously planned to extort the furs from him.

"Well, now," said Mitchell. "Tell you what I'm going to do." Jacques walked over to the counter to where his furs were. The other clerks stood by to watch the fleecing.

"I will trade you that rifle for all these furs. That rifle is made in the colonies," said Mitchell, as he smugly looked at Jacques. The clerks all smiled in agreement.

Jacques felt anger building up inside. He had been warned that this unscrupulous person would try to take advantage of him. He reached over and grabbed Mitchell by the lapels and half pulled him over the counter.

"Listen here, you little worm," said Jacques. The sudden movement caught everyone by surprise. A clerk dropped his broom and stepped away from the fray. Mitchell, gripped by sudden fear threw his arms up for protection, and pleaded with Jacques. Jacques tossed him back over the counter where he struck his back against the shelves behind.

"How much you pay?" screamed Jacques, scowling at the cowering Mitchell.

"Forty Pounds, gold," stammered the frightened proprietor. He just wanted Jacques to leave. One of the clerks ran out the store to fetch the local British patrols nearby. Two armed English soldiers accompanied the frightened clerk back to the store. The English soldiers hated the local Indians and when informed there was a mad Indian in the store they welcomed the challenge to arrest him. As they entered the store, they saw Jacques about to leave, with the gold coins in a pouch and carrying the rifle. Jacques looked at the British soldiers with such force that they were momentarily stunned. His piercing gaze put the fear of God in them. He was so much bigger than they were. They lowered their rifles, and stood aside letting him pass, not knowing if the rifle he was carrying was loaded. The sight of the knife he was also carrying gave them second thoughts. Here was someone they did not want to mess with.

"Let him go," shouted Mitchell. He wanted him out of his store before anybody got hurt.

The merchants at the square, seeing the English soldiers rush into the store, were all eyes on the Micmac as he left. They thought for sure he would be arrested and taken to the fort for punishment.

"Who was that?" was the question going around after Jacques left.

CHAPTER SEVEN

Coureur des bois

Jacques spent the summer of 1714 at the Heberts. There was always plenty to do around the farm; crops had to be planted, additions made to the farmhouse, furniture to be made, etc. With eleven children in his home, mostly girls, Antoine needed all the help he could get. He was grateful for the help he got from Jacques.

Tension between the French settlers and English soldiers was always present. Since the French had been told to either sign the oath of allegiance or leave and since the English did not grant any more land titles to French families, many of the local farmers did not bother to plant crops that year, figuring on leaving.

The Roman Catholic missionaries in the area had their problems also. It was, and still is, the custom in the Catholic Church for anyone contemplating marriage to have their intentions made known throughout their respective parishes by special announcements made at Sunday services. These bans of marriage, as they are called, are announced three weeks in a row. You will find in many of the marriage certificates drawn up by the missionaries during this time proclaim that only one, or two, bans were announced due to the uncertainty of the situation between the French and English.

After France ceded Nova Scotia to England, France determined to build a strong fortification at Cape Breton to safeguard what remained of her Canadian territory. The fortress under construction was called Louisville, in honor of France's King Louis XIV. Many of the French settlers opted to leave Nova Scotia and relocate at Cape Breton. The land in Cape Breton, mostly barren rocks, was not very good for farming. Still it was better than being under the control of the English.

Colonel Nicholson, the victor of the battle at the fort in 1710, had cause to be concerned. If all the French left Nova Scotia for Cape Breton the buildup would have greatly increased the strength of the French forces in the area. Thousands of armed settlers would then be free to support their French cousins. This would have posed a formidable threat.

Lieutenant Governor Samuel Vetch wrote to England and announced:

"The accession of such a number of Acadians to Cape Breton will make it at once a very populous colony. So it is to be considered that one hundred of the Acadians, who were born upon this continent, and are perfectly at home in the woods, can march upon snow-shoes and understand the use of birch canoes, are of more value and service than five times their number of raw men newly arrived from Europe.

"So their skill in the fishery, as well as the cultivating of the soil must make at once of Cape Breton the most powerful colony the French have in America, and to the greatest danger and damage to all the British Colonies as well as the universal trade of Great Britain."

To alleviate the situation, Colonel Nicholson put off demanding that the French sign the oath of allegiance. He didn't want a build up of forces at Cape Breton. For the time being peace was at hand.

When the snows came in late 1714, now that the Heberts were well provisioned for the winter, Jacques determined to spend the winter months by himself in the wilderness. His fur trading had brought him a small fortune, and now he planned to increase it. He would become a coureur-des-bois, a courageous individual who traveled deep into the wilderness trading with the Indians.

He bought many things he knew the Indians desired and would use these to trade for furs. His canoe loaded, plenty of warm clothing made by the Hebert Girls, he set out. He had to make it to the far end of the river before it iced over. Reaching his destination he unloaded the canoe and submerged it into the river. This would not only keep it safe, it preserved the birch bark from rotting.

In the fading light, snow falling, before venturing into the Forrest he opened a leather pouch and removed some ground tobacco leaves. He sprinkled some into the wind and said, "Migamawesu, Great Spirit of the wilderness, it is I, Jacques. I have come to be with you. I have brought many gifts for my friends. Help me Great Spirit and guide me." A strong wind blew, dispersing the tobacco leaves deep into the woods.

Carrying as much as he could, safely hiding what remained to be retrieved later, he entered the deep forbidding darkness of the forest knowing full well that nothing could harm him now; he was under the protection of the Great Spirit of the wilderness.

He headed in an easterly direction, knowing that most of the Indians would be wintering nearby. By late afternoon, he stopped to build a shelter for the night. The stand-by A frame shelter was quickly assembled. Placing many branches against the lean-to, he sealed the cracks as best he could with moss and clay. He stocked as much wood as he could before it got dark. As daylight faded, he was ready. All his supplies were safely in the shelter, his bed was made, and he had a nice fire going. Outside, the wind howled, and snow fell. The temperature was near freezing. He could hear the wolves calling each other in the distance.

Exhausted from the trip and the work in setting up the shelter, he wrapped a heavy fur piece around himself and quickly fell asleep. He slept soundly until near dawn when he was jolted awake by a bad dream. He dreamt he was on a small island with many people. The island floated out to sea, far, far away. He was very sad on this island and the people with him wept.

Wide-awake now, he built a fire and while eating some dried beef, he contemplated the weird dream. "What could that mean?" He thought to himself. Outside, snow was still falling, but it was still not too deep. He loaded his supplies on his backpack and set out. Soon, he came to a Micmac shelter. They greeted him warmly and offered him some food, which he accepted. This shelter was reminiscent of his friend Paul. There were the parents, a young son, and grandparents.

"What are you carrying?" they inquired.

"I have many things," said Jacques. He opened his backpack and displayed his wares. They were excited when they saw the many items he had. The young boy picked up a knife and said, "I would like to own such a knife."

"Have you any furs?" he asked the young boy.

"Yes," answered the father, "we have many beaver skins."

"I will give you the knife for two beaver skins," said Jacques.

The boy's eyes lit up. He was very happy to trade what nature provided for a beautiful knife. Jacques felt a twinge of remorse after making the deal, he felt he was taking advantage of the family, but they were so happy to get the knife for the boy that he overlooked any sense of guilt.

The grandmother eyed a pot Jacques had and asked how much he wanted for it.

"One beaver," Jacques replied. The grandmother sent the youngster out to gather all the skins they had. She would do some trading.

The father and grandfather traded for some hatchets, pans, and tin cups. The Micmacs had traded nearly all their furs for things they sorely needed. Everyone was happy. The grandfather lit his pipe and offered Jacques a few puffs. The young boy gleamed over his new knife, holding it up for all to see and behold. The grandmother used her new pot to brew some tea, which she passed around for all to drink, using their new tin cups. Jacques brought some happiness to this family while at the same time enriching himself. They had him stay for more food later, enjoying his visit. He told them he spent many months with Paul and his family and the many hunts with them.

The grandmother asked him many questions about the land across the deep pond, meaning Europe. They were interested in the Great White Father, King Louis XIV.

The grandmother, it turned out, was known among the Micmacs as a Shonan, a person who has a special gift, sort of a fortuneteller. When the grandfather told Jacques that his wife had this power he was very much interested. Maybe, thought Jacques, she might be able to interpret his dream. The Indians were big believers in the Great Spirit talking to them in dreams.

"Grandmother," said Jacques. "I had this strange dream. It even woke me up."

"Tell me about your dream," she said. The others in the shelter all wanted to hear about his dream also.

"Grandmother, I dreamt I was on a small island with many people. We were all sad. The island drifted out across the deep pond, far, far away."

Grandmother's eyes opened wide when she heard that. She shook her head from side to side. Her look gave Jacques cause for concern. He didn't like her reaction.

"Grandmother," continued Jacques, "what do you think that means?"

"That is a bad omen, my son," said grandmother. "There is deep trouble for you in the future. But, the Great Spirit will be with you and guide you."

That unnerved Jacques a bit. He put a lot of faith in the Indian ways, and heard that they could see into the future. He was relieved to hear that he would be protected. He thanked his host for their hospitality; loaded his furs, and left.

Back at his shelter, he stocked the furs inside and before losing any more daylight continued to patch up the shelter as best he could. With the little bit of daylight left, he chopped and stacked his firewood. That had been a very profitable day. He was happy with his trading and could see where that would be a good way to amass a big fortune.

The next few days he spent doing some hunting and scouting. Not too far from his shelter, he came across a small pond that was iced over. He broke through the ice near the shore and set a beaver trap. He would check his trap daily. Game was plentiful and he spent a lot of time building drying racks and curing the meat.

He constructed a trap known amongst the Micmacs as a 'tomber', a French word meaning 'to fall'. Locating a large fallen tree, trimming the branches, and using a tall lever made from another large branch he was able to lift up one end of the heavy log. He placed a two-foot piece of wood under the log, about twenty-four inches from the end, to hold it up. This was the trigger piece. He planted small branches on either side of the log to keep it from rolling off the trigger piece. Attached to the trigger piece was bait made from meat. He planted twigs to form a narrow passageway leading to the meat. Any animal that crawled under the log to retrieve the meat was instantly dispatched when the trigger gave way as the animal pulled on the bait. It was a crude but humane way to trap fur-bearing animals. Martins, foxes, otters, mink, and even some wolves fell prey to this device. There was no shortage of food while he lived in the wilderness. He made several trips back to his cache of goods near the river's end to use for trading with other Micmacs wintering nearby.

He found the days very busy; there was always something to do. He had pelts to skin, stretch, and air dry. He broke a hole through the ice in the nearby pond and did some ice fishing. He did a lot of hunting, and he spent a great deal of time tanning the skins he had. He learned the secret of tanning from the Micmacs where they showed him how to use the animal's own brain in a mixture to soak the skin in. His pelts were prime.

He didn't mind the days, but the nights were very lonely. He was not used to being alone. Each night, as he sat by his fire, his thoughts were always on the pretty little blond haired girl back at the Hebert farm. He pictured her in his mind constantly, remembering the way she looked, the way she smiled, the way she would make him hold her yarn while she rolled it into a ball, and always he delighted looking into her eyes. She was becoming a woman. He pictured her curves showing through the linen bodice she wore. Her graceful hips were evident even thou she always wore a long gown. Her sensuous lips were enticing when she spoke to him. He wished with all his heart that she could be with him now.

If I can make enough money from this trip, he thought, maybe I could buy a piece of land from Antoine. He already had more than was needed to buy land from his last trade with the English. He thought about how he would approach the Heberts and ask for their permission to court Magdelaine. Would they accept him? What if they rejected him! No, he would not dwell on the negative side of the issue. He knew he could support a wife; he was a good farmer, a good Catholic, a good Frenchman, why wouldn't they accept him?

The long winter wore on and he collected more and more skins. His shelter was so full he could hardly move. The skins inside the shelter provided plenty of insulation from the cold outside as he stacked them against the walls.

Living in the wilderness in the summer months is relatively easy. There is plenty of game about and plenty of vegetation to eat; then also one does not have to worry about freezing. In the wintertime though, things are far different. The cold nights are extremely harsh and everything freezes. The birds are gone, the bears hibernate, and strangely, there is a serene quietness everywhere. Sound seems to travel further in the wintertime.

After a few weeks in the wilderness, he felt he had made a big mistake in attempting that venture. He wanted to make money, but the loneliness was getting to be more than he could bear. He seemed happy only when he met the Indians living in the big woods. The nights were the worse time, so he tried to keep as busy as he could treating his skins and fixing his meals. He swore that if he ever attempted anything like this again, he would   first buy a dog for companionship. He loved Paul's little dog, the one that chased the moose, however the Micmacs did not take their dogs with them when they set their traps and collected the pelts. They felt the dogs might get caught in the traps, or worse...leave a scent that would chase the fur bearing animals away.

He arose early one morning and went a short distance into the interior.

The sun was just starting to rise, and it was still a little dark out. He heard branches being broken nearby and that startled him.

"Migamawesu, is that you?" he shouted. He heard tromping noises coming towards him. He grabbed for his knife, not knowing who or what was out there. His heart began beating faster as he felt the adrenalin rush. Crouching low, he crept closer to the source of the noise. As he peered through the thicket he saw the antlers of a large male moose. The large animal picked up his scent and charged. Quickly, Jacques made for the safety of his shelter but the animal was right behind him. Fearing that the enraged bull would tear down his flimsy shelter, Jacques only had a few seconds to reach inside for a weapon. The only thing close at hand was a rope. He grabbed the rope and ran to the safety of a nearby oak tree. The moose had stopped and was stomping its leg, lowering its head preparing to charge. Jacques only had the rope and his knife. What was he to do?

"Migamawesu," said Jacques, "Great Spirit of the forest. Tell this moose person I am alone and to go away."

Still, the moose stayed there eyeing Jacques behind the oak tree, contemplating how to charge, seemingly very angry.

Looking around, Jacques saw a fist size rock nearby. He picked up the rock not knowing what to do with it, probably he could throw it at the enraged animal and scare it off, but then he thought that might just make it angrier. Then he remembered something that Paul had showed him last year and he was inspired to give it a try. He tied one end of the rope around the rock, remembering how Paul had used this same technique as a bolo.

He stepped out from behind the oak tree exposing himself to the moose. The moose quickly lowered its head and charged. Just as the animal approached him, he stepped aside and tossed the rock in front of the beast. The rope tangled the moose's front legs. The rock, still tied to the rope, carried around the legs and held them securely. The moose took a nosedive and tried desperately to right itself. As soon as it went down, Jacques was on it with his knife in hand. He quickly cut the jugular vein on the right side, jumping away to safety. While it was trashing about, he ran to the other side and at the first opportunity slashed the left vein. In a few moments the ground was covered with deep red blood. It only took a few minutes before the animal stopped kicking and the spirit of the animal left.

"Moose person, I asked you to leave before, now you have forced me to take your life. You will feed many people. We will honor your spirit."

Jacques cleaned the animal, skinned, and quartered it. He made a drag and carted some of the meat to the nearest Micmac camp, where the Shonan lived. They came back with him and took more meat for the other Indians camped around. He kept a hindquarter, the bladder, intestines, and the skin. He hoisted the hindquarter to a large branch so it would not be accessible to marauding animals. The cold winter air would preserve it for months. The hanging hindquarter must have attracted many animals because his tomber had more than the usual kills in it after that.

He found that walking in snowshoes for a long time caused pain in his feet. The awkward bending of the toes led to a painful condition. He was glad to remove the snowshoes in his shelter and stretch out a bit. He also found that the glare from the white snow hurt his eyes. He fashioned some protective eyewear from a piece of flat birch bark with tiny slits, which reduced the amount of light entering his eyes. He had been warned by the Micmacs never to venture out in the snow alone without the snow glasses. Should he get snow blindness he was doomed unless someone was with him to guide him home.

Alone in his shelter at night he could hear a wolf howl in the distance. Soon, he would be joined by another wolf, and then another. The cold weather had reduced their food source, and they were hungry.

Looking at the northern sky at night, Jacques saw the Northern Lights flickering, casting strange looking bands of brightly colored clouds.

He enjoyed a hot cup of tea in the evening after cutting and stacking his firewood. He would melt a piece of ice from the nearby pond over his fireplace in a small kettle and brew some pine needles.

The nearby pond provided him with fresh fish after he broke a hole through the ice with his hatchet. He learned from the Micmacs how to preserve his fish by cutting a trough in the ice and placing his fish in it, then pouring water over the trough, which quickly froze over. Anytime he wanted fresh fish, he had merely to cut into the top layer of his ice preserve. He enjoyed watching a hungry wolf trying to scratch the ice away from one of his fishes.

The long winter months passed slowly for Jacques, even though he kept himself busy; it was the constant thought of the little blond haired girl that kept tormenting him.

When the weather warmed a bit, it was time for the maple sap to flow. Jacques fashioned a little wooden pipe made from alder. The alder wood has a soft center which can be easily removed providing a ready made conduit, which he stuck into the trunk of a maple tree after drilling a hole with his knife. He collected the sap in a birch bark container that he fashioned into a cup. He let the sap freeze at night, which separated the water from the syrup. He enjoyed the syrup in his tea, and he also made candy by pouring the syrup into the snow to harden.

In the spring of 1715, loaded with furs, twenty-year-old Jacques left the wilderness, returning to the Hebert farm. Approaching the farm, the Hebert's dog announced the approach of the visitor.

At first the Heberts did not know who this bearded stranger was beaching his canoe on their landing. The stranger had a full load in his craft so they mistook him for a peddler. When he waved to them, they suddenly saw that it was Jacques. All the girls ran out to greet him.

Marie Hebert, Magdelaine's eighteen-year-old sister, threw her arms around Jacques's neck and gave him a big hug. She was a stunning brunette, the envy of all the young ladies in the village. She smiled at him and said, "Hello, Jacques. How have you been?"

"Very well," he replied, but he was looking for Magdelaine.

Magdelaine was furious when she saw Marie brazenly make an advance on the object of her affection. She stared hard at her older sister not wanted her to steal her heart's desire. He could sense the apprehension in Magdelaine so he reached out and grabbed her by her waist, pulling her close to him. Feeling confident in his arms, she stuck her tongue out at Marie when no one was looking.

Antoine came out to greet Jacques, and look over the load of furs.

"Another nice catch," said Antoine.

When Jacques entered the house, Jeanne greeted him with a big hug. She was in a family way again. Her youngest was just a year old. After lunch all the family wanted to know how he spent the winter in the wilderness. The children enjoyed hearing about his adventures; they were fascinated with the incident dealing with the moose.

Later, sitting by the fireside, the young boys asked a million questions. "How did you get so many furs?" asked thirteen-year-old Louis.

"Well, I bought things I knew the Indians would want and traded with them."

"You got all those furs by trading?" asked twelve-year-old Pierre.

"No," replied Jacques, "I hunted and trapped a lot myself."

He explained about constructing a tomber and trapping many animals that way. "When the animal pulls on the stick holding the heavy log, bammmmm, down it goes!"

Young Pierre winced when he heard the gory details.

"I can assure you that when that log falls on an animal, it dies instantly."

After lunch, Magdelaine had put on her favorite dress to impress Jacques. She need not have bothered; she was beautiful in whatever she wore.

The following day, dressed as a typical French settler, Jacques paddled across the river to the market square. He drew a lot of attention from the merchants as he carried his furs to the trading post. He entered the same store owned by the English merchant who had tried to cheat him before. Dressed as he was, and with a full beard the proprietor did not recognize him, nor did any of the other clerks. Still, the owner eyed him with apprehension. There was something about him that the owner could not quite figure out, whether it was in the eyes, the mannerism, or the great size. He felt he had met him before but could not remember. Whatever it was the owner thought best not to trifle with this individual.

Jacques placed his furs on the counter as he had done before. Quickly the clerks gathered to look at the treasures before them. The owner could not believe his eyes. That was indeed a big load of prime pelts.

When Jacques saw that he was not recognized and there would be no soldiers rushing in to arrest him, he spoke to the owner.

"Do you buy furs, Sir?" asked Jacques, in fluent French.

"Yes," replied the owner, who also spoke very good French.

The owner looked very carefully at each pelt, looking for defects. Finding them all in excellent condition he smiled and said, "Very nice furs!"

"Yes," replied Jacques.

"Where did you get them?" asked the owner.

"I have a brother who trades with the Indians. I supply him with goods."

The owner looked at Jacques and remembered the incident with the Micmac with the blond hair from last year.

"I think we dealt with him last year. We don't want him in here anymore!"

"Yes, my brother can be troublesome, at times."

"What is your name?" asked the owner.

"Jacques."

"What is your brother's name?"

"Paul."

"Well Jacques," said the owner. "We will do business with you, but not with your brother!"

They went over the furs piece-by-piece and arrived at a satisfactory conclusion. Jacques received two hundred Pounds, in cold coins, a rather large sum in those days. After concluding their business the owner informed Jacques that he would be glad to get as many more furs as he could. Jacques purchased cloth for the Hebert girls and hard candy for the young Hebert boys before leaving. The Hebert girls were very grateful for the cloth, and the youngsters truly enjoyed the candy. The girls would make handsome dresses for themselves and their mother.

That evening after supper, Antoine and Jacques went into the barn to milk the cows. Alone together, while Antoine was getting his bucket and milk stool, Jacques said he wanted to speak to him.

"Yes, Jacques," said Antoine, "what's on your mind?"

"Antoine," began Jacques, not knowing how to start.

"Yes," replied Antoine.

"Antoine, you've known me for many years now."

"Yes, Jacques,"

"Antoine, may I have your permission to call on Magdelaine?" he blurted out.

Antoine's face lit up. He was delighted. He could not have picked a better suitor for his daughter. "Yes, of course, Jacques."

"I didn't know how to ask you, and I was afraid of what you might say."

"Well, I am delighted, and I am sure Jeanne feels the same way. Of course, the other girls will be disappointed."

"Oh, I'm sure the other girls will find beaus."

"Now, there is just the problem of getting a piece of ground. The British will not grant any more land to us, so I'm afraid we will have to relocate to New Brunswick," said Jacques.

"Nonsense, you can have a piece of my land."

"I could not just take a piece of your land, but I would be more than happy to buy a parcel of land from you."

"You don't have to buy the land. If you marry Magdelaine, the land will be part of her dowry."

"Thank you Antoine. You are very generous."

"That's quite all right. You can have the land next to the potato garden. It needs to be cleaned up. There is about ten acres there but its mostly weeds and brushes."

Just then the girls came into the barn to help with the milking so the conversation dropped off, but they couldn't help noticing that Jacques was happily singing as he milked the cows.

Later that night, Jacques went to Magdelaine while no one was around and asked her if he could call on her. She smiled at him approvingly and said that it would be up to her parents, but she would love to have him call on her.

"I've already asked your father and he gave me his blessings. Now, I will ask your mother." Said Jacques.

That evening he approached Jeanne and asked for her permission also. She already knew from Antoine, and readily agreed. There was a lot of joy at the Hebert farm that evening as they celebrated the betrothal of Magdelaine to Jacques.

In the following days, Jacques and Antoine were busy clearing the land and preparing to build a new home. Jacques and Magdelaine enjoyed quiet evenings leisurely drifting in his canoe on the river, making plans for their future.

With the death of Queen Anne in 1714, a German dynasty replaced the House of Stuart when the dull son of Sophia, King James' granddaughter, George was crowned King of England in 1715. Lieutenant-Governor Caufield of Nova Scotia took advantage of the situation to renew the demand that all non-English residents take the unqualified oath of allegiance. The French living more than three miles away from the fort at Annapolis Royal refused to take the oath claiming that negotiations were even now under way between France and England regarding their situation. Those living near the fort were pressured to sign or suffer the consequences.

When the King of France, Louis XIV, died on September 1, 1715, his nephew the Duc d'Orleans assumed responsibility for all major decisions. The new king, Louis XV was just a child incapable of ruling. The Regent was more interested in peace, and rebuilding than the sword, which gladdened the hearts of the British. The Regent sent ships to Cape Breton to beef up the deplorable conditions at Fort Louisburg. It was anticipated at that time that help would come from the French settlers living in Nova Scotia. This gave the French settlers in Nova Scotia cause for concern. They wanted to be left alone to live in peace, and declared themselves neutrals.

Costabelle, the French governor of Cape Breton was adamant that the French living in Nova Scotia should leave and resettle in Cape Breton. He sent officers to speak to the settlers encouraging them to relocate. It was easy for him to say 'leave,' but for those who spent their whole lives, even generations, clearing and tilling the soil, raising families, and caring for livestock, the prospect of leaving was hard to bear.

The British sent soldiers to all the families living near the fort with an ultimatum; sign or get out. In Port Royal on January 13, 1716, thirty-six Acadians signed the following conditional oath.

"I sincerely promise and swear that I will be faithful and maintain a true allegiance to His Majesty King George, as long as I shalll be in Acadie or Nova Scotia and that I shall be permitted to withdraw wheresoever I shall think fit with all my moveable goods and effects, when I shall think fit, without any one being able to hinder me."

It was the intention of the French settlers to pack up and leave at the first opportunity due to the callousness of the Governor of Nova Scotia, Colonel Nicholson. This tyrant was so ruthless that his subordinate, Colonel Vetch, wrote the Board of Trades (England's ruling assembly) complaining.

Letter dated September 2, 1715.

"M. Nicholson's discouraging, or rather discharging all Trade there to the Acadians, and causing keep the gates of the fort shut against them night and day, that they may have no manner of commerce with the garrison, and having by proclamation discharged their harbouring or resetting any of the natives, with whom they used to have a considerable trade for peltry, hath so discouraged them from staying that they had built abundance of small vessels to carry themselves and effects to Cape Brittoun, which was what the French officers so much solicited."

Concerning this situation, Lieutenant-Governor Caufield wrote to Colonel Vetch on November 2, 1715.

"I am but too senceable (sic) of Col. Nicholson's unprecedented malice, and had his designs taken their desired effect, I am perswaded (sic) there had not been at this time an inhabitant of any kind in the country, nor indeed, a garrison: when I recollect his declaration to the Acadians and afterwards to the soldiers, wherein he told the latter that the French were all rebels and would certainly cut their throats if they went into their houses, telling of us that we must have no manner of correspondence with them, and ordered the gates of the garrison to be shut, tho, at the same time he was senciable (sic) that we could not subsist the ensuing winter, but by their mains, there being no other prospects left to us, if the whole seine of his administration here was plainly laid down, it would be very difficult to find one instance of all his proceedings, whereby the garrison or colony could receive the least benefit."

So, the French were not permitted to leave. They had been assured that they would be allowed to depart with all their goods within one year of the signing of the peace treaty in 1713. But their departure would leave the garrison at a disadvantage, and without the French presence the Indians would have no one to hold them in check.

When the French settlers started building ships to transport their goods away from Nova Scotia the English would not supply them with the necessary rigging material, so that caused another delay.

For years the French had lived here and enjoyed the fruits of their labors. They reclaimed land from the swamps by building dykes. They tilled the soil, planted fruit trees and crops. They raised horses, chickens, cattle, pigs, sheep and even oxen. They traded with each other and utilized the services of artisans such as carpenters, cobblers, blacksmiths, and wagon makers. They hunted and fished, and traded with the local Indians. Infant mortality was extremely rare, and longevity was the norm.

That is not to say that they did not quarrel with each other. The missionaries settled their differences. The English were amazed at the utopian atmosphere present when they took possession of the former French colony.

The differences in religious beliefs, however, were the main cause of dissention between the French and English. The Protestant English did not tolerate the Roman Catholic French who were under the control of the Pope. When the Protestants living in the colonies at that time were approached to war against the French in Nova Scotia, they jumped at the chance. "We are doing the will of the Lord!" said the colonist. How many people perished throughout history by nations doing battle with other nations, all under the name of the Lord.

The English soldiers stationed in Annapolis Royal treated the local French settlers with condescension and derision. The always-armed English soldiers walked about as Lords of the land, ever quick to push elderly settlers out of their way as the latter traded at the market square.

One day, in the spring of 1716, Jacques and Paul, both dressed as Micmacs, took their furs to the market square to sell. After selling the pelts they walked about the market square looking to purchase goods for the Micmacs. An English sergeant, named Eric Mitchell, accompanied by an unknown private, was patrolling the area. They witnessed the sergeant brutally and arrogantly pushing an elderly peasant out of his way. There was plenty of room to go around, but the sergeant wanted to make his presence known and to instill fear in the hearts of the French.

"Did you see that?" said Paul.

"Yes," replied Jacques, who felt his temper building and the adrenalin starting to rush.

"You get the little one," said Paul. "I will deal with the ass-hole sergeant!"

They approached the soldiers head on. The soldiers, seeing the pair approaching, raised their rifles in front of them to use as a battering ram to separate the pair. Quickly, Paul grabbed the sergeant's rifle with both hands and kicked him in the groin, doubling him up. The sergeant let go of his rifle and leaned forward, bending to protect himself. With the sergeant's rifle in his hands, Paul bashed the soldier in the face with the butt end, splitting his lips and knocking out some teeth. The sergeant dropped to the ground. Paul smashed the rifle to the ground breaking the stock to pieces, ruining the firing mechanism. He used what was left of the rifle to whack the stricken soldier over the head, and tossed the pieces at the sergeant. The Indians had a way of dealing with their enemies, which made them think twice about exacting revenge. As he lay there, bleeding profusely, the sergeant glanced at Jacques. Something about Jacques made him take notice. It might have been the fact that this Micmac had blond hair. He would remember this man's face. Meanwhile, Jacques grabbed the private's rifle and wrested it away from him, smashing the butt end into his stomach knocking the wind out of him. He also went down. Seeing what Paul had done to the rifle, Jacques also smashed his to the ground breaking the stock and rendering the gun useless. He also tossed his gun to the hapless soldier. The French merchants were stunned when they beheld the mayhem. Never had anyone defied the hated English before.

When a few English soldiers were seen approaching from the fort, the merchants gathered together to form a barrier, preventing the soldiers from seeing their stricken comrades.

"Go!" shouted one of the merchants to Jacques and Paul. The pair nonchalantly turned and made their way to the river and the safety of their canoe.

"That was the same Micmac that was here a while back trading his furs," said one of the merchants, remembering the havoc Jacques had caused.

"He's going to get himself killed," replied another.

A few weeks later sergeant Mitchell was seen, accompanied by four armed soldiers, patrolling the market square, minus some teeth. He seemed to have learned some manners as he no longer bullied his way through the crowd, and he no longer carried a rifle.

In the summer of 1716 while Jacques visited the Micmac camp along the Annapolis River, he was informed by Paul that the Catholic Missionaries in Nova Scotia, Quebec, and Cape Breton had called for a great pow-wow of all the tribes to meet at Cape Breton. The occasion was the distribution of gifts from France to be doled out to all the friendly tribes allied with France. The meeting would take place in October. Jacques accompanied the Micmacs to Cape Breton to witness the event. Hundreds of Indians showed up. They quickly erected shelters. They were treated with delicious food including bread and all manner of meats. Liquor was also distributed to which the Indians quickly consumed turning a somber affair into one of gaiety. The hated Kenebecks were there, which the missionaries were able to control.

Jacques met Father Michel, a Recollect missionary priest, who lived among the Indians the last twenty years, eating raw meat like them, sleeping in the cold and even fasting when food was scarce.

"I haven't had fresh bread in six years," said Father Michel.

He could scarcely speak French now without mixing it with Indian words. The Indians gave him the honour and respect due a priest. Games were played with opposing tribes. The Micmacs won most of the games. After the games it was the custom of the losing team to pay the winning team. The Micmacs won so much it took large blankets to carry it all. After this affair, the Kenebecks became friends with the Micmacs, and a lasting peace ensued.

Jacques learned that there were about four hundred Indians living on the island. They were a tall, olive-skinned people with long black hair. Their women were also tall and fat. Their cabins were covered with oil-treated birch bark, which they rolled up and carried with them in their boats. Isadore was one of their leaders; he spoke French and was a most wily man. His daughters were quite handsome even though they wore animal skin dresses: that is, their bodies were covered but their arms, legs and thighs were naked.

Jacques had more interesting stories to tell the Heberts when he arrived back home after the pow-wows. There was never a dull moment in his life.

CHAPTER EIGHT

Beautiful Magdelaine

In the summer of 1716, the French Sieur de Verville, an engineer skilled in the art of fortifications, was sent to Cape Breton to lay out the plans for the construction of the fortress to be known as Fort Louisbourg. The following year, July 1717, construction started in earnest.

At this time, some of the French settlers at Annapolis Royal, in Nova Scotia, eager to get out from under the rule of the British government, were informed that French ships would arrive to transport them to nearby Cape Breton. Anticipating their departure, they did not bother to plant crops. The ships never arrived, so they were dependant on their neighbors for sustenance.

The same year, John Doucette, a French Huguenot, became governor of Nova Scotia. He sent troops out to outlying areas to compel the French settlers to sign the oath of allegiance. The French were willing to sign providing a clause was inserted indicating that they would not be required to take up arms against anyone. Failing to get the Acadians to sign, John Doucette was exasperated. He wrote letters to the Roman Catholic missionaries of the outlying districts asking them to intercede, and use their influence to induce the French to sign the oath.

Felix Pain, a Catholic priest at Mines, wrote back stating:

"I have received the letter, with which you honored me, under date of December 5, 1717. I have the honor to signify to you, sir that these Acadians must be sufficiently acquainted with their duties and obligations without needing my help for what you desire me to do with regard to them. Allow me to declare to you, so that you may have nothing to say against my behavior in this matter, that I am resolved to give no advice for or against the measure: thus you will recognize their natural intentions."

The French governor of Cape Breton wrote the governor of Nova Scotia asking why the French had not been allowed to leave. The English governor wrote back stating that the French settlers had been given one year in which to make up their minds to either leave, or stay. Since the year had come and gone, they were no longer entitled to the provisions of the peace treaty.

When it became obvious that should the French setters leave there would be no one to provide food for the garrison and the few English settlers, and to keep a tight control on the Indians, they were, of course, denied permission to leave during the period specified.

The French governor wrote back:

"Concerning your complaints that the inhabitants of Acadia had not departed as agreed upon, and that this delay has caused loss to His Britannic Majesty, you must have known, sir, the impossibility in which Mr. Nicholson and other rulers of Acadia have put them to executing what had been agreed upon; some not wishing to let them carry away their effects, and the others not wishing to send them the rigging to equip the little ships they had built, and which in consequence they were obliged to sell almost for nothing to English merchants. I will not fail to inform the King my master of all your remarks to me thereon, so that he may give the orders that he will judge proper."

Signed..deBrouillan, Governor of Cape Breton.

With all that was happening, the British governor decided, for the time being, to let things quiet down. Throughout all the years, whenever the British were victorious in conquering land, they had little difficulty subjugating the inhabitants and eliciting an oath of allegiance from them. The French settlers in Nova Scotia were, however, a different lot. Never had the English seen anything like it. The English had little trouble when they took New York from the Dutch, thus establishing the British Empire in the New World, in compelling them to take the oath of allegiance. However, the Acadians, being very well armed and with the Micmacs as allies, were a force to contend with.

The soldiers stationed at Annapolis Royal actually feared the French settlers. They had been warned by their superiors to be on guard against the Catholic Acadians who would just as soon slit their throats as look at them. When Jacques and Paul attacked the two English soldiers, there was no retaliation for fear of an uprising since the Acadians and Indians greatly outnumbered the British garrison.

Something had to be done to guarantee the safety of the garrison at

Annapolis Royal. The English governor, Doucet, tried again to illicit the signing of the oath by the French. In desperation the French settlers, or Acadians as they were better known, wrote to the French governor of Quebec.

"You are, sir, aware of the difficulties opposed to our departure when we petitioned for it, and the impossibility in which we were to accomplish what was demanded of us. And yet now, they wish to constrain us to take the oath or to abandon the country, and it is impossible to do either. We are resolved not to take this oath imposed upon us, but we cannot quit the country without suitable facilities such as were promised to us by the court of France and refused by the court of England. Our situation is painful and perplexing and we beseech you to assist us."

The French governor then wrote to Colonel Richard Philipps, Governor-in-Chief of Nova Scotia, the following:

"Allow me to state that the inaction of the Acadians neither can nor should be imputed to them, both on account of their want of the assistance essentially requisite for their transmigration, and on account of the obstacles which the Governors, General or Local, who preceded you put in their way.

"I cannot, moreover, refrain from representing to you that the clauses of your proclamation that refer to the term and the circumstance of their departure seem to me but little in keeping with ordinary kindness, especially after a treaty and an agreement of mutual good faith between Queen Anne and King Louis XIV, a treaty that has been executed in its entirety by France and partially by England, and I have the honor to represent to you that nothing could be harsher than the extremity or rather the impossibility to which these poor people would be reduced, should you not consent to be less severe for the time and the manner in which you exact their departure."

At a meeting with his officers Colonel Philipps was all for evicting the Acadians, but a captain named Paul Mascarene said, "If the Acadians leave they will destroy the dikes that had been constructed after years of labor, causing irreparable damage. The Indians will wreak havoc with us. Cape Breton will be greatly strengthened," said Mascarene.

Colonel Philipps wrote to England for instructions, meanwhile he issued a proclamation to the Acadians.

"It is expressly prohibited to those who will choose to leave the country to sell, dispose or bring with them any of their effects."

That devastating news caused a great stir amongst the Acadians. Those conditions were of Colonel Phillips's own making --- cruel and unjust. Forcing someone to sign a document does not make that morally binding.

Jacques's plans for establishing himself and his family in Nova Scotia were uncertain and tenuous at best.

The next time the Catholic missionary visited Annapolis Royal the Acadians met with him to discuss their future. The priest drafted a letter to Colonel Philipps:

"We cannot take the oath which you demand of us, and the question is still more difficult with regard to the Indians than to the French because the former daily threaten us with revenge if our reservations do not extend to them. Since you cannot grant us this reservation, there only remains to us the alternative of retiring from the country even on the hard conditions you impose, life being dearer to us than all our goods. As the sowing season has just elapsed and there remains hardly any more grain to nourish our families, the only favor we beg of you is to prolong the delay a little, so as to give us time to gather in our grain and permission to carry it away with us, and also to make use of the vehicles that we own or of those we might make or otherwise procure hoping that Your Excellency will permit us to send to Cape Breton Island to ask help for our departure."

The dastardly Colonel Philipps replied to the response by informing the Acadians that the only right they had was to sell or dispose of their effects should they desire to leave. He knew that since they were the only inhabitants, they could hardly sell to each other.

More meetings between the Acadians were held trying to determine the next course of action. The British had denied them the use of the river for transportation, or even constructing ships for that purpose. To use the overland route seemed impossible since there were no roads.

The Acadians had large stores of food besides livestock to take with them, which would not only benefit them in their new location, Cape Breton, but would help the French forces there also. How to get it there was the problem.

The French forces at Fort Louisburg had engineers skilled at road building, i.e., cutting through the forest to clear avenues. The Governor of Cape Breton decided to use his engineers to clear a path through the woods from Cape Breton to Annapolis Royal. If the Acadians could not use the river route, they would use the new road. Construction of the road began at the far end of Nova Scotia, near Cape Breton. Every able-bodied French settler pitched in to help.

Word of the road construction reached Colonel Philips. He flew into a rage. He quickly got a letter off to England telling the Lords of Trade that the French were constructing a road from Cape Breton to Annapolis Royal with the intention of using this road to invade and destroy Annapolis Royal. He knew full well that the real purpose of the road was for the convenience of the Acadians to be able to transport all their belongings and livestock.

The Lords of Trade replied to Colonel Philipps:

"As to the Acadians of Nova Scotia, we are of the opinion they ought to be removed as soon as the forces which we have proposed to be sent to you shall arrive in your province; but as you are not to attempt their removal without His Majesty's positive order for that purpose, you will do well in the meanwhile to continue the same prudent and cautious conduct towards them."

This profound document will henceforth haunt the English for years to come. Many will blame the Governor of the American Colonies, Phipps, and the Governor of Nova Scotia, Colonel Lawrence, to be the instigators of removing the French from their homeland, but the truth is that the Crown of England is directly responsible for this inhuman, and dastardly act. Further proof of this atrocious and shameful deed on the part of England comes from a letter written by the Secretary of State of the British Kingdom, Secretary Craggs to Colonel Philipps.

"My dear Philipps:

"I see you do not get the better of the Acadians as you expected before your departure. It is singular all the same that these people should have preferred to lose their goods rather than to be exposed to fight against their brethren. This sentimentality is stupid.

"These people are evidently too much attached to their fellow countrymen and to their religion ever to make true Englishmen. It must be avowed your position was deucedly critical; it was very difficult to prevent them from departing after having left the bargain to their choice. However, you did well to act thus, it was your only resource. The treaty be hanged!

"Don't bother about justice and other baubles any more than Nicholson and Vetch did; those thing will not advance our interests.

"Their departure will, doubtless, increase the power of France; it must not be so; they must eventually be transported to some place where, mingling with our subjects, they will soon lose their language, their religion, and the remembrance of the past, to become true Englishmen."

Now Colonel Philipps must come up with a ruse to prevent the Acadians from leaving, fearing for the build up at Cape Breton. He conveyed a false message to the Acadians that they would no longer be molested or hindered and would not be required to sign the oath of allegiance. Upon hearing this, the road-building project came to an end.

An uneasy peace settled between the Acadians and the English. The Acadians did not trust the English and knew full well that any time they could turn and deal badly with them.

It was under these conditions that Jacques courted and came to marry his lovely Magdelaine. In the fall of 1720 after the planting and harvesting were done, missionary Father Charlemagne Couvier performed the marriage ceremony at St. Joseph's Church at Annapolis Royal.

Since the English hated the Catholic missionaries, there was always pressure to oust them from Nova Scotia, and not knowing when he might be forced to leave, Father Couvier performed the ceremony after publishing the bans of marriage only twice, instead of the usual three.

On November 25, 1720 with half the Micmac tribe in attendance and with thirteen of her brothers and sisters taking up most of the seats in the tiny church, Jacques and Magdelaine were wed.

A copy of the actual marriage certificate is on file at the Canadian Archives in Halifax, and at the University of Moncton, in Moncton, New Brunswick, Canada. Translated from the original French:

"On the twenty-fifth day of November of the year seventeen hundred twenty, I the undersigned, in charge of priestly functions at Port Royal of Acadie, after having published only twice, for unavoidable reasons, without there having been found any impediment, I have joined together before witnesses present, Jacques Maillet, son of deceased Antoine Maillet, making a living in Paris, and of the deceased Francoise Choppart, to Magdelaine Hebert, daughter of Antoine Hebert and of Jeanne Corporon, living in Port Royal, in faith of which I have signed with the groom and the bride, the parents and witnesses the day and the year mentioned."

Signed: Father Chalemange Couvier, Missionary
Signature of Groom: Jacque Malliet (sic)
Signature of Bride: X

The reception was held at the home of the bride's parents. The music, festivities, and food lasted till the late hours of the night. Later, the newlyweds entered their new home adjacent to the Hebert homestead. Magdelaine's sisters assisted her in removing her wedding gown, and left.

Alone at last they retired for the night. After the lantern was extinguished, the commotion started outside; pots banging, cow bells clanking, whistling, shouting, hands clapping…the usual saturnalia following a wedding reception. All Jacques could do was sit up in bed while she hid under the blankets. When the revelry finally died down and the noisemakers went home, she peeked from under the cover, and in the dim moonlight saw Jacques fast asleep in a sitting position.

The following week the Micmacs left the Annapolis River to winter in the interior. The first heavy snows arrived shortly thereafter. Jacques and Magdelaine lost themselves in complete ecstasy.

As the snow fell and covered the ground, Jacques and Magdelaine gazed out the front window to behold the gentle flowing river, spread out in front of their farm, glistening like a jewel. The whole countryside was covered in a white blanket. Here and there could be seen smoke rising from the chimneys, pinpointing the homesteads. The Hebert children next door gleefully played with their homemade sleds in the snow.

The cold winter months kept the Acadians indoors most of the time so by the time spring arrived in 1721 it was a welcome relief to spend a little time outdoors. The Annapolis River had warmed enough to melt the ice and open the vital waterway once again.

One evening, as Jacques sat by the fireside, Magdelaine, who had been cooped up all winter and felt she wanted a change of scenery, approached him and sat on his lap. She wrapped her arms around him and looking longingly into his eyes asked, "What is it like, living with the Micmacs in the woods?"

"There is nothing like it in the world."

"Can we visit the Micmacs?"

Jacques looked at her. The question caught him completely off guard, and he couldn't believe she was asking something like that. He thought she was joking.

"You mean you want to travel into the woods and visit with Paul?"

"Yes, darling," she said, as she brushed her face against his, her hair falling over his eyes. She had not been feeling well lately and felt she wanted to get out and breathe some fresh air. Maybe a trip downriver would help. He could hardly resist her. She was soft all over and he felt he was like putty in her hands. He looked into her beautiful blue eyes, and thought to himself, "what a woman."

"Well, if you really mean it, when would you like to go?" He asked.

"Would tomorrow be too soon?"

Jacques laughed and replied, "If you want to go tomorrow, you had better get your things ready now."

She gave him a kiss, jumped off his lap and made for the bedroom to pack her belongings. She had this planned all the while because she had just finished baking more bread than usual. Fresh bread was something the Indians dearly loved, and it made a wonderful gift.

The following morning, Jacques got the canoe ready and loaded the supplies. The sun was shining brightly this day as if to add to the pleasant atmosphere of the trip.

With the canoe in the water he picked up his lovely bride and carried her, placing her gently in the front of the canoe, then he pushed off and jumped in behind her.

She was dressed in a warm woolen parka with a heavy hood, long woolen pants, and mukluks made by the Indians. He was dressed in his Micmac moose skin jacket and pants, also wearing heavy boots, called mukluks. Both were wearing heavy woolen mittens. Although the sun was shining, the temperature was still near freezing. As they paddled along, she turned to look at him, her face resplendent in a rosy glow. Her hair protruding from the sides of the hood added to her picturesque beauty. She smiled at him with that smile that just melted his heart, that irresistible smile that beckoned him to hold her, to love her and want her. He smiled back, thinking to himself that he was the luckiest man in the world.

Overhead, the geese were returning to their summer homes, their long V formations were a sight to behold. All along the river farm animals were enjoying the new greenery and grazing contentedly. A dog, from one of the farms, ran up to the edge of the river to bark at them as if to warn them away from his property.

Jacques had taught Magdelaine how to paddle a canoe, placing the paddle even with her waist, then dip and push back, giving the paddle a slight twist at the end of its travel. She could keep this up for hours. He sang as they paddled keeping time with the cadence of the song. They floated past the beautiful Acadian farms nestled along the river. There lived the Saulniers, there the Doucettes, there the Boudreaus. They followed the twists and turns in the river till they arrived at a large stream leading into the woods. At the end of the stream, in the shallow water, Jacques jumped out and carried Magdelaine on to dry land. After beaching the canoe, he reached into the supplies and pulled out a small leather bag. He removed some dried tobacco leaves and proceeded to sprinkle them into the air, letting the wind carry them away, and said, "Migamawesu, it is I, Jacques. I have come to visit my brothers. I have brought my bride with me. Be with us and protect us."

Magdelaine was surprised at this ceremony. She knew Jacques to be a good Catholic, not prone to praying to strange gods, but at the same time she was excited with this performance. Somehow, she was starting to feel part of what he was, a free roaming spirit.

They loaded their supplies onto their backpacks and headed into the deep forbidding forest. He had his black powder musket ready for any danger. He carried it with his left hand. His knife, in a sheath, was at his right side, also ready. Along the way, startled deer ran for cover. Black squirrels, common in the North Country, darted about the branches of tall trees. They could feel the presence of wild animals observing their movements.

"See this print," said Jacques, pointing to a deep hoof print in the soft sand. "A moose passed this way not more than an hour ago."

"Darling," said Magdelaine, "how can you tell it was an hour ago?"

"The print is still dark, compared with the light colored soil surrounding it. It still has moisture in it. As the print ages, it dries and will become the same color as the soil around it. The Micmacs know that this would be a good print to follow to get that moose."

Continuing on, she said, "Darling, what happens if we get lost?"

He chuckled at her question realizing that to her this must be a strange environment. He also felt that way when he first ventured into the wilderness.

"Always look for low lying ground. There you will probably find water, then just follow that stream. They all empty into the Annapolis River."

After a two-hour hike, he pointed out smoke rising above the trees ahead.

"That's the camp, up ahead," said Jacques.

"Thank God," she replied.

Jacques gave a loud yell to announce his arrival.

"Who is it?" came the response from the camp.

"It is I, Jacques!" He replied.

Paul ran out to greet his friend. Meeting them half way, he took the heavy load off Magdelaine's back. "Here, let me help," said Paul.

Inside the wigwam, Paul's mother, Mary, gave Magdelaine some hot tea made from evergreen needles. "This should take the chill from you."

Mary then told Anne, Paul's sister, to prepare a bed for Magdelaine. When it was ready, they encouraged Magdelaine to rest a while. In short order, she fell asleep, tired from the long walk and the canoe paddling. They covered her with a large moose skin blanket. She slept soundly.

Awakening the following morning she could not eat breakfast, claiming she was not feeling well. Alarmed, Jacques did not know what to do. How could a trip make her ill, he wondered. Mary noticed Jacques's concern for his wife and took him aside.

"You will soon be a father," said Mary.

CHAPTER NINE

The oath of allegiance

In May of 1721, Paul was to get his chance at bringing down a moose by himself. Out hunting one day he saw the spoor of a large moose, evident by the deep depression. He followed the trail and came across the large bull moose in a small clearing. Getting as close as he could, downwind, he was able to loose an arrow and strike the beast in the hindquarter. The moose quickly ambled away, limping as it went. Paul trailed the animal for a whole day firing arrows at every chance. Eventually, the animal tired and Paul was able to get close enough to finish him off. He thanked the animal's spirit for giving up its life so that he may obtain nourishment. It took him most of a day to get back to his camp. Back at camp, his father, Jean-Pierre, decided it would be better to move the whole wigwam to the kill sight rather than trying to move the large animal. The Micmacs set up their camps such that with little notice they can simply pick up and move, which they often did when a kill was made at great distances.

In the spring of 1721 the Micmacs returned to their summer homes along the Annapolis River. Paul and his family set up camp near old friends of theirs. There was a beautiful Indian maiden living at this camp. Paul had known her for many years, but never paid much attention to her, now seeing her again he could hardly believe his eyes. She had blossomed into a woman almost overnight. He watched her one day, as she went to a fresh water stream for water. He grabbed a gourd and dashed to the stream on a pretense of fetching water. They met at the stream and he exchanged pleasantries. She smiled at him and he asked if he could call on her. She dropped her eyes and bashfully nodded her head in assent. He was elated, grabbing her water carrier; he said he would help her.

Paul's parents were gladdened with the news that he would be courting the young girl, next door so to speak. Paul visited the girl's parents and made his intentions known to them. They accepted him and with that he proceeded to move his things from his own wigwam to his intended's. He would live with them for a year or so, all the while providing her family with food from his hunts and fishing trips. He had to prove to her parents that he was capable of taking care of her not only by providing food, but also by showing that he was skilled at making various things, such as tools and even a canoe. She had to prove to him that she could cook, treat skins and make clothing.

After the long courtship was over, sometimes lasting two or three years, the families would get together and arrange for the wedding. The feast would last for days. There were games to play, songs to sing, and the traditional dancing.

Jacques and Magdelaine were busy with their new life together. He now had crops to plant, animals to tend, furniture to make, provide meat, etc. He also had the hated British to contend with.

As usual, the Micmacs were causing great problems for the English. They would capture British couriers and hold them for ransom. Skilled at boating they would venture out into the Atlantic Ocean and capture large numbers of

English ships. They delighted in sailing these prizes, then selling them back to the English. They captured numerous ships in the Bay of Fundy all to the consternation of the British. Paul reported all these events to Jacques as they occurred.

In the fall of 1721 a blessed event occurred when Jacques became a father. Magdelaine bore him a son, born on November 29, 1721. They named him Jean-Jacque. Because they now had so much at stake it was very difficult to abandon everything and move, so hoping for the best they decided to stay and see what the outcome would be.

The Micmacs were taking so many English vessels that finally England declared war on the Indians. The English were fighting on Indian territory, not a good choice when you consider that the Indians knew every nook and cranny in Nova Scotia. The Indians stepped up their attacks taking a total of 25 vessels in the Bay of Fundy and off the coast of Nova Scotia in 1722.

On one of their raids just off the coast of Nova Scotia, in the Atlantic, the Indians spotted a ship from New England. This ship was carrying sixty armed men. The Micmacs, with fifteen men aboard, took after the vessel. They fought for two hours. Greatly outnumbered and under armed, the Micmacs relented and escaped by abandoning their vessel and swimming to shore leaving five dead behind. The English put the heads of the dead men up on pickets at the port of Canso for all to see. In retaliation, the following year, in July of 1723, all the Micmacs in all of Eastern Canada took part in a raid on Canso. They captured 17 sailing ships.

In the summer of 1723, Paul married his sweetheart, Babette, on the shore of the Annapolis River. There was feasting, singing, and dancing for days. Jacques and Magdelaine were the guests of honor. Jacques was his best man. The wedding was also officiated by missionary Father Charlemagne Couvier who performed the Catholic sacrament.

On September 13, 1723 Magdelaine gave birth to their second child, another boy. They named him Antoine Solomon.

The following year, in the summer of 1724, the Micmacs attacked the fort at Annapolis Royal. They were able to surprise the British Police force at the market square and captured, of all people, sergeant Eric Mitchel, and a few English soldiers. They shot and scalped sergeant Mitchel. They also killed an English private and wounded several British officers who managed to make it back to the safety of the fort. They destroyed some of the homes belonging to the English settlers, killing their farm animals along the way. They took away with them several men, woman and children. Those were ransomed later and returned to their homes unharmed.

Lieutenant-Governor Doucet later ordered that a Micmac prisoner be taken to the same spot where sergeant Mitchel was killed, and there executed. After the execution, he ordered that the Micmac be scalped!

A British officer named Murdoch, wrote later:

"The execution of the hostage or prisoner I cannot but regard as a blot on the fair fame of our people; while great allowance should be made for the feelings of the English, exasperated as they doubtless were by the barbarous cruelties exercised on their countrymen in New England and Nova Scotia, and the treachery they found at work everywhere. However this execution may be palliated, I see no grounds on which in any way it can be justified."

Still seething with revenge, Doucet ordered some of the Acadians homes nearby destroyed. "I know the priest put the Indians up to this," said Doucet. He ordered Recollet Father Charlemagne Couvier out of the country.

Father Couvier, who had performed the wedding ceremony for Jacques, Paul, and many others, beloved by all Acadians at Annapolis Royal, left Nova Scotia and established himself at Cape Breton.

On December 6, 1724, Magdelaine brought another child into the world, another boy. They named him Gregoire.

Construction of the fortress at Cape Breton by the French, better known as Fort Louisburg was booming. Louisburg was becoming a major port with an ever-increasing population. While Louisburg was strengthening itself, Annapolis Royal was falling into disrepair. This scenario gave the local French inhabitants at Annapolis Royal a false sense of security. They turned their backs on the English conquerors. Many Acadians left Annapolis Royal to settle on the isolated island of Ile Saint-Jean (now known as Prince Edward Island) across the Northumberland Strait. One of the first white settlers there was a man named Michel Gallant and his wife Anne, nee Cormier. It is said that all of the Gallants in Canada are descendants of this couple.

In October 1723, Paul's wife, Babette, bore him a male child. He named his son Joachim.

In the spring of 1724, Paul and Babette visited Jacques and Magdelaine. Babette carried little Joachim, completely covered, in a special sling she carried on her back. She would carry Joachim wherever she went all day long, even while doing her work around the lodge. Jacques's children were fascinated with little Joachim. He had the darkest hair they had ever seen, a stark contrast to their light hair.

It is interesting to note that with the birth of these children, under British Territory, they automatically became British subjects entitled to English protection. However, the French determined to maintain their allegiance to their French Monarch, King Louis XV, and retain their Roman Catholic teachings.

As to the signing of the oath of allegiance, the Acadians were willing to sign provided there were clauses inserted, which excluded them from taking up arms, and giving them freedom of religion. The difference in religion was the main sticking point, and the Catholic priests in Acadie made sure that the French kept to their religious beliefs. The Catholic priests reminded the Acadians repeatedly that should they decide to sign the oath of allegiance, the Micmacs would burn their houses and kill their livestock. The Catholic missionaries ruled the Micmacs with an indomitable spirit.

The English also tried to rule with a resolute spirit. An account is on record of a servant of Governor Armstrong who had insulted his master. The servant was sentenced to sit upon the gallows for a half hour, three days in a row, with a rope about his neck from which hung a sign that read "Audacious Villain." When the three days were up, he was taken out and led from the fort to the end of the pier and back again receiving five lashes on his bare back with a cat-o-nine whip every one hundred paces.

On April 26, 1726 Jacques was again blessed with the birth of another boy. This fourth child he named Charles. This would be the boy who would most closely follow in his father's footsteps.

The fort at Annapolis Royal at this time was in shambles. It would have been an easy matter for the Acadians, assisted by the Micmacs, to charge and take the fort. Fearing this, Mr. Doucet, Lieutenant Governor of the province, decided he had better do something to avert a catastrophe. War with the Micmacs was wreaking havoc with the garrison. The English soldiers feared for their lives. Mr. Doucet either had to acquiesce or face defeat. The war had to cease.

In June of 1726 Paul visited Jacques to discuss events.

"Mr. Doucet wants to meet with us and sign a truce," said Paul.

"He better do something because he has no choice."

"We have arranged to meet with him, and we want you to be there with us," said Paul.

"We had better get Mr. Robichau to interpret what the English are saying," said Jacques. Mr. Robichau, an educated person, spoke English very well, and was well respected in Annapolis Royal. He would be the ideal choice to deal with the British.

On June 15, 1726, the gates of the fort were lowered and the chiefs of the Micmacs entered accompanied by Jacques, Prudent Robichau, and Abraham Bourg, who also spoke very good English. Paul and other braves escorted the entourage.

It was an eerie feeling, entering the fort again after so many years, for Jacques and Paul. They fought there sixteen years ago. They remembered leaving the fort exhausted, beaten and demoralized. Now, they were being received with military honors. English soldiers, resplendent in their red tunics, were lined up with the traditional presentation of arms. Mr. Doucet met the entourage and led the way to the center of the fort, where the English flag was flying.

"This place is a wreck," said Jacques to Paul, as they looked around. The walls were crumbling and buildings were in a sad state of disrepair.

"We could have taken this place and kicked their asses out of here," said Paul.

"I think Mr. Doucet knows that. That's why he wants to sign a peace treaty with you."

As Mr. Doucet read the terms of the peace treaty, Mr. Robichau did the interpreting. The Micmacs, conversing with each other and coming to an agreement, gave their assent to each of the demands. They signed the peace treaty.

Following the signing of the peace treaty, gifts were presented to the chiefs, and finally all Indian hostages were released. The freed Indians shouted in jubilation upon being released and reunited. The war hoops put the fear of God in the English garrison. The Indians were treated to a feast, and left the fort holding their heads high.

The Lieutenant Governor of the Province, Mr. Doucet, who had engineered the peace treaty, died shortly thereafter on 19 November of that same year. Colonel Armstrong arrived to take over the reins of Government on December 17, 1726.

The first order of business for the new governor was to have the Acadians sign an unconditional oath of allegiance. Colonel Armstrong sent for Acadian delegates; people chosen by the French to represent them. The delegation was to meet at the fort. At this meeting Armstrong gave a stern warning that should they refuse to sign, their properties would be confiscated. They indicated they would sign provided a clause was inserted indicating they would not take up arms. Armstrong wrote the clause along the margin, and they signed.

In September 1727 King George of England died and was succeeded by his son, King George II. Now, all British subjects had to sign a new oath of allegiance to the new monarch. As if Colonel Armstrong didn't have enough problems to get the Acadians to sign before, he now has to rescind the old oaths and have new ones signed. The Acadians figured that if they were able to sign on condition before, they might be able to gain more concessions on this go round. The Acadian deputies presented a list of demands, which infuriated Armstrong. He had two Acadian deputies jailed for contempt and disrespect to His Majesty's government.

British Ensign Robert Wroth was assigned the task of visiting the French in the far reaches of Nova Scotia and induce them to sign the oath of allegiance. Anxious to get the Acadians to sign, he promised them certain concessions. Among those concessions was the provision exempting them from bearing arms. They were also led to believe that they could leave the province whenever they wished and would be free to practice their religion.

Since Armstrong was just Lieutenant Governor of Nova Scotia, the real governor, Colonel Richard Philipps, now in England, had to leave his plush office and sail for Annapolis Royal to resolve the dilemma of the signing of the oath. He was extremely upset when he read the report that Ensign Robert Wroth had granted such liberties to the Acadians.

Colonel Philipps wrote to England later reporting that he had managed to get all the Acadians to sign the oath of allegiance. How had he done it? By a verbal promise! To back this promise the priests wrote the promise down and kept records.

"We, Charles de la Goudalie, priest missionary of the parish of Minas, and Noel Alexandre de Noinville, missionary and parish priest of the Assumption and of the Holy Family, of Pisiquid certify to whom this may concern, that His Excellency Richard Philipps...has promised to the inhabitants of Minas and other rivers dependent thereon, that he exempts them from bearing arms and fighting in wars against the French and the Indians, and that the said inhabitants have only accepted allegiance, and promised never to take up arms in the event of a war against the Kingdom of England and its Government."

The oath the Acadians signed is as follows:

"I promise and swear sincerely as a Christian that I will be entirely faithful, and truly obey His Majesty King George II, who I acknowledge as Supreme Lord of Acadia or Nova Scotia. So help me god."

The report sent back to England caused a concern amongst the scholars and grammatists. The Board of Trades wanted Philipps to go back and do it again. This time, do it right! The French had promised to be faithful, but to whom? Grammatically, as Philipps had constructed the oath 'faithful' had no object! The English feared that some Jesuit might see the flaw. Philipps wrote back arguing that the conjunction 'and' took care of the problem. He explained that no matter how the oath was written, the Jesuits could get around it. So the matter rested.

On November 9, 1727, Magdelaine brought another boy child into the world. They named him Louis Cyrille. Jacques had wanted one or two boys to help on the farm, now he had more than he could hope for. The boys loved the farm and enjoyed when Jacques took them fishing on the river. They intermingled with the Micmacs and learned the Indian tongue at an early age. Paul and Babette were also fruitful, and she bore him many sons.

Jacques and Paul still managed to hunt and trap animals. They sold their furs at the market and always received a good price. The English mainly kept to themselves at this time and spent their time at the fort, never venturing too far out. The British bought goods from the Acadians and for a time it seemed that they might actually get along. English ships regularly stopped at Annapolis Royal and traded there. Many ships came from the Caribbean loaded with fruits, and molasses, which the Acadians loved. Ships headed back to the islands in the Caribbean carried mostly lumber and dried codfish. Nova Scotia was noted for its fine trees used for making masts and spars in shipbuilding.

There was an uneasy peace in Nova Scotia at this time. The Acadians had signed the oath of allegiance with the proviso that they be declared Neutrals. The English accepted this, for now.

On February 17, 1729, Magdelaine delivered another child. To the immense joy for Jacques, this was a girl! The sweetest little baby girl in the world, and they named her Marie Magdelaine. Jacques carried this little bundle everywhere he went. He was so proud of her. Magdelaine had to admonish Jacques not to show so much favoritism to little Marie for fear the boys would be jealous, but it was hard putting her down. Jacques couldn't wait to tell Paul of his new daughter.

The Acadians were increasing in great numbers, to the concern of the English overlords. In the past ten years they had doubled in population in Nova Scotia. The English were not granting any more land to the Acadians, so the French had to subdivide what land they had, as was the case for Antoine and Jacques. Because they could no longer obtain space for farms, the newlyweds were relocating across the Bay of Fundy to New Brunswick. There were so many French settlers now moving to New Brunswick that the region near Nova Scotia was named Nouvelle Acadie Francaise. Many other newlyweds were migrating to Prince Edward Island.

Colonel Philipps had a conference in his office at Fort Anne in Annapolis Royal with his subordinate officers in the summer of 1729.

"Gentlemen," said the Governor, "something has to be done about these Acadians." He looked across the conference table to all the officers seated there. Orderlies dressed in white tunics, were standing by with refreshments for the officers.

"What do you propose, Colonel?" asked Major Cosby.

"Well, that is why I have called for this council," said Philipps.

"We are greatly outnumbered here, and the French have constructed a huge fortress on Cape Breton. We need reinforcements to be able to do anything," said Captain Taylor.

"I agree with you, Captain," said Philipps. "We need to get these people out of here so that we can replace them with proper English people from our own country."

"Sir," said Major Henry Cope, "no one from England wants to migrate and live where there are savages, and French Papists all around. Their lives would be in constant danger."

"So, that is the crux of the matter!" said Philipps.

Philipps placed ads in the New England papers offering free land to all Protestants settlers who wished to come. No one took him up; such was the fear they had of the French.

The question of what to do with the Acadians was left to the Board of Trades in England. Mr. Philipps left for England and Armstrong assumed command of the province.

On December 6, 1733 Jacques became a father once more. Magdelaine gave birth to another boy. They named him, Joseph.

Also in December of 1733 the English near the fort arrested a man named Francis Meuse. It seems Mr. Meuse had chopped some trees and placed them in the road leading to the fort, such that it prevented the supply wagons from reaching the fort. For this offense, Mr. Meuse was tied to a post at the entrance to the fort, stripped to the waist, and given forty lashes with the cat-o-nine-tails.

There was no more mention of signing the oath of allegiance for the time being. Jacques remained busy on his farm in the summer and hunting with Paul in the winter. Together, they were able to amass quite a handsome sum of money

On August 11, 1735, Magdelaine's beloved father, Antoine, died. He was sixty-five years old. Jacques was heartbroken. He dearly loved his benefactor. He owed just about everything he had to this kind man. This was the man who took him in, fed him, clothed him, gave him shelter, and eventually gave him his daughter to wed.

Generations follow generations. On November 12, of that same year, a few months after the passing of Antoine, Magdelaine brought another child into the world. Another boy, they named him Jean-Baptiste. Jacques now had seven boys, and the darling of his eye, little six-year-old Marie Magdelaine, the only girl.

The Acadian (French) population at this time in Nova Scotia was roughly about 1,400 at Annapolis Royal, 4,000 at Grand Pre, and about 2,000 at Beaubassin, the border town between Nova Scotia and New Brunswick. The Acadians were increasing in population yearly. The English Governors were upset that no British subjects were migrating to Nova Scotia, the land of plenty.

Jacques's oldest son, fifteen-year-old Jean-Jacques, accompanied him everywhere. Jean-Jacques was an accomplished woodsman; completely at home everywhere he went. He spoke fluent Micmac and had many Indian friends.

"I remember when I was your age," said Jacques to his son, Jean-Jacques, one day in late December of 1735, while a snowstorm howled outside. Jacques seated in his comfortable chair by the warm fireside, holding little Marie-Magdelaine on his lap. "We were young soldiers fighting the English at the fort." The children, eager to hear the stories, gathered around. "How many Brits did you kill, Papa?" asked twelve-year-old Antoine.

Magdelaine, who hated violence and did not want to see her children become soldiers, concerned for their safety, interrupted and looked sternly at Jacques to get him to talk about something else. "The children don't want to hear your old war stories," said Magdelaine. "Tell them how you came over here on the big ship." So, Jacques had to change the subject and delighted the children with his sea adventures.

On February 22, 1737 Magdelaine gave birth to another of Jacques's delight. Another girl they named, Marie Elisabeth. Little seven-year-old Marie Magdelaine was delighted to have a baby sister. Her brothers were always teasing her. Now, she would have someone who would play with her.

On January 5, 1738, Magdelaine gave birth to another boy. They named him Euphrosie. Jacques's family was increasing by leaps and bounds. It was at this period of time in Nova Scotia that the Acadian population, in general, was also increasing at a tremendous rate, so much so that the English governors were concerned. Instead of becoming British subjects, as natural born citizens, these children were being raised, first Roman Catholic, secondly French.

On February 8, 1739, Magdelaine gave birth to another boy. The named him Etienne. Also in 1739 a strange event occurred. Lieutenant Governor Armstrong, either due to ill health, or deep depression, committed suicide. Some say he had been acting very strange prior to his death, and some say he had been a lunatic. John Adams assumed the command, but was replaced shortly thereafter by Mascarene.

In the summer of 1739 Jacques and his son, Jean-Jacques, visited Paul at the Indian summer camp along the Annapolis River. Seventeen-year-old Jean-Jacques and Paul's fifteen-year-old son, Joachim, took the canoe out to do some fishing while the elders talked.

"Have I missed anything lately?" asked Jacques to his old friend, Paul.

"Well, we had some fun a few nights ago," replied Paul.

"Still harassing the English are you," said Jacques.

Paul starting laughing and said, "We swam up to one of their vessels anchored in the bay at night, and cut the anchor rope. The ship floated away!"

"Oh, that must have been great."

"It certainly was. They couldn't stop if from floating away and all hell broke out on deck when they gave the alarm."

Jacques told Paul that a new missionary had arrived at Annapolis Royal. His name was Nicholas Vaquelin.

Any missionary assigned to Nova Scotia by the Bishop of Quebec had to appear before the British governor for permission to work there. This order was instituted to keep the missionaries from overstepping their bounds. They were not permitted to travel from one parish to another without first obtaining permission.

"This new missionary is soft on the British. He favors signing the oath of allegiance and submitting to British authority," said Jacques.

"He sounds like the complete opposite of the new missionary that our brothers speak of. We have been hearing about a most unusual missionary camped at Shubernacadie (situated in the heartland of Nova Scotia)."

"What's so unusual about him?" asked Jacques.

"Well, for one thing. He carries a gun instead of a cross!"

"A missionary with a gun?"

"Yes," replied Paul, "his name is Father LeLoutre. Our brothers tell us that this missionary can walk further than any Micmac, can carry a heavier load, and he can go longer than we can without food."

"This is no ordinary missionary, indeed," said Jacques.

"This missionary speaks better Micmac than we do, and he has only been here about two years."

"Well the missionaries are supposed to be intelligent people. They are the only ones here who can read and write French."

"They say he has an intense hatred for the British, and tells our people that the English Protestants are devils to be eliminated."

Abbe Jean-Louis LeLoutre, was born in 1709. He graduated from the Seminaire des Missions Etrangeres, Paris in 1736 and was sent to Nova Scotia in 1737. He carved himself a niche in Canadian history as the most notorious person ever to have set foot on those shores. A bane to the British, he was, nevertheless, a hero to the French. He never bothered to check with the British authorities for permission to work in Nova Scotia.

The English anchorless vessel, that Paul set afloat, arrived at Annapolis Royal for repairs about a week after the Indians cut the anchor rope. Her captain, Trefry, requested an anchor be removed from a derelict ship tied up at the port.

The derelict ship that Captain Trefry mentioned was the brigantine Baltimore. This ship was found abandoned at a nearby port. Upon investigation it was determined that the crew of this ship had all been murdered (bodies were found on the shore) and that the lone survivor was a woman named Mrs. Buckler, wife of the captain. She managed to make it to shore and was taken care of by the local Indians. The ship's cargo was completely removed by the Indians. Mrs. Buckler was eventually taken to Boston.

Upon the death of Lieutenant-Governor Armstrong in 1739, Paul Mascarene succeeded him. Mascarene was a French Huguenot, who had been driven from his country by religious persecution.

The fort at Annapolis Royal was in bad shape. The earthen walls were crumbling, and the buildings were rotting away. Mascarene wrote to the Board of Trades in London advising them of the necessity of repairing the fort. He was informed that little could be done as this time and in fact danger was looming in the near future, and so he should do whatever he could to beef up the fortifications as best he could.

The peace treaty signed in 1713 gave the British limited trading rights on the Spanish sea-lanes. The British exceeded this limit and forced the Spanish to retaliate. In one of the clashes between England and Spain, an Englishman named Jenkins, lost an ear. Jenkins preserved his ear in a bottle and presented it to the English Parliament. Angered at the sight of the ear, the British declared war on Spain. This war became known as the War of Jenkins's Ear. The English feared this would eventually lead to a confrontation with France, so Mascarene was advised to be careful.

As the population of Acadians was increasing, Mascarene looked to England for advice. He wrote to the Board of Trades in November of 1740.

"The increase of the Acadians calls for some fresh instructions how to dispose of them. They have divided and sub-divided amongst their children the lands they were in possession of. They applied for new grants which the Governors Philipps and Armstrong did not think themselves authorized to favor them with, as His Majesty's instruction prescribed that grants be given to Protestant subjects only. This long delay has occasioned several of them to settle themselves on some of the skirts of the Province, pretty far distant from this place, notwithstanding Proclamations and orders to the contrary have been often repeated. If they are debarred from new possessions, they must be made to withdraw to the neighboring French colony."

The Board of Trades replied to Mascarene that only Protestant subjects were to be given grants of land.

The fort being constructed at Isle Royal (Cape Breton) by the French was being beefed up. This force kept the fishermen from the colonies from fishing at the Grand Banks, famous for its cod. The American colonists were angry at being denied access to this abundance of food. Resentment against the French was building in the colonies. Besides the incursions of Indians into the colonies, raiding and pillaging, now they were being denied a source of food. They were seeking revenge.

On August 5, 1741 Magdelaine gave birth to another child, a girl. They named her Ange. The following year, 1742 she bore another child, a girl. They named her Louise. This gave Jacques thirteen children.

The situation in Europe at this time was tenuous. Nations were rising against nations. Eventually, France and England were involved. On March 18, 1744 France declared war on England. Now the garrison at Annapolis Royal was concerned. How the Acadians would react, was questionable.

CHAPTER TEN

Father LeLoutre

Early on the morning of June 12, 1744, before the sun came up, while carrying eggs from the barn, Jean-Jacques, Jacques's twenty-three year old son, caught a glimpse of dark shadows approaching in the river. He quickly ran to the house to inform his father.

"Papa, there are hundreds of men on the river coming this way!"

Jacques looked at him in disbelief, and then he ran out to see for himself.

He was stunned to see that this large group of men had stopped at his landing, and were beaching their canoes on his farm. In the dim early morning light, he recognized Paul leading a large group of Indians. He ran to greet his friend.

"Jacques," said Paul, "we need to camp here for a while."

"Of course, come in."

Jacques recognized the Indians, and he greeted them. In the midst, standing there as tall as could be, was a black robed priest. Jacques had never seen this man before. The Indians stood around the priest as if guarding a scared cow. Jacques's sons came out to see what the commotion was all about. Magdelaine sent the girls to their room, fearing for their safety.

"Jacques, this is Father LeLoutre," said Paul, as he introduced the notorious priest to his friend.

Father LeLoutre stood out from the Indians. He had a full facial beard, and long pitch-black hair that seemed to match his frock. He wore a wide sash at the waist from which could be seen a cross neatly tucked in. He was dressed completely in black, except for a tiny white collar that signified his saintly profession. The thirty-five year old priest had piercing eyes that seemed to penetrate ones inner soul. Towering the Micmacs, the six-foot-three priest looked fearless and carried himself with an air of authority.

After the introductions, Jacques surveyed the entourage. There were three hundred Indians in this group led by Father LeLoutre, and they had designs on attacking the fort!

"We need to rest for a short spell till daylight," said Father LeLoutre.

"Of course, Father. My house is your house. Please come in."

Jacques had wanted the good father to come into the house for food and to rest a spell.

"I will stay with my children in the barn," said Father LeLoutre.

Father LeLoutre and the chiefs went into the barn to construct their plan of action while the rest of the group hid behind the barn, out of sight of the river. Jacques had Magdelaine and the girls prepare a breakfast for their guests. The boys carried the food to the barn, along with kettles of hot tea.

By providing shelter for this renegade group, Jacques was violating his neutrality status, something the Acadians insisted on when asked to sign the oath of allegiance. After refreshing themselves they thanked Jacques, and left. They crossed the river to lay siege to the fort. They stealthily crept up to the unwary guards outside the fort and killed them.

Father LeLoutre had made plans in advance with Captain Duvier from Fort Louisburg about attacking Fort Anne at Annapolis Royal. The attack was to be coordinated such that Father LeLoutre would attack by the river, while Duvier would attack from inland, south of the fort. Father LeLoutre did not wait for Duvier to arrive before he commenced the attack.

Duvier arrived the following day and joined forces with Father LeLoutre. Duvier was assured a large French fleet would come to the assistance of the raiders. Confident they could take the fort, the French began a siege. A few days later, under a flag of truce, they sent a message to Governor Mascarene to surrender the fort. He defiantly refused their request.

"We will wait them out, and take care of them when our ships arrive," said Father LeLoutre.

The attackers had no heavy guns needed to persuade Mascarene to surrender. A few days later sails were spotted at the entrance to the Annapolis River.

"Our ships have arrived," said one of the French soldiers.

Their jubilation quickly faded when it turned out to be an English force approaching, bringing supplies to the fort. With the arrival of British reinforcements, Father LeLoutre had no choice but to abandon his quest, and retreat.

The expected French fleet did arrive later and captured some English vessels in the Annapolis River, but because Duvier had left with Father LeLoutre and there were no ground forces available, they retreated.

Governor Mascarene held a conference with his officers and newly arrived soldiers. The fort now replenished and more heavily fortified, he could afford to relax.

"Gentlemen, we had a narrow escape. It is only by the providence of God that we managed to hold on. We lost a few men to the Indians who came upon us unaware. I must state for the record that the local Acadians were indeed true to their oath. Had they not taken the oath of allegiance they could have easily joined forces with the Indians and wiped us out."

Mascarene wrote to the Secretary of War in England on July 2, 1744:

"The Acadians of this river have kept hitherto in their fidelity, and no ways joined with the enemy, who has killed most of their cattle, and the priest residing amongst them has behaved also as an honest man. They helped in the repairing of our works to the very day preceding the attack."

With the outbreak of war in 1744, the French forces at Louisburg attacked and secured the nearby English port of Canso. The French took 250 English prisoners to Fort Louisburg. The French did not have enough provisions to take care of their prisoners so they released them under the promise, as gentlemen, that they would not take up arms against the French for the period of one year. When the English agreed, they were transported to Boston.

The English representative or Governor of the colonies, as he was known, was an English gentleman named William Shirley. When the repatriated soldiers informed Shirley that they would not take up arms for one year he was furious, and flew into a rage. No matter what Shirley did or said, they were adamant and refused to take up arms. They did inform Shirley that Fort Louisbourg was in shambles, badly in need of food and supplies and only had a few hundred soldiers there. With this intelligence, Shirley opted to attack Fort Louisbourg. He had little trouble in amassing an army from the colonist who had been denied access to the Grand Banks fishing ground, not only that but they would be wiping out the hated Catholic Papist. The following year the colonial army was ready, and assisted by English gun-ships they attacked and took Fort Louisbourg.

In seven weeks of fighting the English took control of Cape Breton and Prince Edward Island and invaded New Brunswick itself. The Canadians living in New Brunswick had not taken the oath of allegiance in any form, so there was no reason to submit to the hated British.

The skirmishes in New Brunswick produced some of Canada's most heroic resistance fighters. Two of the most outstanding heroes were Joseph

Broussard, better known as BeauSoleil, and Jacques's own son, nineteen-year-old Charles. These men had a price on their heads. Other Acadian defenders with a price on their heads were: Joseph LeBlanc, better known as Maigre. Raymond LeBlanc, Louis Gautier, Louis Hebert, Pierre Guidry and Amand Bugeau. They were wanted, dead of alive.

The English forced all the Acadians in the captured lands to sign an oath of allegiance, or leave. They signed with the proviso that they would not take up arms. They wanted to be neutral.

The dastardly Governor Shirley of Massachusetts, who had a great influence in Canadian management, wanted to evict some Acadians in Nova Scotia from their lands and hand that land over to Protestant settlers with the idea of separating the French Catholics from their religion and have them intermingle with Protestants with the hope of eventually accepting the Protestant faith. He offered a reward of money to any of the Catholics in Canada who would renounce their faith and become Protestants. He further offered rewards to any of the Catholics who would send their children to English schools and churches.

In November of 1744, Paul and his son, Joachim, visited Jacques. He had some horrific news to report. He was very upset and angry.

"My cousins, Jean-Baptiste and Pierre, camped together near the tall timbers. We found Jean-Baptiste's eleven-year-old son, Laurent, wandering alone through the woods. We thought he was lost. He told us English soldiers had attacked his camp, but he escaped. We gathered a party and went to see for ourselves."

Paul had to stop and recompose himself. Jacques knew the worst was yet to come. He could read his friend very well and understood him. Paul went on, "Laurent had gone into the woods away from the camp. He heard the British soldiers attacking so he crept closer to see what was happening. He saw the British shoot into the wigwams killing those inside. Jean-Baptiste's wife, Marguerite, and Pierre's wife, Rose, were both Prégnant."

Paul had to stop again, and shook his head from side to side, as if trying to force the horrid details out. Tears were streaming down his face. Magdelaine told the girls to leave the room, she had heard enough.

"Jacques," sobbed Paul, "we found their bodies with their stomachs ripped open. They killed my two cousins and their wives, and their children, and burned the wigwams with the bodies inside."

"Good Lord in Heaven!" said Jacques, shocked at what he heard.

"We will never forget this!" said Paul. "And they call themselves Christians, attacking defenseless women and children. When we fight with them, we deal with their soldiers, not their women."

The ire of the Micmac nation had now been aroused. So frightened were the British that they had Mohawk Indians from New York brought in to keep the Micmacs away from the fort. The Mohawks proved to be so uncontrollable that they were soon sent back to New York.

The French Acadians living in Nova Scotia at this time found themselves in an unhappy situation. Those born after 1714 were technically British subjects, and as such, England wanted them, but because of the influence of their Catholic priests, they were prevented from enjoying their birthrights. Father LeLoutre made it known throughout Nova Scotia that any Frenchman who sided with the

English would have his home burned to the ground by the Micmacs.

The Acadians were an illiterate lot. Few could sign their names. Since they could not read, they knew little of what was happening in the world around them. They had no leaders other than their priests, and wanted only to be left alone. They never argued with their neighbors, but on the contrary were always there to lend a helping hand. They were industrious in their farms. A hardy bunch, they were very prolific and all had large families.

The French population in Nova Scotia had risen to around thirteen thousand. There were only about two hundred English soldiers at Fort Anne to oversee this large population; a situation that made it tenuous for the English. If the English should attempt to oust this large population, they would indeed have an excessively large force to contend with once they joined the other French in nearby territories.

During the year 1745, Jacques's son, Gregoire, married Marie Aucoin, daughter of Rene and Magdelaine Bourque of Grand Pré. The newlyweds were not granted title to any land in Nova Scotia. The parents of either party would sometimes divide their own land, but Jacques did not have that much to begin with, neither did Rene Aucoin. This situation often times forced the newlyweds to move to neighboring New Brunswick for land.

Before Gregoire married, he and his brother, Charles, made many trips to New Brunswick looking for land. They found suitable property in Cran, near present day Moncton. On one of their trips, the brothers decided to stop at an inn for food and refreshments. Inside, as they were enjoying their meal, a group of locals had come together for a meeting. One of the locals approached the brothers.

"Where are you boys from?" he asked, as he looked the strangers over with a quizzical look.

"We are from Annapolis Royal," answered Gregoire.

"What brings you here?" asked the local.

"We are looking for a homestead. I am getting married soon, and the god damn British won't grant us any more land," said Gregoire.

The local, a man named Charles Belliveau, looked at Charles and said, "How about you. Are you getting married soon?"

"Hell, no," replied Charles. Charles Belliveau chuckled at the quick and defensive reply.

"We are forming a militia here and we need all the help we can get. If you men want to live here, you had better be prepared to defend your land. There is land available along the river. The English have been sending patrols nearby."

Gregoire obtained a large tract of land in Cran. He and brother Charles busied themselves preparing a place to live. One day, while constructing the house with the help of neighbors, a British patrol approached along the river. Work stopped as all the locals ran to their respective homes for their guns.

"Get your guns and hide," said the locals to the brothers, before they left.

The English patrol sailed up river a short distance, turned and sailed back downriver to the Bay of Fundy.

Later, as the brothers were having their meal at the inn, they were introduced to the captain of the local militia, who also frequented the inn.

Charles Belliveau made the introductions. The captain was none other than Beausoleil himself.

"Captain," said Mr. Belliveau, "meet Gregoire, and his brother Charles."

"It's a pleasure, gentlemen," said Beausoleil. "May we join you?"

During the meal, they discussed the situation in Cran and the nearby region. Beausoleil told the brothers that he had formed a regiment of French locals and was looking for more volunteers. Since many of the regiment consisted of Micmacs he was looking for someone fluent in their language to coordinate their attacks. When Beausoleil head Charles could speak the Micmac language, he was delighted.

"I would be more than happy to join your group, Captain," said young Charles. "Maybe we can stop them from sailing up river."

Captain Beausoleil had found his right hand man at last.

The following year, Masacarene had assembled a large force of regular soldiers. This army ventured to the far end of the Bay of Fundy to Grand Pré. At Grand Pré, they forced the local Acadians to billet the British soldiers in their homes. The English hoped to bring a strong presence to what was the most heavily populated area of French settlers in Nova Scotia.

When the snows came that year, the Micmacs were ready. Father LeLoutre led his people to the area and was successful in killing most of the five hundred soldiers. Those not killed outright were made prisoners. Not a single Acadian had warned Mascarene of the attack.

France, smarting under the loss of Fort Louisbourg, determined to regain control of Cape Breton and retake the fort. The French king sent a large naval force to Canada, but the elements were against this large fleet. Of the sixty-five ships that set out, only a few reached Canada. Those that reached the shores of Nova Scotia were in such bad shape that they had to disembark and bivouac ashore. Typhus decimated the crews. There were dead bodies all over the shore. Some three thousand sailors perished on this expedition. The Indians who took the dead sailors' clothes for their own soon contracted the disease themselves. The Indians spread this disease to seventy-five percent of the Micmacs in Nova Scotia.

The leader of the expedition, Duc d'Anville, also succumbed to typhus. Vice-Admiral d'Estournelles, who took command after d'Anville's death, probably in a state of high fever, took his own life.

There is an interesting story about a large dog belonging to the French sailors. This animal was rescued from this disaster. A Micmac, named Cope, saw the dog near the dead bodies. He took the animal away to his own home a fair distance from where he found it. He lived along the coast where a river entered inland. This river snaked its way around a piece of land that jutted out into the ocean.

A family with small children lived on this small piece of land. This point of land was almost completely surrounded by water. The dog would swim the river and play with the children. This area is famous for having the highest tides in the world. One day, in midwinter, the tide rose exceptionally high completely isolating the family at the point. This precarious piece of land was about to be swept out to sea on the receding tide. No one could survive the frigid waters for more than a few minutes. Huge ice floes were everywhere. The family looked doomed. No one wanted to venture to the point in canoes for fear of the ice floes.

The Micmac, Cope, and his dog looked forlornly on the hapless stranded children. In desperation, Cope instructed his dog to swim over to the children. The father tied the youngest child on the dog's back. The dog swam back to Cope carrying the child to safety. The dog made two more trips each time carrying children back to safety. Cope sent the dog back over again, this time pulling a rope in its mouth. The father secured the end of the rope to a toboggan. While the mother sat in the sled, Cope and some other Indians pulled the woman to safety. They managed to get the father to safety in the same manner.

The French governor of Canada, Beauharnois, in Quebec, had been informed before the sailing of the ill fated fleet that an attack on Nova Scotia was being planned. He organized a small army under the command of Nicholas-Roch de Ramezay to march to Nova Scotia to join up with the fleet. Ramezay set up camp at Grand Pré and waited for news of Duc d'Anville's arrival. When word of the disaster reached Ramezay he decided to remain in the area hoping for more reinforcements to attack Annapolis Royal with the force he had.

Mascarene must have learned of the presence of Ramezay at Grand Pré because he organized a British regiment consisting of 470 men to go to Grand Pré to keep an eye on Ramezay. As this regiment was leaving Annapolis Royal, Jacques and the other Acadians were observing it.

Jacques remembered the last time a large detachment left the fort, when he informed the Micmacs that an invasion was being planned. He had saved the Micmacs of certain death. He wasted no time in paddling to the Micmac camp to warn Paul that another sortie was taking place.

"Paul," said Jacques, "I counted about 400 soldiers, boarding ships."

"I will warn my brothers," said Paul.

"If they are using ships that must mean they will sail the Bay of Fundy to Grand Pré," said Jacques.

"My brothers in Grand Pré will hear about this before their ships arrive. We will be ready."

On January 8, 1747, Ramezay received word of the approaching English. The news had reached him through a system of Micmac relays in a matter of hours. This would give him plenty of time to arrange for resistance fighters to amass and attack.

The British soldiers were put ashore at Grand Pré. They took up residence in the homes of some of the Acadians.

In some of the coldest weather ever, the resistance fighters gathered to do battle. Father LeLoutre led his Indians to the scene. The snow fell very heavy, the blistery wind blew, feet and faces froze. They had to traverse ice-covered ground. Many of the resistance fighters lived as far as twenty-five miles away; still they braved the bitter cold and hardships to join forces. They met along the way, joining with groups from other areas.

Early in February, they had amassed near Grand Pré. The plan of attack was laid out with groups having certain objectives. Nearing Grand Pré the small army stopped for the night. It was still snowing, the wind was still blowing, and bodies were still freezing. Someone spotted smoke rising in the distance so the army made for source. It was an Acadian farm and incredibly, there was a wedding feast taking place. Needless to say the guest were more than stunned to see this rag tag army barge in on them. The resistance fighters welcomed the warmth of the fire and the nourishments provided. The guests were able to tell the Acadians where every English soldier was billeted; a stroke of pure luck.

The English had taken over twenty-four of the houses in Grand Pré. The Acadians set up their plan of attack. The Acadians were assembled into groups of ten each. The groups were each assigned to a house as described by the wedding guests. The guests opted to lead the different groups to point out the houses mentioned. Father LeLoutre gave absolution to all the Indians and Acadians who were to take part in the raid. At 3:00 AM the raid started.

In the darkness, as snow was falling, a British sentry outside one of the houses thought he saw something so he yelled, "Halt, who goes there." The Acadians quickly threw themselves flat on the ground. Another sentry inside the house, hearing the outer guard, opened the door to see what was going on. Seeing nothing, he dismissed the alarm and went back in. The Acadians crept closer until they were almost at the front door. Covered with snow, they opened fire and killed the outer guard. The inner guard opened the door again only to be surprised by incoming shots. The Acadians rushed the house, killing twenty-four Englishmen inside. Hearing the shots being fired the other Acadians rushed their assigned houses. By early morning, it was over. The British casualties were 130 killed, 15 wounded, and 350 captured.   The Acadian casualties were about forty killed, and many wounded.

The captured English were accorded military honors, and allowed to depart after they promised they would not take up arms against the Acadians for six months; their wounded would be taken care of and returned later. Therefore, one of the most gallant exploits of Acadian history ended.

On February 5, 1748 Jacques's oldest son, Jean-Jacques, married Ursule Blanchard, daughter of Rene and Marie Savoie, at Annapolis Royal. They also had to seek a homestead away from Annapolis Royal.

On October 18, 1748, the war between France and England ended with the signing of the peace treaty at Aix-la-Chapelle. The treaty called for England to return Cape Breton to France in exchange for Madras.

With France and England now at peace the governor of the colonies, William Shirley, pressed the home government in England to send English settlers to Nova Scotia.

"The French will rebuild Fort Louisbourg. We need to establish a fort of our own to offset the French fortress. Besides, our settlers will expand the sovereignty of England," expounded Shirley.

Bolstered by this grandiose allusion to the grandeur and splendor of the British Empire the Duke of Newcastle thought it was a grand scheme.

The new president of the Board of Trade was Lord Halifax, a protégé of the Duke.   He was instrumental in having a public notice printed in the Gentlemen's Journal, a London publication, expounding the merits of obtaining free land in Nova Scotia. The prospective settlers would be transported to the new world, given assistance for one year, and provided with the tools they would need to cultivate the land. To the starving masses, this was a utopian gesture indeed.

Lord Halifax had hoped that the proper gentry of England would apply; the carpenters, stone masons, blacksmiths, farmers, physicians, etc... Instead, he was deluged with requests from people that Cornwallis would describe as "the King's bad bargains."

Colonel Edward Cornwallis was selected as the man in charge of this expedition. The shore of Chebucto (Now known as Halifax) was the place selected to plant this seed of settlement. This was the same place the ill-fated French fleet found itself following the disastrous crossing earlier.

On July 21, 1749, Cornwallis and two thousand immigrants landed at Chebucto. John Bruce, the expedition's engineer and Charles Morris, the surveyor, laid out the plan of the city. The immigrants were all granted plots of land.

The hamlet of Chebucto, now garrisoned with British soldiers, was renamed Halifax in honor of Lord Halifax, head of the Board of Trades in England. The newly arrived British immigrants busied themselves planting their crops and preparing to survive through the winter.

Father LeLoutre kept his Indians busy harassing the English immigrants. The Indians inflicted many casualties among the new arrivals.

Cornwallis appointed one of his officers, Major Charles Lawrence, to sail around Nova Scotia to the Bay of Fundy and on to Chignecto Bay to construct a fort and thereby maintain British authority and security in this forlorn region. Upon his arrival, from his ship, Lawrence witnessed a huge migration of Acadian settlers away from Nova Scotia into Cape Breton. They were driving their cattle before them and carting all their possessions away. They left a scorched earth behind. Everything went up in flames. Unknown to Lawrence, it was Father LeLoutre and his Indians responsible for this mass destruction of property. Father LeLoutre had forced his own people out of Nova Scotia and into Cape Breton. He had the farms destroyed to make sure the Acadians would not return.

With the heavy presence of British soldiers nearby, Father LeLoutre was instrumental in the building of the French fort, Beausejour, which was situated at the demarcation line between Nova Scotia and New Brunswick.

By this time there were about 10,000 Acadians living in Nova Scotia. The Micmacs were numerous also, and they were not too pleased to see English settlers moving into their hunting grounds. The Indians did what they could to keep settlers from encroaching on their territory. Father LeLoutre and Beausoleil also did their parts.

In order to counterbalance Fort Beausejour, the British constructed a fort of their own on the western bank of the Missiquash. British Captain Howe, who was said to be a charming man who also spoke fluent French, commanded this outpost.

Captain Howe spoke with the Acadian settlers nearby, convincing them of the folly of their ways. He was able to bring most of the Acadians around to see that if they continued with Father LeLoutre, all would be lost. Captain Howe was well liked by the local Acadians, which did not bode well with Father LeLoutre. The priest saw that the Acadians were siding with the British, even supplying them with supplies and labor. Something had to be done.

On October 15, 1750, a lookout at the British fort saw a white flag waving on the French side of the river.

"Captain Howe," reported the sentry, "the French are waving a white flag across the river."

"Very well," said Captain Howe. "I'd better go see what they want."

He left the safety of the fort and walked to the water's edge. The French sent someone over to talk to him. After a brief exchange, the Frenchman turned to canoe back to the other side. As soon as the two men separated, a shot rang out from the French side. Captain Howe died instantly, shot through the heart.

News of this filled the French Commander, La Corne with anger and shame. It was Father LeLoutre who had ordered an Indian to fire on Captain Howe.

"Now, he will not influence the Acadians any more," said Father LeLoutre.

This shameful act was so repulsive to the Acadians; many of them now opted to sign an unconditional oath of allegiance with the English!

Governor Cornwallis wrote to the Board of Trades and called it "an act of treachery and barbarity not to be paralleled in history."

In New Brunswick meanwhile, construction on Gregoire's house was completed. His brother, Charles, stayed with him to get him started. Charles met the lovely Marie Babineau while staying with his brother. On one of his visits to Nova Scotia to see his parents, Charles recounted his activities.

"We've been very busy in New Brunswick," said Charles.

"A lot has been going on here, also," said Jacques. "We were ordered to send some of our representatives to Halifax to talk to Governor Cornwallis. He demanded that they sign the oath of allegiance, but they refused. They told him that they had to talk it over with the other members of their respective parishes."

"Well, we also paid a visit to Halifax," said Charles. "Beausoleil led a raid on the English settlements, and I went with him to interpret for the Indians."

Magdelaine was very upset when she heard that her son took part in a dangerous raid. "You could have been killed," said Magdelaine.

"Father LeLoutre was there with us, and he gave us all absolution, so had I been killed, I would be in Heaven."

"What happened over there?" asked Jacques.

"I can tell you that we put the fear of god in the English farmers. I don't think they will be staying there very long."

Charles told his parents that Gregoire's house was very big and they had just completed the barn. He also mentioned the girl he met in New Brunswick.

"The only thing that bothers us," said Charles, "is that the English sail their vessels up the river to harass us. Beausoleil is going to take care of them, soon."

The English governor knew that the Micmac nation was indeed powerful, and a proper menace to his government. In the American colonies, the British were successful in obtaining the Native Americans as allies by buying their loyalty, if you will, by giving them trinkets. Cornwallis opted to try this in Nova Scotia. He had the word spread throughout that if the Micmacs would present themselves at Halifax and sign a peace document, they would receive gifts.

Father LeLoutre sent a delegation of about one hundred warriors to Halifax. Cornwallis was delighted. He entertained them well, and they affixed their marks on the peace document. They received lavish gifts and were sent home in an English ship. On the way, they captured the ship, killed and scalped the crew. Father LeLoutre paid one hundred dollars for each English scalp. These poor misguided Indians were used by Father LeLoutre to vent his hatred on the English Protestants.

When once, these proud natives enjoyed the freedom of all of Nova Scotia, and indeed all of Canada, those free spirits who enjoyed each others company, who hunted only for their survival and not for the sport of it, who had lived in this harsh country for thousands of years, who respected the dignity of life, even of the animals and plants, now found themselves pawns in a struggle between the super powers of Europe.

Cornwallis understood that the Indians were being used by the French clerics to prevent the British from exercising their rights as owners of this land. He wrote to the Bishop of Quebec,

"Was it you who sent LeLoutre as a missionary to the Micmacs? And is it for their good that he excites these wretches to practice their cruelties against those who have shown them every kindness? The conduct of the priests of Acadia has been such that by command of His Majesty I have published an order declaring that if any one of them presumes to exercise his functions without my express permission he shall be dealt with according to the laws of England."

France, at this time, was building a few fortifications at Cape Breton. Supplies were badly needed at these forts, along with the manpower to fend off attacks.

Father LeLoutre demanded that all Acadians leave Nova Scotia and relocate to Cape Breton. He promised them, under the name of the Governor of Cape Breton, to support them for three years. If they refused to obey him, he would have all Catholic priests removed from Nova Scotia and they would no longer be able to receive the sacraments. This meant, they could not marry, confess their sins, or receive absolution when death seemed imminent. He also threatened to have their wives and children removed from them, and the Indians would lay waste their farms. A mass exodus ensued.

Paul paid a visit to Jacques after hearing what Father LeLoutre had planned.

"Jacques," said Paul, "Father LeLoutre wants us to threaten our friends to force them to relocate to Cape Breton."

"Yes, so I have been hearing. However, do you realize that if the Acadians leave, you will be at the mercy of the British? Who will stand by you?"

"I've thought about that. We haven't forgotten the butchery they committed on my cousins."

"Father LeLoutre has been causing nothing but trouble since he arrived. We were living in peace with the English. They were not bothering us; in fact, we were trading with them. I made a fortune selling my furs to the English traders. Our lives here have been very good. My children were all born here, our farm is here. We have all signed the oath of allegiance with the provision that we do not take up arms. If we leave, the English will surely attack my Micmac brothers. I don't think we should relocate just to please Father LeLoutre."

"You are absolutely right. It would be better if all Acadians stayed. I will speak to my people."

Two thousand Acadians were compelled by Father LeLoutre and the Indians to leave their homes. They lived a life of misery in Cape Breton. Their homes were whatever shelter they could find under a large tree. Father Girard, a Catholic priest, who had moved to Cape Breton rather than violate the oath of allegiance that he signed, wrote:

"Many of them cannot protect themselves day or night from the severity of the cold. Most of the children are entirely naked; and when I go into a house, they are all crouched in the ashes, close to the fire. The run off and hide themselves, without shoes, stocking, or shirts. They are not all reduced to this extremity but nearly all are in want."

Had it not been for the assistance given them by the French Governor at Cape Breton, most of them would have perished.

Governor Cornwallis in a proclamation to the Acadians at Annapolis Royal said that he was aware of the situation that had been forced upon them.

"Great advantages have been promised you elsewhere, and you have been made to image that your religion was in danger. Threats even have been resorted to in order to induce you to remove to French territory. The savages are made use of to molest you; they are to cut the throats of all who remain in their native country, attached to their own interests and faithful to the Government. You know that certain officers and missionaries, who came from Canada last autumn, have been the cause of all our trouble during the winter. Their conduct has been horrible, without honor, probity, or conscience. Their aim is to embroil you with the Government..." He went on to say:

"Our determination was to hinder nobody from following what he imagined to be his interest. We know that a forced service is worth nothing, and that a subject compelled to be so against his will is not far from being an enemy. We confess, however, that your determination to go gives us pain.

"We are aware of your industry and temperance and that you are not addicted to any vice or debauchery. This province is your country. You and your fathers have cultivated it; naturally you ought yourselves to enjoy the fruits of your labor. Such was the design of the King, our master. You know that we have followed his orders. You know that we have done everything to secure to you not only the occupation of your lands, but also the ownership of them forever.

"We have given you also every possible assurance of the free and public exercise of the   Roman Catholic religion. But I declare to you frankly that, according to our laws, nobody can possess lands or houses in the province that shall refuse to take the oath of allegiance to his King when required to do so.

"You know very well that there are ill disposed and mischievous persons among you who corrupt the government, and your habit of following the counsels of those who have not your real interests at heart, make it an easy matter to seduce you. In your petitions, you ask a general leave to quit the province.

"The only manner in which you can do so is to follow the regulations already established and provide yourselves with our passport. In addition, we declare that nothing shall prevent us from giving such passports to all who ask for them, the moment peace and tranquility are re-established."

Cornwallis knew that anyone leaving Nova Scotia had to pass the French and Indians at the border, and once at the border, they would be required to take up arms against the British.

These were trying times for the Acadians and Micmacs.

CHAPTER ELEVEN

Fort Beausejour

In the early 1750s, the situation in Nova Scotia had not changed much for Jacques and his family. His son, Charles, was engaged to the lovely Marie Babineau from New Brunswick. His other son, Louis-Cyrille, was engaged to Theotiste Bourgeois, a local girl. They had to seek homesteads away from Nova Scotia in preparation for their nuptials.

Charles and Louis Cyrille married in 1752. Charles settled in the village of Peticoudiac, near present day Moncton. He volunteered his services with the militia under the command of Captain Joseph Broussard. Louis Cyrille settled in Annapolis Royal, sharing land given by his father-in-law.

Charles took up military training at Fort Beausejour. His services were especially needed since he could speak fluent Micmac. He was like a mirror image of his father. He went on many raids with Beausoliel and the Micmacs.

Of all her sons, Magdelaine worried most about Charles. He was the one with the free roaming spirit. She knew he detested the British and would fight them at a moments notice. He was taller and brawnier than his father, with the same light hair and blue eyes. Charles also spent a lot of times with his Micmac friends, much as his father had done in his youth.

For the poor Acadian souls that were forced to leave their homes earlier and relocate in Cape Breton, life was a different matter. They found living conditions there intolerable. They could not grow crops in Cape Breton, as they did in Nova Scotia. The soil was mostly rocky terrain. They also signed an oath of allegiance to the French monarch once they had reached Cape Breton, renouncing their former oath of allegiance to the King of England.

"We want to go back to Nova Scotia," cried the Acadians in Cape Breton.

Those miserable souls selected a few men and sent them to Fort Edward in nearby Nova Scotia to seek permission to return to their old homesteads. The English informed them that the matter had to be taken up with Cornwallis at Halifax, and they would get their reply later.

Father LeLoutre stationed himself at Fort Beausejour. He ruled both the French and Indians with an iron determination. He became the most powerful person in Nova Scotia. In desperation, some of the starving French refuges living in Cape Breton escaped and went to Halifax. They willingly signed an unconditional oath of allegiance! Swearing to be good British subjects, they were given provisions, tools, and land well within the safety of the British garrison.

"We have had enough," said Paul, on a visit to Jacques. "Father LeLoutre will destroy us all."

"There is nothing we can do," said Jacques, "he has everyone running like scared rabbits."

"He has no regard for human life."

"I agree, even the local missionaries fear him."

"We have decided to go to Halifax and see if we can have a meeting with Cornwallis and settle this war," said Paul.

In autumn of 1752, Chief Jean-Baptiste Cope broke with Father LeLoutre and signed a peace accord with the British in Halifax. News of the hardships faced by the refuges in Cape Breton reached the Acadians still living in Nova Scotia.

"There is no way I am going to leave my warm home, my stock of food, my farm, to relocate to Cape Breton just to please Father LeLoutre," said Jacques to Magdelaine.   Other Acadians living in regions near Cape Breton also opted to remain.

In September 1752, Peregrine Thomas Hopson replaced Governor Cornwallis, who was on a leave to England. The new governor was said to be more humane than his predecessor. He saw the difficulties in trying to persuade the Acadians to sign the oath demanded by Cornwallis. He also saw the potential these Acadians had and how they could benefit the Royal Crown by providing badly needed assistance for the British subjects willing to relocate to Nova Scotia.

Hopson issued the following orders to his officers:

"You are to look upon the Acadians in the same light with the rest of his Majesty's subjects, as to the protection of the laws and the government; for which reason nothing is to be taken from them by force, or any price set upon their goods but what they themselves agree to; and if at any time they should obstinately refuse to comply with what His Majesty's service may require of them, you are not to redress the wrong yourself by military force, or in any unlawful manner, but to lay the case before the governor and await his orders. You are to cause the following orders to be struck up in the most public part of the fort, both in English and French:

1. No provision or any other commodities that the Acadians shall bring to the fort to sell are to be taken from them at any fixed price, but to be paid for according to a free agreement made between them and the purchasers.

2. No officer, non-commissioned officer, or soldier, shall presume to insult or otherwise abuse any of the Acadians who are upon all occasions to be treated as His Majesty's subjects, and to whom the laws of the country are open, to protect as well as punish."

The Acadian population of Nova Scotia at this time was probably around eleven thousand. Some of those Acadians were of the third or even fourth generation living there.

This was a time of peace for all peoples of Nova Scotia. Fur bearing animals were in abundance providing food and clothing. Game birds were plentiful, providing the hunter with great sport. The rivers and oceans provided still more abundance. They grew their own food and planted orchards of apples, peach, pear and even cherry trees. The warm summer months were for sowing and reaping. In the fall, the lovers married, and the long winters were spent visiting and enjoying each other's company. There were always dances, singing, and many games.

After the signing of the peace pact between Chief Cope and the British, Governor Hopson at Halifax felt he could at last relax a bit.

However, in April of 1754 two men named John Connor and James Grace arrived at Halifax with a horrendous story. In a meeting with Hopson they began:

"At evening, our schooner lay at anchor at Torbay, along the eastern coast," said John Connor, still visibly shaken. The tall, very strong man was dressed in tattered clothing. His beard was badly matted and unkempt. His long thinning hair looked like a mass of dried seaweed.

"Indians attacked us and forced us ashore," injected James Grace, his partner. He was also an extremely powerful man, who from his appearance was not one to trifle with. He was holding a satchel.

"What have you there?" asked Governor Hopson, as he eyed the satchel being held so diligently by Grace.

"Scalps, Your Grace," replied James Grace.

"Scalps!" gulped the Governor. "What are you doing with scalps? Where did you get those?" stammered the stunned governor.

"If Your Grace will permit me," said Connor.

"Yes, go on."

"The Indians attacked our ship while we were at anchor. They forced us to go ashore with them. As soon as we landed, some of our men turned on the Indians, but we were outnumbered. The Indians killed two of our men outright with their hatchets, and then they proceeded to scalp the poor unfortunates. We were forced to march inland to their camp. Later on, four of them they took Grace and me back to the landing. They had an Indian woman and a young Indian boy with them. At the landing, the four Indians canoed out to the schooner for more loot, leaving the woman and the boy to guard us. We knew we were done for so we took our chance. They had not tied us very securely so we were able to free ourselves. When the woman and boy were not looking, we crept up to them and killed them. When the others returned we fought with them and managed to kill them also. We proceeded to scalp them as they had scalped our men. We have six scalps here."

Governor Hopson was shaken by the news. He was hoping that there would be no more incidents with the Indians.

"There is going to be hell to pay when the Indians find those dead Micmacs, especially when they see they were scalped," intoned Governor Hopson.

"We were fighting for our lives, Your Grace," said Connor.

"Yes, yes, quite right," said the Governor.

Shortly thereafter, Governor Hopson appointed an Englishman named Anthony Carteel, who could speak fluent French, to travel inland to find Chief Cope and try to amend the situation. Carteel took six men with him.

Chief Cope was delighted when he met Carteel, an Englishman who could speak French. He saw in Carteel an important individual, probably worth money. He would hold him for ransom. All six of Carteel's men were killed and their scalps sold. Chief Cope took Carteel to Fort Louisbourg where he sold him for a rather large sum of money.

Father LeLoutre happened to be at Fort Louisbourg at that time. Carteel had to endure the verbal abuses of the priest.

"You English can build all the forts you want, but you had better not leave them or my Indians will deal with you," said Father LeLoutre. Carteel was visibly shaken at that tirade.

Carteel was released back to the English in a prisoner–of–war swap. His report to Governor Hopson of his ordeal was very unsettling.

"These damn Acadians and their Indians are too much. Something has to be done," declared Governor Hopson.

In November of 1753, Governor Hopson returned to England due to a serious problem with his eyes. Charles Lawrence assumed command.

On November 19, 1753, the apple of his eye, Marie Magdelaine, Jacques's first-born daughter, married Rene Saulnier, son of Rene and Marie Josephe Trahan. Rene was the brother of the girl that Jacques's son, Antoine Solomon, married. Therefore, two members of one family married two members of another family.

In December of 1753, Lawrence had to deal with not only the Acadians and the Micmacs, but also now with the unruly German setters in Lunenburg. A rebellion broke out in the German community led by a man named Johan Hoffman.

Lawrence sent Lieutenant-Colonel Robert Monckton to Lunenburg to quell the riots. Lieutenant-Colonel Monckton returned to Halifax with Johan Hoffman in irons.

"What is your problem?" asked the Governor to the German instigator.

"We want to be treated as the Acadians are. We want to be accorded the status of Neutrals."

"I'll treat you as a neutral. You can be a neutral on George's Island for two years!"

George's Island was the place of confinement for prisoners. Governor Lawrence later said, "I know him to be a restless fellow. I heartily wish the colony were rid of him."

In the spring of 1754, another settlement was opened for twenty British immigrants ten miles east of Dartmouth. This was called Lawrencetown in honor of Governor Lawrence. Each family was granted one thousand acres. To safeguard these new arrivals, Lawrence assigned two hundred regular soldiers. A blockhouse was erected in Lawrencetown, and soldiers patrolled the perimeter of the twenty thousand acres.

Word of the new settlement reached Beausoleil in New Brunswick by way of the Micmac communication system.

"We have to do something to stop these English dogs from settling here," said Beausoleil at a meeting in Coude (present day Moncton). A plan was drafted and put into action.

"Charles, where are you going?" asked Marie, when she saw her husband saddling his horse, early one morning.

"Hunting," said Charles.

She knew something dreadful was going on because he had also packed a large amount of supplies and taken all his black powder and shot along with extra rifles. His bedroll was slung behind the saddle.

"Don't go, darling," she pleaded, "we have plenty of food." She was holding eleven-month old, Jean-Baptiste.

"Your parents will be over later today to help you if you need anything," said Charles. He gave Marie and baby Jean-Baptiste a kiss, hugged them, and left. She had tears in her eyes as she watched him gallop away. She knew she could never tame him; he was too much like his father.

They met at the inn in Coude. A ragtag army of resistance fighters with their Micmac allies all mounted and heavily armed. The local missionary gave them absolution and they rode off for Lawrencetown. They rode about thirty miles to Fort Beausejour the first day and rested. Leaving the fort, they rode for four days, averaging about thirty miles per day till they arrived at Father LeLoutre's camp in Shubernacadie in the heartland of Nova Scotia, where they rested for a few days. After gathering more Micmacs at Father LeLoutre's camp, they set out for Lawrenctown, reaching their destination two days later. On the outskirts of Lawrencetown, they camped for the night. Early the following morning they attacked.

"Burn everything!" ordered Beausoleil.

Before the English settlers knew what was happening, before they even got out of bed, their barns went up in smoke. The immigrants were horrified to see Indians attacking them. They saw the white men with them, leading them.

When it was over, four settlers and three English soldiers had been killed. Most of their property destroyed. Everything in sight was going up in flames.

"It was Beausoleil," said one of the surviving English soldiers to Governor Lawrence. The settlers in Lawrencetown were so unnerved from that experience, they left the settlement. Lawrencetown remained unsettled until years later. Beausoleil, with his protégé, Charles, had achieved their mission.

Governor Lawrence wrote the Board of Trades in England after the Lawrencetown raid, detailing the events. The Board of Trades replied, stating they had concluded that since the Acadians refused to take the required oath of allegiance, and due to their obstinate behavior, it might be prudent to somehow remove the whole lot from Nova Scotia. The Board stressed the importance of not sending them to neighboring Cape Breton or New Brunswick else they would form a powerful army with the regulars already there.

The Board of Trades wrote to Governor Lawrence on March 4, 1754 as follows:

"The more we consider this point, the more difficult it appears to us; for, as on the one hand great caution ought to be used to avoid giving any alarm and creating such a diffidence in their minds as might induce them to quit the province, and by their number add strength to the French settlements, so on the other hand, we should be equally cautious of creating an improper and false confidence in them that by a perseverance in refusing to take the oath of allegiance, they may gradually work out in their own way a right to their lands."

This was England's way of saying, 'appease them now, we will deal with them later.'

With Halifax growing rapidly with an influx of new immigrants, supplies were badly needed to feed these people. Governor Lawrence looked to the Acadians to furnish the foodstuffs needed. The Acadians on the other hand were sending all their supplies along with manpower to French Fort Beausejour, against the orders of the English Governor, needless to say, Lawrence was furious.

In Annapolis Royal, the Catholic Acadians were stunned to learn that their missionary, Abbé Jean Baptiste Desenclaves, a good-natured priest, who gave the English no cause for alarm, was to be replaced by none other than the irascible Abbé Henri Daudin. Father LeLoutre had the change made because he thought Father Desenclaves was too soft on the British.

At Fort Edward, in Piziquid, the Acadians found it advantageous trading with the British garrison stationed there. When Father LeLoutre heard of this, he assigned Abbe Daudin to the area. When Abbe Daudin arrived, he forbade the Acadians to deal with the British, using threats of Indian reprisals. With the little manpower available at the fort to deal with Abbe Daudin, the matter rested. Happy with the results that Abbe Daudin achieved at Piziquid, Father LeLoutre then had him transferred him to Annapolis Royal. As soon as Abbe Daudin left Piziquid, the Acadians there resumed trading with the English.

One of Father LeLoutre's Indian messengers brought news to Father Daudin in Annapolis Royal, that the Acadians from his old parish were again selling wood to the British.

"We will see about that!" ranted Father Daudin. He traveled back to Piziquid.

Soon after the arrival of Father Daudin back at Piziquid, the British storekeeper at Fort Edward informed the commander, Captain Muray, that the Acadians stopped working for them again.

"Sir," said the sergeant, "our supply of firewood is almost depleted, and the Acadians inform us that they will not supply us with any more."

"What seems to the problem?" asked Captain Muray.

"The Acadians tell us that Abbe Daudin is back, and he informed the Acadians to cease all transactions with us."

"Arrest that scoundrel, and bring him here!" ordered Captain Muray.

Father Daudin was arrested and brought before Captain Muray.

"Have you ordered the Acadians to stop selling us wood?" asked the captain.

"Yes, I have," replied Father Daudin, defiantly, "and I'd like to see you try to do something about it."

"Oh, we will definitely do something about it," said Captain Muray. He called the sergeant-of-the-guards, and had the priest locked up.

Captain Muray sent Captain Cox to Halifax to inform the Governor about the situation in Piziquid.

"Now," said Captain Muray, "I will deal with these Acadians." He issued orders to have the Acadians bring in firewood or the British army would arrest the whole lot. The Acadians resumed the lucrative practice of supplying the British at Fort Edward.

Captain Cox returned from Halifax with orders to bring Father Daudin, and a few select Acadian elders to the Governor's office. Father Daudin and four Acadians were marched to Halifax. In Halifax, they were held on King George's island for a few days.

Separated from Father Daudin, the Acadians realized the folly of their adventure with him.

"We may never get out of here," protested Jean Poirrier.

"I have animals to care for," said Francois Thibodeau.

A week later, the distraught Acadians were brought before Governor Lawrence.

"We were pressured by Father Daudin, Your Excellency," said Jean Poirrier.

"I will release you if you promise you will return and resume work at Fort Edward. If you do not deliver the supplies we need, you will be brought back here for a much longer stay, I can assure you," said the governor.

They agreed, and returned to Piziquid where work had already started. As for Father Daudin, once in the presence of the governor a week later, he was not so cocky. He was released, and he returned to Annapolis Royal a changed man.

In Massachusetts, Governor Shirley wrote to the Board of Trades in England extolling the dangers that presented themselves in the American colonies.

"If we do nothing about the French in Canada, we face the possibility of annihilation. The French have sent large armies of Indians to raid the colonies killing many settlers. If this keeps up, the Indians we have as allies might join with the Canadian Indians and kill us all. The negro slaves we have will undoubtedly join in this rebellion and aid the French and Indians. The German settlers in Pennsylvania will most likely join forces with the French. We cannot count on the Quakers in Pennsylvania for support, they will not fight. The Dutch in New York will also join the Canadians."

Communications between the governor of the colonies, William Shirley, and the governor of Nova Scotia were intensifying. The French seemed to be everywhere. They ranged from Canada to the Gulf of Mexico. The Ohio valley was patrolled by French and Indians and it was not safe to venture past Pennsylvania. The French had forts constructed all along the interior of the American colonies. The main purpose for all this was to trade with the Indians for the lucrative furs, and they wanted no outsiders coming in and encroaching on this bounty.

The British Earl of Holderness wrote to Governor Shirley:

"In the case the subjects of any foreign Prince of State, should presume to make any encroachment on the limits of His Majesty's dominions, or to erect any forts on his majesty's land, or commit any other act of hostility, you are immediately to represent the injustice of such proceeding, and to require them forthwith to desist from any such unlawful undertaking, but if notwithstanding your requisition, they should still persist, you are then to draw forth the armed force of the province, and to use your best endeavors to repel force by force."

Governor Shirley appointed General Edward Braddock to form an army with the purpose of capturing the French fort at Crown Point. Shirley had other officers assigned to capture Duquesne, Niagara, and Beausejour.

A young British officer named George Washington, who would later become the first president of the colonies, was assigned to assist General Braddock.

Governor Shirley had waited for this moment. Now, he would vent his anger against the French Roman Catholic Acadians. It is strange to note that Governor Shirley at one time was an official in France and even married a young Catholic French girl!

At a place near present day Uniontown, Pennsyvlania, a detachment of Virginians led by George Washington fought an all day battle on July 3, 1754 against the French. By nightfall, George Washington surrendered. It was the start of what history now calls, "The Seven Years' War." The following year, also in July, General Braddock was killed fighting the French and Indians.

The board of Trades in England wrote to Governor Shirley in Massachusetts and Governor Lawrence in Nova Scotia detailing their plan of action as regards the Acadians in Nova Scotia. The one obstacle in the plans for eradicating the Acadians was the French stronghold, Fort Beausejour.

"The fort must be taken," wrote the Board of Trades.

Therefore, the most despicable act of cruelty by one nation on another was conceived. The Acadians were a peace-loving nation, not given to war. There were innocent women and children involved. According to civilized rules of engagement, armies fought armies; not women, children, and the aged.

At Fort Beausejour, the British had their spy working for them. He was none other than Thomas Pichon, the Commissary of Stores. Born in France, his mother was English, which probably explained his leaning towards the British side. He kept the British informed with all aspects of Fort Beausejour. At the fort, Pichon had to deal with Father LeLoutre who controlled everything in the fort. Pichon sarcastically referred to Father LeLoutre as Moses because the Father had led his people out of bondage and into the Promised Land.

The people that Father LeLoutre had led to the so-called 'promised land' had a meeting at one of their shelters.

"I have called for this meeting so that we can discuss our situation," said Pierre Theriot.

"What can we do?" asked the hapless Acadians.

"Do you want to stay here or go back to Nova Scotia?" asked Theriot.

"We want to go back..." came the overwhelming response from the group.

"Then I propose we draft a petition, everyone here sign it, and hand it to Father LeLoutre."

Pierre Theriot drafted a petition asking permission to leave Cape Breton and return to Nova Scotia. Those that could, signed their names, the others simply made an X alongside their written names, which were attested by witnesses. The petition was delivered to Father LeLoutre.

He flew into a rage when he read the petition. His face became beet red, the veins in his forehead looked as if they were ready to burst, his eyes glared at the shaken Pierre Theriot. He ranted at Theriot, spraying him with spittle.

"If you don't tear this up you will not receive sacraments in this life, nor heaven in the next!" shouted Father LeLoutre.

Pierre Theriot stood his ground. He and the others had endured enough.

"If you refuse to approve this petition, I shall personally take it to Governor Duquesne at Quebec," said Theriot.

Governor Duquesne was the top administrator for all Frenchmen in Canada and all its provinces.

Father LeLoutre told Theriot to have a seat, he would return shortly. He went into the other room and wrote a letter to Governor Duquesne explaining the difficulties with the unruly Nova Scotian Acadians. He sealed the letter and gave it to Theriot with instructions to hand it to the Governor. Theriot and another Acadian traveled to Quebec for an audience with the Governor. They handed him their petition along with the letter from Father LeLoutre.

The Governor of Quebec was not too happy with the Acadians from Nova Scotia. It seems they would not rise up against the British, nor were willing to leave the comfort of their farms to assist the French in nearby Cape Breton.

Pierre Theriot and his companion returned to Cape Breton, two broken men resigned to their fate. They delivered a letter to Father LeLoutre from the Governor.

"I think that the two rascals of deputies whom you sent me will not soon recover from the fright I gave them, notwithstanding the emollient I administered after my reprimand; and since I told them that they were indebted to you for not being allowed to rot in a dungeon, they have promised me to comply with your wishes."

Such was the power of Father LeLoutre that even the Governor of Canada acquiesced to his wishes.

Between the colonial Governor, Shirley, and Nova Scotia Governor Lawrence, plans were drawn for the conquest of French Fort Beausejour. Colonel Robert Monckton was appointed by Lawrence to head the expedition.

On May 22, 1755, the attacking fleet left Boston, Massachusetts. They arrived at Annapolis Royal on the 26th.

Returning from a trip across the river to the market square for supplies, Jacques entered his house visibly shaken. He seemed all out of breath.

"What's wrong, darling?" asked Magdelaine. She could tell he was not his usual self.

"I have counted about forty English schooners, and three frigates coming into the Annapolis River," said Jacques to Magdelaine.

A sense of foreboding crept over her. She did not like what she was hearing.

"God help us, now what is going to happen?" asked Magdelaine.

"It looks like they are planning an invasion someplace," said Jacques. "I had better warn Paul."

Jacques mounted his horse and put out for the Micmac camp along the lower Annapolis River. He found his friend, Paul, and informed him of the large fleet arriving.

"Paul, what do you think they are up to?" asked Jacques.

"Looks like an invasion someplace," he replied. "We had better warn Father LeLoutre." The Indian relay system quickly warned Father LeLoutre of the large English fleet at Annapolis Royal. Father LeLoutre gave the news to Fort

Beausejour Commander, Vergor.

Vergor, visibly shaken said, "We better warn Fort Louisbourg and have them help us."

"How many men do you have here?" asked Father LeLoutre.

"I have 160 regulars. The rest are just local farmers."

"I will get the Acadians to fight for us," said Father LeLoutre.

The poor Acadians who were forced to leave their homes, who had their petition to leave Cape Breton denied, and even threatened with excommunication, now were being asked to take up arms against the British.

"If we take up arms against the British and they take us prisoners, we will be shot," claimed the hapless Acadians.

"The English will never take this fort," said Vergor. "If they do, I will swear that I forced you to take up arms."

With this assurance, hundreds came to the aid of Fort Beausejour. Others were armed and hid in the woods. They awaited the inevitable onslaught.

CHAPTER TWELVE

The dastardly plan

The year 1755 was the darkest year in Acadian history. The Acadians call the event that took place that year, Le Grand Derangement; or better known in English as, The Expulsion.

In early 1755, communications between England, Nova Scotia, and the Colonies grew in intensity. The British powers formulated plans for the destruction of the Acadians in Nova Scotia. They even contemplated using clothing contaminated with smallpox to eradicate the Acadians and Indians.

Sir Jeffry Amherst wrote to Colonel Bouquet.

"Might we not try to spread smallpox among the rebel Indian Tribes? We must in this occasion make use of every device to reduce them."

Colonel Bouquet replied:

"I will try to introduce smallpox by means of blankets, which we will cause to fall into their hands.

Sir Jeffry Amherst wrote again:

"You will do well to try to spread smallpox by means of blankets, and by every other means which might help to exterminate that abominable race."

The main obstacle in the path of total British conquest of Nova Scotia was Fort Beausejour. Therefore, the first step in the plan was to capture that fort. Colonel Robert Monckton was placed in charge of the expedition. He had two capable officers to assist him; namely Captain Scot and Colonel Winslow.

Colonel Winslow was a colonial officer, not a regular British officer. The British government paid him 800 pounds to lead his colonial forces in Nova Scotia.

On the other hand, the French had the misfortune of having Louis De Vergor du Chambon in charge of Fort Beausejour, a most incapable officer. Compounding this miserable character was the traitor, Thomas Pichon, keeping the English well informed of everything going on at the fort.

Early on the morning of June 2, 1755, the fleet neared Fort Beausejour. The hour the Acadians dreaded had arrived. The English dropped anchors in Maringouin Cove, about a mile from Fort Beausejour, near their own fort.

Fort Beausejour commander, Vergor, sent troops out to compel the local farmers to report to the fort immediately. Two thousand reluctant peasants reported. Vergor took three hundred into the fort, and stationed the rest outside to ambush the enemy.

Vergor put the farmers to work building a stronger bastion. Father LeLoutre stood over them in his shirtsleeves with a pipe in his mouth, ordering them to 'toil for the Lord.' Those poor wretches, in the open, were easy targets for the British; they did not stand a chance.

"The first chance I get," said one of the farmers, "I'm getting the hell out of here!"

"You won't be alone!" said his neighbor.

When the fighting started, indeed, many of the local farmers escaped. They had signed a qualified oath of allegiance that they would not take up arms against the British. Should the British capture them, armed as they were, they would have to forfeit their farms, or might even be shot.

Colonel Monckton had landed at his own Fort Lawrence, unopposed. His troops were bivouacked close to the safety of the English fort. He could see Fort

Beausejour in the distance, and formulated his plans.

Early on the morning of June 4, 1755, the British garrison advanced. The local farmers lay hidden from view. As the English force approached, the Acadians jumped up and opened fire. This small battle lasted until the English brought up some field pieces and raked the area ahead of them. Greatly outnumbered, the Acadian farmers retreated. The English advanced to within a half mile of the French fort where they camped for the night. During the dark hours of the night, the sky was illuminated. The Acadians torched all the buildings outside the fort.

The following day the English began constructing trenches. The trenches weaved from side to side getting closer and closer to the fort. In this manner, they were protected and able to bring up their heavy artillery pieces to bear on the fort.

A French officer, named Vannes, boasted that he could drive the invaders away.

"Give me about one hundred regulars, and I will deal with these English pigs!" said Vannes, to Father LeLoutre.

The priest was impressed with his rash statement and eager to dispatch the English.

"Take your men and deal with the Protestants," said Father LeLoutre.

Vannes and his men marched out to face the enemy. When he saw the large force before him, he quickly retreated to the fort. The Acadian fort broke out in laughter. He was the laughing stock of the Acadians.

The English, using oxen, hauled large pieces of artillery to within range of the fort. Then the shelling began in earnest.

Inside the besieged fort, the local farmers begged Father LeLoutre for permission to leave. The priest, in his shirtsleeve, still smoking his pipe, ranted and railed against the defenders. He ran around encouraging the French to stand and fight.

Later, one of the shells from a large artillery piece, fired from the English trenches, went through a bombproof shelter in the fort killing six officers and a British captive. Near the destroyed shelter was another, occupied by the commanding officer, Vergor, Father LeLoutre, and some French officers. They all felt they were next. Vergor ordered a white flag immediately. Father LeLoutre, fearing for his life at the hands of the English, with nothing to loose said, "It is better to be buried under the ruins of the fort than to give up!"

Vergor, nevertheless, hoisted a white flag. He sent an officer to the English side to negotiate the terms of surrender. Many of the local farmers had escaped earlier as they had planned so there were not too many Acadians left in the fort when the British marched in. The battle lasted only fourteen days. On June 16, 1755, the British hoisted the Union Jack at Fort Beausejour.

Colonel Monckton and Vergor sat at table and discussed the terms of the capitulation. Vergor showed a document in which he attested that he forced the inhabitants to take up arms or he would have shot them himself. Monckton realized the farmers had no choice.

The truce stipulated:

(A) The repatriation of the French regulars to Fort Louisbourg.

(B) A general pardon to the Acadians for taking up arms.

Vergor prepared a supper for the English and dined with them that evening.

Father LeLoutre escaped in disguise and made his way to Quebec. From there, he boarded a ship to return to France. While at sea the British captured the ship.

When the English discovered they had captured their worst enemy, he was incarcerated on the Island of Jersey where he spent the next eight years.

While in jail, he narrowly escaped death when one of the guards tried to run him through with a bayonet. It seems that this particular guard, along with his regiment, had fallen into the hands of Father LeLoutre when they served in Nova Scotia. The guards on duty at the time of this incident prevented the angry guard from carrying out his designs.

"This is the Catholic Pig that led a band of Indians that captured our regiment," said the soldier. "He was the one that took out his knife and started to scalp me alive!" This so unnerved the warden that he had the guard removed.

"I'll get him if it takes the rest of my life," shouted the guard, as they escorted him away.

In Nova Scotia, Fort Beausejour was renamed Fort Cumberland by the British. Colonel Monckton ordered Vergor, along with the French regulars, out of the country. The regulars went to Fort Louisbourg while Vergo returned to France where a court martial awaited him. Somehow, he was let off with a slight reprimand.

The Beausejour campaign costs the British 20 men killed, and about 25 wounded. With the fall of Fort Beausejour, the Governor of Nova Scotia, Charles Lawrence, had free reign to do as he pleased with the Acadians.

On June 11, 1755, British Admiral Boscawen, commanding a large English fleet near Newfoundland, captured two French ships, the Alcide and the Lys; commanded by French Admiral Hocquart. Upon investigating the supplies in the French ships, the British were stunned to see huge amounts of hatchets, knives, guns, powder, and other items of war.

"This cargo can only be construed as supplies to be given to the Acadians to overthrow the English," said Boscowen.

This evidence prompted Lieutenant-Governor Phipps of Massachusetts to write to Governor Lawrence the following:

"I must on this occasion also propose to your consideration whether the danger with which His Majesty's interest is now threatened will not remove any scruples which might heretofore have subsisted with regard to the French Neutrals, as they are termed, and render it both just and necessary that they should be removed unless some more effectual security can be given for their fidelity than the common obligation of an oath."

Governor Lawrence summoned Acadian representatives to assemble in Halifax for a conference. A barrage of accusations and mistrust greeted the delegates upon their arrival.

"You people have been disloyal for the past forty years," screamed the governor. The delegates were stunned.

"But, Your Excellency..." stammered one of the Acadians.

"You have helped the King's enemies. You are ungrateful and unworthy!"

"Your Excellency...we are indeed loyal," said another delegate.

"Then prove it...sign the oath of allegiance...now!"

"Your Excellency," begged another of the delegates. "We need time to go home and discuss it with our people."

"I will give you until tomorrow morning!"

The governor had the men locked up for the night. The following morning they appeared before the governor.

"Well, what have you decided?" asked the governor.

"Your Excellency, as we have said yesterday. We need time to discuss this with our people."

With that the governor jumped up and shouted, "You will all be deported!"

The stunned delegates looked at each other with horror in their eyes. They had given the wrong answer. They thought they could put off signing the oath of allegiance as they had done previously. The governor was in no mood to trifle with those Acadians. Seeing the mood the governor was in, and realizing the power this man yielded, they acquiesced and said they would sign the oath of allegiance.

"It is too late," screamed the governor. "You don't get a second chance. You are nothing but Popish recusants!"

Governor Lawrence had all the delegates incarcerated. He would make an example of them. He wrote a letter to the Board of Trades in England.

"As the French inhabitants of this province have never yet, at any time, taken the oath of allegiance to His Majesty, unqualified, I thought it my duty to avail myself of the present occasion, to propose it to them; and, as the deputies of the different districts in Mines Basin, were attending in town upon a very insolent Memorial, I was determined to begin with them.

"The oath was proposed to them; they endeavored, as much as possible, to evade it, and at last desired to return home and consult the rest of the inhabitants, that they might either accept or refuse the oath in a body; but they were informed that we expected every man upon this occasion to answer for himself.

"The next morning, they appeared and refused to take the oath without the old reserve of not being obliged to bear arms, upon which they were acquainted, that as they refused to become English subjects, we could no longer look upon them in that light; that we should send them to France by the first opportunity, and till then, they were ordered to be kept prisoners at George's Island, where they were immediately conducted.

"They have since earnestly desired to be admitted to take the oath, but have not been admitted, nor will any answer be given them until we see how the rest of the inhabitants are disposed.

"I have ordered new deputies to be elected, and sent hither immediately, and am determined to bring the inhabitants to a compliance, or rid the province of such perfidious subjects."

Lawrence had already planned the expulsion of the Acadians, but he wanted something concrete as evidence for the record.

He said, "I will propose to them the oath of allegiance a last time. If they refuse, we will have in that refusal a pretext for the expulsion. If they accept, I will refuse them the oath by applying to them the decree of Parliament, which prohibits from taking the oath all persons who have once refused to take it. In both cases I shall deport them."

When the second group of deputies arrived at Halifax and faced Governor Lawrence, they also refused to sign the unqualified oath of allegiance. They ended up on George's Island, along with the others.

A few days later, Governor Lawrence visited George's Island. He asked one of the Acadians if he persisted in refusing to sign the oath of allegiance.

"Yes," he replied, "now more than ever. We have God on our side."

The red-faced Lawrence, seething with hate, withdrew his sword. "You insolent fellow, you deserve that I run my sword through your body!"

The Acadian bravely exposed his chest to Lawrence. "Strike, if you dare. I shall be the first martyr of the land. You may kill my body, but you can not kill my soul!"

All the Acadian prisoners shouted the same thing. Seeing he was losing face, Governor Lawrence left in a huff. He was determined to get even with them. He ordered all missionaries rounded up and arrested.

"Bring them here," said Lawrence.

The British arrested Father Daudin at Annapolis Royal, Father Lemaire at Canard, and Father Chauvreulx and marched them to Halifax. In Halifax, Governor Lawrence had the missionaries stripped to the waist and tied to pillars; subjected to taunts, jeers, and mockery.

Feeling vindicated, he had the priests transported to England and jailed. They made their way to France following their release years later.

Governor Lawrence met with his council to determine the fate of the Acadians. Admiral Boscawen and Admiral Mostyn, in Halifax at this time, also attended the conference.

"Gentlemen," said Lawrence. "We have to get rid of these Acadians and turn this land over to proper English subjects."

"What do you propose?" asked Admiral Boscawen.

"Ship them all back to France!" replied Lawrence.

"I agree with you, Your Excellency," said Admiral Mostyn. "Didn't they take up arms against His Majesty's forces when they defended Fort Beausejour?"

"Absolutely," replied the governor.

Secretary of the province, William Cotterell, then reminded Governor Lawrence of something that Peter Warren had recommended back in 1745.

"Your Excellency, a few years ago Peter Warren had suggested to the Board of Trades that should the Acadians refuse to take the required oath of allegiance, rather than forcing them out to join their countrymen in Cape Breton or New Brunswick where they would increase in strength and pose a serious threat to our sovereignty, would it not be better to scatter them to the wind, so to speak, by placing them in the several colonies. In this manner, the King would not lose his subjects and in time the French Catholics would intermingle with English Protestants and eventually, without the influence of their papist priest, they would see the folly of their way and adopt the proper English Protestant views."

"Excellent suggestion," said Chief Justice Jonathan Belcher.

Those in attendance that day included Governor Charles Lawrence, Chief Justice Jonathan Belcher, Admiral Boscawen, Admiral Mostyn, Secretary Wiliam

Cotterell, Captain John Rous, Merchant Benjamin Green, and Settler John Collier, et al.

Admiral Boscawen said, "Now is the proper time to oblige the said inhabitants to take the oath of allegiance to His Majesty, or to quit the country."

"Your Excellency," said Admiral Mostyn, "now is also the time to strike. We have a strong force still here in Nova Scotia. Our fleet has not returned home from our battle at Fort Cumberland. The 2,000 men from New England are also still here."

"Yes, quite so," replied the governor.

On August 1, 1755 the governor wrote to Colonel Monckton:

"The order is given to send in all diligence to the Bay a sufficient number of transports to embark the population. You will at the same time receive the instruction relative to the measures to be taken in regard to the deported and the places assigned to them and all that will be necessary in the premises. In the meantime, you should act with the greatest secrecy; for fear that, they will flee with their beast. And to put this project into execution, you should have recourse to a few stratagems so as to place the men in your power, young men and old, and especially the heads of families. You will detain them in order that all may be ready to embark upon the arrival of the transports; after that, there will be no danger of the women and children fleeing with the livestock."

The British formulated the most despicable act ever recorded against human rights. Governor Lawrence ordered Secretary William Cotterell to dispatch orders to his field commanders; John Winslow at Grand Pre, Robert Monckton at Fort Cumberland, Alexander Murray at Piziquid, and John Handfield at Annapolis Royal.

"As it had been before determined to send all the French inhabitants out of the province if they refused to take the oaths, nothing now remained to be considered but what measures should be taken to send them away, and where they should be sent to.

"After mature consideration, it was unanimously agreed that to prevent as much as possible the attempting to return and molest the English settlers that may be set down on their lands, it would be most proper to send them to be distributed amongst the several colonies on the continent, and that a sufficient number of vessels should be hired with all possible expedition for that purpose."

Ships were hired in the colonies to transport the Neutrals to all parts of the world.

John Winslow at Fort Cumberland (old Fort Beausejour) wrote later:

"We are now hatching the noble and great project of banishing the French Neutrals from this province; they have ever been our secret enemies, and have encouraged our Indians to cut our throats. If we can accomplish this expulsion, it will have been one of the greatest deeds the English in America have ever achieved; for, among other considerations, the part of the country which they occupy is one of the best soils in the world, and, in that event, we might place some good farmers on their homesteads."

"Seize all Acadian weapons," ordered Governor Lawrence to his subordinates.

The English troops in the Grand Pré area entered the Acadian homes, two by two, late at night, waking them and taking their arms. The following morning showed the cowardly deed accomplished without any resistance. The English even took all their boats.

When the Acadians later asked the Governor for the return of their firearms, he replied, "Catholics are not permitted by English law to own weapons."

The Acadians in the Grand Pré area drafted a petition to Governor Lawrence:

"We, the inhabitants of Minas, Piziquid, and the River Canard, take the liberty of approaching Your Excellency for the purpose of testifying our sense of the care which the Government exercises over us.

"It appears, Sir, that Your Excellency doubts the sincerity with which we have promised to be faithful to His Britannic Majesty.

"We most humbly beg Your Excellency to consider our past conduct. You will see that, very far from violating the oath we have taken, we have maintained it in its entirety, in spite of the solicitations and the dreadful threats of another power. We will entertain, Sir, the same pure and sincere dispositions to prove, under any circumstances, our unshaken fidelity to His Majesty, provided that His Majesty shall allow us the same liberty that he has granted us. We earnestly beg Your Excellency to have the goodness to inform us of His Majesty's intentions on this subject, and to give us assurances on his part.

"Permit us, if you please, sir, to make known the annoying circumstance in which we are placed, to the prejudice of the tranquility we ought to enjoy. Under pretext that we are transporting our corn or other provisions to Beausejour and the River Saint John, we are no longer permitted to carry the least quantity of corn by water from one place to another.

"We beg Your Excellency to be assured that we have never transported provisions to Beausejour or to River Saint John. If some refugee inhabitants from Beausejour have been seized with cattle, we are not on that account by any means guilty, inasmuch as the cattle belonged to them as private individuals, and they were driving them to their respective habitations.

"As to ourselves, sir, we have never offended in that respect; consequently, we ought not, in our opinion, to be punished; on the contrary, we hope that Your Excellency will be pleased to restore to us the same liberty that we enjoyed formerly in giving us the use of our canoes, either to transport our provisions from one river to another, or for the purpose of fishing; thereby providing for our livelihood.

"This permission has never been taken from us except at the present time. Moreover, our guns, which we regard as our own personal property, have been taken from us, notwithstanding the fact that they are absolutely necessary to us, to defend our cattle which are attacked by the wild beasts, or for the protection of our children and ourselves.

"Any inhabitant who may have his oxen in the woods and who may need them for purposes of labor, would not dare expose himself in going for them without being prepared to defend himself. It is certain, sir, that since the Indians have ceased frequenting our parts, the wild beasts have greatly increased, and that out cattle are devoured by them almost every day. Besides, the arms that have been taken from us are but a feeble guarantee of our fidelity. It is not the gun, which an inhabitant possess that will induce him to revolt, nor deprivation of the same gun that will make him more faithful; but his conscience alone must induce him to maintain his oath.

"An order has appeared in Your Excellency's name given at fort Edward, June 4, 1755, by which we are commanded to carry guns, pistols, etc. to fort Edward. It appears to us, sir, that it would be dangerous for us to execute that order before representing to you the danger to which this order exposes us. The Indians may come and threaten and plunder us for having furnished arms to kill them.

"We hope, sir that you will be pleased, on the contrary, to order that those taken from us be restored to us. By so doing you will afford us the means of preserving both ourselves and our cattle.

"In the last place we are grieved, sir, at seeing ourselves declared guilty without being aware of having disobeyed. One of our inhabitants of the river Canard, named Pierre Melancon, was seized and arrested in charge of his boat, before having heard any order forbidding that sort of transport.

"We beg Your Excellency, on this subject, to have the goodness to make known to us your good pleasure before confiscating our property and considering us in fault. This is the favor we expect from Your excellency's kindness, and we hope you will do us the justice to believe that very far from violating our promises, we will maintain them, assuring you that we are, very respectfully, Sir, your very humble and obedient servants."

Twenty-five of the most prominent men of the area signed this petition.

In the American colonies at this time, the devastating news that General Braddock was killed while engaging a French and Indian force caused a great deal of concern to Governor Lawrence. Lawrence feared that English rule in the colonies was ending. Besides having to deal with the French Neutrals, he also had the 2,000 colonials, whom he did not trust, on his hands. He did not think the colonials were worthy of being in the King's Service.

The colonial forces, led by Winslow, and the regular British troops did not see eye to eye. There was much rivalry amongst them. The British, being professional soldiers, thought they were way above the lowly colonial conscripts.

The colonials did most of the dirty work. Governor Phipps, of Massachusetts, informed them that they would serve their country by going to Canada where they could eliminate the hated papists. These colonials sought every chance they could to fire on a French habitant, male or female, young or old.

In Halifax, Governor Lawrence dispatched a most horrific order to Colonel John Winslow at Chignecto ---"Clear the Acadians from their land."

Colonel Winslow issued the following summons:

"To all the male Acadians of Minas.

"All males over ten years of age are to repair to the church at Grand Pré on Friday, September 5, 1755, at 3 o'clock in the afternoon so that we may impart what we are ordered to communicate to them, declaring that no excuse will be admitted on any pretence whatsoever, on pain of forfeiting goods and chattels in default."

He also ordered that the French reap their harvest immediately. He wanted them to do the dirty work of picking their crops so he could more easily collect it for his own troops. They assumed he wanted them to harvest the crop so they could take it with them when they left the province for Cape Breton, which is what they had been led to believe would happen. The Acadians were deported before they could benefit from their labors. The English took all their crops

At Grande Pre, before the Acadians arrived, Winslow ordered his men to remove all sacred objects from the church before the colonials could get their hands on them and desecrate them. He had his troops set up a camp around the church. He asked for and received the key to the church. He set up his quarters in the priest's own house, evicting him. He requested that the local inhabitants supply his troops with provisions, which they gladly did.

Once situated, Winslow looked about the countryside. He observed the serene beauty of the Grand Pré region. He marveled at the dikes, and enjoyed seeing the prosperous farms and the children playing. Here and there, the hard working Acadians tended to their farms while the women busied themselves with laundering.

He later wrote "Are these happy and prosperous people really the enemy we have to worry about?"

On the day that the Acadian men were to report to the church, Winslow looked out the window of his quarters and saw the dust rising in the distance, indication that there was movement coming his way along the dirt road. In every direction, he observed their movements.

On September 5, 1755, four hundred and eighteen Acadians assembled within St. Charles Catholic Church at Grand Pré. They thought it strange that no sacred objects were in sight. Upon arriving at the church, they had found it heavily guarded by a large militia, which gave them cause for concern. As they entered the church, they saw Winslow sitting at a table at the front, attired in his best uniform, flanked by his officers. Although there were no sacred objects in view, as they entered, they genuflected from force of habit before entering the pews. Once all were inside, the doors were shut and armed guards stood at the ready to prevent any from leaving. An interpreter stood by Winslow's side.

As Winslow spoke, the interpreter relayed the information to the amazed Acadians.

"Gentlemen, I have received from His Majesty's Commission, which I have in my hand and by whose orders you are convened together, to manifest to you His Majesty's final resolution to the French inhabitants of this his province of Nova Scotia, who for almost half a century have had more indulgence granted them than any of his subjects in any part of his dominions. What use you have made of them you yourself best know.

"That your land and tenements, cattle of all kinds and live stock of all sorts are forfeited to the Crown with all other your effects saving your money and household goods, and you yourselves to be removed from this his province.

"I shall do everything in my power that all those goods be secured to you and that you are not molested in carrying of them off, and that whole families shall go in the same vessel and make this remove which I am sensible must give you a great deal of trouble as easy as His Majesty's service will admit, and hope that in what ever part of the world you may fall you may be faithful subjects, a peaceable and happy people.

"You will remain in security under the inspection and direction of the troops that I have the honor to command. You are declared the King's Prisoners."

Upon hearing this, the Acadians looked about for an avenue of escape, but the guards were plentiful and well armed, bayonets at the ready. There was nothing they could do. There was a great deal of murmuring. One can only imagine the thoughts going through the minds of the Acadians.

Winslow wrote later:

"They were greatly struck, though I believe they did not imagine that they were actually to be removed."

One of the Acadians stood up and begged Winslow to be allowed to return home and inform his family of this catastrophe so his poor wife and children would not be worrying about his safety.

"How many men have children here now?" he asked.

Most of the Acadians raised their hands. Winslow selected twenty men with children in the church.

"You twenty men are allowed to leave and inform your families. Your sons will remain for security. Should you fail to return, they will suffer the consequences."

The released Acadians informed their worried families of what had just transpired. The news quickly spread to all the surrounding villages and eventually to Annapolis Royal. The men had to return to the church and await further action by the British. The wives and daughters gathered outside the church unable to assist in any way. Some gathered in prayer groups while others wailed away. Mothers held their infant children; young girls clung to their mother's aprons, and the younger women supported the elderly gray-haired ones. All around the church stood the armed colonials waiting for any provocation to use their weapons. This recruited militia from Massachusetts had an intense hatred for the Roman Catholics, and thoroughly enjoyed what they were doing.

The ships needed to transport the captives had not arrived by September 5, so Winslow had to keep the Acadians locked up in the church.

For six days, they waited all confined in the tiny church. Winslow allowed a few at a time to go out, under heavy guard. On one of these brief releases, one of the Acadians made a dash for the woods whereupon four of the colonials fired at him killing him instantly. The Acadians looked on in stunned horror. The four colonials congratulated each other.

When the transports finally arrived, Winslow ordered the Acadians out of the church. All the women from the villages had gathered; they stood around praying, weeping and pleading. Armed guards prevented the women from approaching their sons, fathers, brothers, and loved ones.

Winslow ordered his troops to separate all the young men from the group. He figured they would be the hardest to handle. They lined up away from the elders. He then gave the orders for his troops to march this group to the waiting boats. They would not budge.

"Use bayonets!" shouted Winslow. Still, they would not budge.

Furious, he grabbed one of the young men and hurled him forward whereupon a colonial was on him ready to run him through. The young man slowly moved away. Seeing the hatred in the eyes of the colonials, the other young men started moving. This group was marched to the shore where rowboats waited, a distance of about a mile. All along the way, mothers followed their sons, wives their husbands. To add to the misery, it started to rain.

Winslow wrote about that situation later:

"Ordered ye prisoners to march. They all answered they would not go without their fathers. I told them that was a word I did not understand, for that the King's command was to me absolute and should be absolutely obeyed and that I did not love to use harsh means, but that the time did not admit of parleys or delays, and then ordered the whole troops to fix their bayonet and advance towards the French, and bid the four right-hand files of the prisoners consisting of 24 men, which I told of myself to divide from the rest, one of whom I took hold, who opposed the marching, and bid march: he obeyed and the rest followed, though slowly, and went on praying, singing, and crying, being met by the women and children all the way with great lamentations upon their knees, praying."

Five ships waited for the human cargo. They placed the young men on one of the ships while placing the elders on separate ships, separating the brothers from each other and sons from the fathers, never to see each other again. The five ships each had different destinations. Once the younger ones were on board and secured, the elders were next. Eighty-nine married men were marched to waiting rowboats and boarded on different ships from the ones their sons were on, also never to see each other again.

One of the young men managed to escape the ship he was on and swam to shore. He did not get very far before he was captured and taken to Winslow.

"We will make an example of him," said Winslow.

The young man was marched to his home, where his mother and sisters awaited.

"Burn the place down!" said Winslow. The colonials were very happy to oblige. The women, forced from their home, stood and watched as their home for many years went up in flames. The colonials took the livestock away.

The young man stood there with tears in his eyes. How hard he had worked to build his home, his barn. He saw his beloved horse led away, but the thing that really broke his heart was watching the colonials shoot his dog; his faithful companion for many years that only gave love, and never asked for anything in return.

They forced the young man to march away, leaving his mother and sisters amidst the ashes, never to see them again.

With little provisions for the Acadians on board, the ships departed leaving the women behind to fend for themselves.

When more transports arrived later for the women, Winslow had his troops round them up. He took great delight in placing the women and children on these ships and sending them to ports other than the ones the men went to.

One of the hapless victims, Jeannette, wife of Antoine LeBlanc, was carrying her nine-month old daughter, Angelique. Being almost at the end of the line, she managed to escape when her guard turned his watchful eye away for a few seconds. She dashed into the thickets and hid until the sorrowful procession was no longer in sight. She rested there, nursing her baby, until she was sure no soldiers lurked about. She watched as the ships sailed away carrying their cargo of human misery, then she made her way back to the church. She was appalled when she arrived at the church and saw the building engulfed in flames. She gazed at the burning structure and sadly remembered the many happy hours she and her family had spent in that house of prayer. This is where she was married, and her children baptized. Now, it was going up in smoke.

She made her way back to her village late in the evening and found it utterly deserted. Arriving back at her home, totally exhausted, she collapsed. The sound of her baby crying early the next morning woke her. With what little strength she had left, she picked herself up and beheld the most tragic sights imaginable.

The cows, waiting to be milked, bellowed pitifully. She managed to milk one of them and drank the milk, which gave her strength to carry on. The pigs were running around squealing for food, uprooting everything in sight. The horses broke out of their enclosures and devoured the greenery in the garden. The oxen, still yoked, ran wildly trying to find food, unable to untangle the yoke holding them together.

Later that day she saw a Micmac Indian canoeing nearby. She ran to the water's edge and hailed him. He saw her and came over to investigate, surprised at seeing the woman.

"How you escape?" he asked.

She explained as best she could how she hid and returned to her home.

"All gone," said the Indian. He helped her get some of her things and brought her to his wigwam. Here, she met the few remaining women who also had managed to escape.

The colonials ransacked the abandoned farms taking all the livestock and booty they could carry. They delighted in slaughtering the faithful dogs and cats innocently awaiting the return of their masters.

When a governing body desires to subjugate its citizens, the first action taken is to disarm the populace. Once the citizen relinquishes his firearms, he relinquishes his freedom. Captain Murray, in Piziquid, ordered all Acadians to turn in their guns and powder. After disarming the Acadians, Captain Murray ordered all Acadian men to assemble at Fort Edward. Unaware of the trap, these Acadians entered.

The fort being as small as it was could hardly accommodate all the prisoners. The crowded condition caused Captain Murray to send a dispatch to Winslow asking him to send the ships quickly. While awaiting the ships, some of the men confined in the underground bunkers dug their way to freedom and escaped. In a strange twist of fate, a colonial soldier, curious to see where the tunnel led, crawled in and was killed when the ground caved in.

In Annapolis Royal, the Micmacs had received the news of the events taking place. Paul canoed to Jacques's home to warn him.

"Jacques," said Paul. "You and your family have to leave immediately."

Jacques and Magdelaine could not believe what they were hearing.

"But, I have my crops to harvest. I have animals to care for," said Jacques.

"I know, but many families downriver are leaving their homes, going into the wilderness to hide. You must do the same!" pleaded Paul.

Still at home were; Jean-Baptiste, aged twenty-three; Joseph, aged twenty-two; Marie Elisabeth, aged eighteen; Euprosie, aged seventeen; Etienne, aged fifteen; Louise, aged fourteen; Ange, aged thirteen.

"Thank you, Paul," said Jacques. "We will get our things together and leave."

"You know where to go and where to find us, my friend," said Paul. "I must go and warn some of the other Acadians." With that, Paul left.

Magdelaine tearfully went next door to her aged mother's home to inform them of the events.

"I won't leave!" cried eighty-three year old Jeanne Hebert.

As quickly as they could, Jacques had his family rounded up some supplies and left the farm for the wilderness. They canoed downriver to where the Micmacs camped and headed into the interior. Jacques led them to where his old camp once stood, the place where he wintered alone many years ago. Some of the frames were still there, but badly decayed and overgrown with shrubs.

They set about building another shelter and settled in for the night. Now burdened with nine mouths to feed, it would be almost impossible to remain there for any length of time. As the days went by, the futility of it all seeped in.

"I wonder what is happening to my animals," said Jacques to his sons.

"Maybe, we should go back, Papa," said Joseph, the oldest boy there.

"Jacques, let us go home," cried Magdelaine.

They all agreed to go back and maybe things would work out. Along the way, they saw other stragglers returning to their homes.

It was good to be home again. They tended to the animals and all seemed normal for the time being.

Major John Handfield, of Annapolis Royal, was greatly distressed when he received orders to round up the Acadians. Having spent many years in Nova Scotia, he had even married a French Acadian girl, now he had the task of rounding up her family and deporting them.

News of this violation of human rights had reached New Brunswick and the resistance movement headed by Captain Beausoleil. The stalwart fighter informed his men, including Jacques's son, Charles, and other freedom fighters to be on alert.

On August 31, 1755, three British ships sailed up the Peticoudiac River towards Coude (Present day Moncton), in the province of New Brunswick. Their movements reported by Micmac Indians all along the way. Beausoleil sent his messengers to notify all his men to meet at the inn at Coude.

"Men," said Beausoleil, "the enemy is even now in our country. This is French soil. They have no rights being here. We must not let them in. Three of their ships are in the river making their way here."

The men were all aroused and ready for a fight. They made plans to meet and attack the ships. Charles rode home for supplies. His wife, Marie, was upset when she saw him stocking up with supplies and taking all his guns and powder with him.

"Charles, where are you going?" she asked. She was holding her three-month old daughter, Marguerite. Little two-year old Jean-Baptiste was at her side.

"We are going to drive the British away from here," said Charles. He kissed his infant daughter, picked up little Jean-Baptiste and gave him a hug and a kiss, then he looked into Marie's eyes and said, "Be brave, darling." He kissed her and left. She wept as he rode away.

They met at a prearranged spot along the river where the water takes a sharp turn westward. This turn, or bend in the river, gave the local village its name, Coude, which means 'elbow' in French. That village changed names later when the British gained possession of New Brunswick. It was renamed Monckton in honor of the British officer who had been in charge of Fort Cumberland, old Fort Beausejour, and was instrumental in rounding up the local Acadians for deportation. A cartographer misspelled the named on his map and called it Moncton.

"Three ships are sailing up river," reported one of the Micmacs to Captain Broussard. In due time most of the resistance fighters had gathered, supported by their Micmac allies.

"This is the plan, men," said Beausoleil. "Let them come up. They will have to turn when they get near the bend. There is a sandbar downriver, when they try to go back down, they will have to cross over it. If the tide has gone out, they won't be able to make it."

They traveled downriver to where the sandbar was and waited, hidden from view. Soon the three ships sailed past, going in a northward direction. After a spell of about an hour, they saw smoke rising in the distance.

"They are torching the farms, the lousy bastards," said Charles.

"Easy boys, we'll get them when they come back," said Beausoleil.

The leader of the British expedition was Major Joshua Frye. He had orders to round up as many Acadians as he could find, and to burn as many farms as he could.

Along the river on either side, the Acadians and Micmacs waited. Towards evening, the ships sailed back downriver to the waters of the Bay of Fundy. This particular area of the world experiences the highest tides ever recorded. The water rises fast, and it recedes fast.

Slowly the three ships navigated the river trying to keep in mid-channel. As the ships approached the sandbar, the lead ship ran aground and halted. British soldiers went ashore to reconnoiter. Beausoleil let the soldiers disembark and waited. The English, carrying lit fagots, were looking for farms to burn. After all the soldiers had disembarked, Beausoleil gave the order to fire. A Micmac high up in a tree fired at the lookout in the lead ship's crow's nest. The soldier fell, hitting the deck with a sickening thud. Pandemonium ensued as black powder rifles opened up on the British. The Micmacs gave their war hoops and proceeded to dispatch the red coats. The British soldiers making for the safety of the ship did not have a chance. The river ran red with blood.

Because the Acadians were all ahead of the ships on either side, the gunners on board could not bring their cannons to bear on them. The ships lined up behind the lead ship could do no better. The riflemen on the ships fired wildly into the wilderness, unable to see the resistance fighters. The blood curdling yells of the Micmacs unsettled the British. They looked all around imagining every shadow an enemy. All Major Frye wanted was to get out of there as quickly as he could. The battle lasted for three hours until the tide rose again to set the ships free. In spite of the terrible damage inflicted to the ships, they managed to make it back to the Bay of Fundy and on to Fort Cumberland. For days after, nerves frayed, Major Frye could not function. The British had torched about two hundred buildings, but at a cost of about 300 men killed. The Micmacs sported their red tunics as trophies after the battle.

"They'll think twice about coming back here again," said Beausoleil.

Charles arrived home, utterly exhausted. He kissed Marie and the children and went straight to bed. Marie stayed at his side, praying on her rosary beads.

"What will become of us?" she thought to herself.

CHAPTER THIRTEEN

The Expulsion

At Annapolis Royal, early on the morning of November 10, 1755, English soldiers on horseback approached Jacques's farm. The moment Jacques had feared had finally arrived. Jacques's barking dog, outside, warned of their approach. He went out to see why his dog was barking. As he watched, soldiers rode towards him. He wondered what they wanted. They dismounted and approached him.

"Your name?" asked the English soldier.

"Jacques."

"Your son's names?" asked the Englishman, while another soldier wrote the answers.

"How many rifles have you?"

"Four, one for myself, and my three sons."

"You will deliver your rifles and all your black powder to the fort tomorrow, or you will be deported. Don't make us come after you, or we will burn your farm." The soldiers left.

"What's going to happen, Papa," asked the boys.

"I guess they mean to deport us."

"It isn't fair," said Joseph, "we've been here all our lives. This is our land." The boy was furious and clenched his fist to make his point.

Jacques looked at Joseph and remembered when he was younger how much fire was in his own blood. Now an older man of sixty, with graying hair, he wished he could return to his younger days to deal with this situation. He would leave the fighting to his young sons. Magdelaine stoically accepted the situation.

The following day Jacques and his sons delivered their weapons to the fort. The quartermaster counted the rifles and checked their names off his list.

While at the Market Square, other Acadians were delivering their arms to the fort. They met later for a meeting at the church. Jacques rose to speak:

"For forty-five years the English have respected our wishes to remain neutral. We have signed an oath of allegiance stating that we will not take up arms against anyone, French or English. Had we signed an unqualified oath of allegiance, they would not have allowed us to practice our Roman Catholic religion, and they would not have allowed our missionaries to remain here. We have signed the oath, swearing to God, that we would not take up arms. Now, they have confiscated our arms, leaving us helpless against wolves attacking our sheep."

There was a general approval of what he had said.

"What can we do?" asked Jean-Baptiste Hebert, one of the younger men there.

"If we unite, and stand together...maybe we can convince them that we will not take up arms against them," replied Jacques.

"We need to file a petition with the English to convince them that we are a peace loving people. We need our guns for protection against wild animals, not against them." Said Jean Pierre Melanson.

A petition was drawn and all present signed it. Jacques along with two other settlers were elected to deliver it to the British governor at Halifax.

Jacques and the other representatives traveled to Halifax and presented their document. The British interpreter translated the paper for Lawrence.

"We unanimously agreed to deliver up our firearms to Mr. Handfield, our worthy commander, although we have not had any desire to make use of them against His Majesty's government. We have therefore nothing to reproach ourselves with, either on that subject, or on the subject of the fidelity that we owe to His Majesty's government.   "For, Sir, we can assure Your Excellency that several of us have risked our lives to give information to the government concerning the enemy, and have, also, when necessary, labored with all our heart on the repairs of Fort Annapolis, and on other works considered necessary by the government, and are ready to continue with the same fidelity.

"We have also selected thirty men to proceed to Halifax, whom we shall recommend to do and say nothing contrary to His Majesty's council, but we shall charge them strictly to contract no new oath. We are resolved to adhere to that which we have taken, and to which we have been faithful so far as circumstances required it; for the enemies of His Majesty have urged us to take up arms against the government, but we have taken care not to do so."

When Lawrence heard the petition he said, "What more do you have to say?" Before anyone could answer he added, "Are you willing to sign an unconditional oath of allegiance?"

Jacques stepped forward and said, "Your Excellency, we appear on behalf of ourselves and all the other inhabitants of Annapolis Royal. We will not take any oath other than what we have taken. If it is your desire to remove us, we ask only that you allow us enough time to prepare ourselves that we may carry our goods away."

The governor's face reddened. He just looked at the group before him and stared long and hard, as if searching for something to say to this unruly and cantankerous assemblage. Finally, he blurted out.

"If you refuse to take an unqualified oath of allegiance now, you will never be able to take it later and you will lose all your possessions! I will give you until ten o'clock tomorrow morning to make up your mind."

The Acadians stood in stunned silence. They could not understand this man's unconcerned appreciation of their feelings.

"Get out!" ordered the governor.

Soldiers escorted them out of the governor's mansion to a locked storeroom at the fort. Provided with meager rations, they spent the night discussing their next move.

The delegates appeared before the governor the following morning, and indicated that they had not changed their minds. Governor Lawrence lambasted them and sent them home.

Back home at Annapolis Royal, the Acadians met again at the church.

"They mean to deport us," said Jacques.

Without their priest to lead them or offer suggestions, they were at a lost.

"What shall we do?" asked one.

"There is not much we can do, they have our weapons," said another.

"I can't just leave my animals," murmured another.

"My brother, Charles, is fighting with Beausoleil in New Brunswick," said Jacques's twenty-year old son, Jean-Baptiste. "I'm going to join him."

"I'm going with you," said Jacques's sixteen-year old son, Etienne.

All the young men agreed that was the thing to do.

Over half the population of Annapolis Royal fled Nova Scotia for the safety of New Brunswick. Jacques opted to stay, unsure of the future.

On August 15, 1755, Governor Lawrence had written the following letter to Major Handfield at Annapolis Royal:

"Instructions for Major John Handfield, commanding His Majesty's garrison of Annapolis Royal in relation to the transportation of the inhabitants of the districts of Annapolis Royal and the other French inhabitants out of the province of Nova Scotia.

"Sir, having in my letter of the 31st of July last, made you acquainted with the reasons which induced His Majesty's council to come to the resolution of sending away the French inhabitants, and clearing the whole country of such bad subjects, it only remains for me to give you the necessary orders for the putting in practice what has been so solemnly determined.

"That the inhabitants may not have it in their power to return to this province nor to join in strengthening the French in Canada at Louisbourg, it is resolved that they should be dispersed among His Majesty's subjects in the colonies upon the continent of America. For this purpose transports are ordered to be sent from Boston to Annapolis to ship on board one thousand persons, reckoning two persons to a ton; and for Chignecto, transports have been taken up here to carry off the inhabitants of that place; and for those of the districts around Minas Basin transports are ordered from Boston.

"As Annapolis is the last place where the transports will depart from, any of the vessels that may not receive their full complement up the bay will be ordered there; and Colonel Winslow, with his detachment, will follow by land and bring up what stragglers may be met with to ship on board at your place.

"Upon the arrivals of the vessels from Boston in the Basin of Annapolis, as many of the inhabitants of Annapolis District as can be collected by any means, particularly the heads of families and young men, are to be shipped on board at the above rate of two passengers to a ton, or as near it as possible. The tonnage of the vessels to be ascertained by the charter-parties, which the master will furnish you with an account of.

"And to give you all the ease possible respecting the victualling of these transports, I have appointed Mr. George Saul to act as agent victualler upon this occasion and have given him particular instruction for that purpose, with a copy of which he will furnish you upon his arrival at Annapolis Royal, from Chignecto, with the provisions for victualling the whole transports. But in case you should have shipped any of the inhabitants before his arrival, you will order five pounds of flour and one pound of pork to be delivered to each so shipped, to last for seven days, and so on till Mr. Saul's arrival, and it will be replaced by him into the stores from what he has on board the provision vessels for that purpose.

"Destination of the inhabitants of Annapolis River, and of the transports ordered to Annapolis Basin:

"To be sent to Philadelphia such a number of vessels as will transport 300 persons.

"To New York, such a number of vessels as will transport 200 persons.

"To Connecticut, such a number of vessels as will transport 300 persons.

"To Boston, such a number of vessels as will transport 200 persons.

"You will use all means necessary for the collecting the people together, so as to get them on board. If you find that fair means will not do it with them, you must proceed by the most vigorous measures possible, not only in compelling them to embark, but in depriving those who escape of all means of shelter or support, by burning their houses and destroying everything that may afford them the means of subsistence in the country; and if you have not force sufficient to perform this service, Colonel Winslow, at Minas, or the commanding officer there will upon your application send you a proper reinforcement."

Meanwhile, at Minas Basin, near Fort Cumberland, the commanding officer, Colonel Monckton, sent his troops out to inform all Acadian males over ten-years of age to assemble at the fort at a designated time.   The Acadians knew not what to expect. The tone of the proclamation was so severe that they dared not refuse. Upon their arrival at the fort, they found themselves incarcerated and subjected to the same decree as Grand Pré.

When darkness approached that day, and the men had not arrived home, the women of the villages worried. Some made their way in the darkness from house to house to see if other families had any information.

"Have you heard anything?" they asked.

"No," was the same answer everywhere.

"His supper is cold."

"The cows have not been milked."

"My little boy is only ten-years old."

"Grandfather is not well."

The following day, a few of the Acadian married men were allowed to visit the villages. The news they gave their women was devastating. Thankfully, the English had not required the missionary priest to report to the fort with the men. It is thanks to this brave priest that the women of Minas Basin rallied and found courage to carry on.

"When you visit your loved ones at the fort, bring them good nourishment, and wear extra clothing," said Father LeGuerne.

Every day the women wore extra clothing and brought food to the fort and visited briefly. After a few of their visits, a head count of the prisoners showed some missing. The women had worn extra clothing and dressed the younger men in bonnets and gowns allowing them to simply walk out past the guards. Colonel Monckton was furious when informed of the escapes. He forbade any more visits. The escapees made their way to New Brunswick where they joined partisan groups.

When the ships arrived, Colonel Monckton marched the Acadian men out to the waiting rowboats. Armed guards flanked the prisoners, providing an escape proof passageway. The women followed on the outside of the English guards. Mothers cried upon seeing their young children being led off to the waiting rowboats, calling their names but to no avail. Wives wailed at seeing their loved ones marched away.

At the shore where the rowboats awaited, hundreds of soldiers circled the group ---all the while women stood helplessly, watching and praying. As the Acadians boarded the first boat, the women burst through the lines and threw themselves into the boats to be with their loved ones. The soldiers turned and faced the rest of the women with fixed bayonets, preventing other women from joining. Then the task of pulling the women out of the boats ensued. Two, and sometimes three, soldiers hauled each wailing women off the boats.

Years later, in his memoir, missionary Father Francois LeGuerne of Minas Basin wrote:

"To save about one-hundred women and their children, whose husbands were put on the ships, I went to them and after consoling and re-assuring them the best I could, I advised them to withdraw to the nearest French territory, which was Ile Saint-Jean (Prince Edward Island.) Many young people, some elderly and five or six men who escaped from Beausejour (Fort Cumberland), began the trek through the swampy woods, a distance of 10 leagues (30 miles) to the sea. They remained out of sight of the English for a month before arriving at Baie-Verte, where they embarked for Ile Saint Jean."

Because of the leadership of the priest, most of the inhabitants of this region escaped deportation.

Captain Murray, commanding officer at Fort Edward in Piziquid, ran into difficulties trying to round up his charges. He wrote later:

"I am happy to learn that things have been so adroitly conducted in Grand Pré and that the poor devils were so resigned; here, they show themselves more patient that I could ever have expected of anyone placed in such circumstances, and that even surprises me, even though those things are to me nearly indifferent. When I think of what happened at Annapolis I dread the moment of execution; I am afraid of the difficulties that may come up when it will be necessary to embark them all. You know that our soldiers despise them, and if they can find an excuse to massacre them, they will do it. I am eager to see the moment arrive when those poor devils will have embarked, then I shall give myself the pleasure of going to see you and to drink to their good voyage."

At a placed called Beaubasin the British met with fierce resistance. This was the domain of Beausoleil and Charles. The luckless commanding officer of this expedition was Major Frye, the same officer who felt the sting of resistance earlier when his ships sailed up the Peticoudiac River. Major Frey knew he would be up against a formidable foe, but his commanding officer, Colonel Monckton, ordered him to proceed.

Major Frye put his troops ashore at Beaubasin. They found most of the farms abandoned. On some of the other farms, they found women huddled together for protection, their men out with the resistance groups. As the English troops went about torching the farms, the freedom fighters gathered behind the English line of retreat. Beausoleil gave the order and the Canadians opened fire. The English fled, taking the women with them.

"Look at the cowards hiding behind women skirts!" said Charles.

When Beausoleil saw the English using the women as shields, he was furious. "Take no prisoners," shouted Beausoleil. The defenders massacred the entire British force.

On September 15, 1755, Captain Lewis sailed into the district of Cobequit aboard the Neptune. He put his troops ashore to round up any Acadians they found. The Acadians, warned by the Micmacs, fled. Angry at not finding any inhabitants the English proceeded to torch everything. Unseen by the revengeful mobsters, a Micmac raiding party canoed out to the ship. They overpowered the crew and set the ship ablaze. Now with no means of escape, the Acadians and Micmacs killed the British Huns.

Of all the districts in Nova Scotia, the one where the English encountered the most trouble was Annapolis Royal. Fierce fighting took the lives of many French and English. Of the three thousand Acadians living here over half escaped, only to be captured and deported later.

Major Handfield issued a proclamation to all male inhabitants over ten-years of age to report to Fort Anne on a certain date. The deportation at Annapolis Royal was about to begin.

The commander of Fort Annapolis had the distasteful duty of arresting all his own in-laws. He had married Elizabeth, daughter of William Winniett of Port Royal.

William Winniett's two other daughters also married British officers. Daughter Anne married Alexander Cosby, while Mary married Edward How. William Winniett's wife, Marie, was the daughter of the famous pirate, Baptiste.

At Annapolis Royal, Jacques had a hunch about what was going to happen. He knew he was about to be deported, but he thought he and his family would be sent to neighboring Cape Breton, or Quebec. He visited Paul before reporting to the fort.

"Paul, the British mean to move us out," said Jacques.

"Yes, I Know. They've been shipping Acadians out all over Nova Scotia."

The Acadians, weary of the British, gave most of their goods to the Indians. Jacques transported items from his own household to the Micmacs. He knew the Indians could use things like knives, hatchets, clothing, pots, pans, iron kettles, etc. At the Micmac campground by the river, Jacques and Paul met, maybe for the last time.

"This may be the last time we see each other, Paul," said Jacques, whose throat was tightening and he found it hard to speak.

"You have been a good friend, Jacques."

"I will never forget you and your wonderful people," replied Jacques, trying to hold back the tears.

"Remember Migamawesu, wherever you go. He will guide you and bring you back home."

"I will pray the Great Spirit be with you after we leave," said Jacques.

They shook hands, looked into each other's eyes, smiled, and held their right arm up as a gesture of peace. The Indians raised their right arm when they met a friend, signifying they held no weapons, and did the same thing when they parted.

Jacques pushed off in his canoe, looked back, waved, and paddled upriver. He knew every twist and turn in the river, having traversed it thousands of times. He also knew all the inhabitants---there was the Bastarache, the Richards, and the Daigles. Making a sharp turn to the left he saw the plot belonging to the Legers, followed by three large parcels all belonging to Heberts. Yes, he knew them all

He was not the same young man that first paddled these waters fifty years earlier. His hair was gray now. His eyes were not as sharp as they once were, but he could still see and hear the sound of the birds chirping happily, perched in the branches. He smiled when he saw a startled deer dash into the woods. He still marveled at the squirrels scurrying up and down trees. He remembered how Paul snatched the goose many years ago at their favorite hunting ground. Thinking about it brought back a little sense of joy in this most trying time. Lost in reverie, he arrived home feeling not the least bit tired; he felt he could have paddled forever.

When the time came for the men to report to the fort, Jacques held Magdelaine for the longest time. They dearly loved each other.

"If I don't go, they will only come and get us and burn our home," said Jacques as he prepared to leave with his sons.

He had instructed Magdelaine to stay with her aged mother till this situation could be resolved.

December 12, 1755, Jacques and his son, Joseph, reported to the fort. His other sons had left earlier to join their brothers in New Brunswick. All the men from Annapolis Royal, over ten-years of age, met at the fort.

Major Handfield was disappointed in the dismal turnout.

"Where are the others?" he demanded. The Acadians just looked at each other without saying a word.

"Any males seen by my patrols will be shot on sight." Still they just stood silently. Major Handfield ordered his soldiers to place the Acadians in the stockade. He later wrote to his commanding officer complaining about the dismal turnout of the inhabitants.

"To: Governor Lawrence

"From Major Handfield

"Sir, one of the transports being arrived from Messrs, Apthrop and Hancock hired to carry of the French Inhabitants of this river, I immediately ordered out a party to bring in about 100 of the heads of families and young men. But, they found the villages up the river destitute of all to male heads of families who are retiered into the woods having taken their beding &c. with them, therefore I am to desire you to send me a reinforcement of men so soon as you can posably spare them that may enable me to bring them to reason.

"I am Sir your most humble servant. J. Handfield."

When the Acadians being held at Fort Anne failed to return home that evening, the women of Annapolis Royal became alarmed. Unfortunately, the women here did not have the spiritual leadership that the other places had.

At Fort Anne, Jacques and Joseph huddled together in the stockade.

"Little did I think forty-five years ago, I would be held prisoner in this fort," said Jacques.

"Too bad the Acadians didn't win that war," said Joseph.

Jacques looked around, and remembered how it was.

"Yes, a lot has happened since I first arrived here," said Jacques. He saw the faces of the young lads. He felt sorry for them, some were openly sobbing.

"I wonder what they are going to do with us," asked Joseph.

"Major Handfield said we were going to be relocated to Cape Breton, or Quebec."

Two days later, a transport arrived at Annapolis Royal. The pier for loading and unloading was only a quarter-mile away, so the prisoners did not have far to walk. Escorted by heavily armed soldiers, the Acadians were marched to the pier and put on board row boats for the short trip to the waiting ship, the Experiment. Later came the hard part, rounding up the women, children, and elderly.

Hundreds of soldiers marched to the furthest reaches on either side of the Annapolis River while hundreds more paddled the river. At the river's end, they burst into the home of Jean Prejean.

Brandishing bayonets, the Massachusetts volunteers pointed their weapons menacingly at Jeannette Prejean, while her children cowered around her for protection.

"Allez...allez," they screamed at her, in the only French word they knew. They made her to understand that she was to leave immediately. She gathered what things she could quickly get her hands on. She dressed her children as warmly as she could; it was bitterly cold in mid December. Little nine-year old Sarah picked up her dog and carried it outside. Once outside, one of the soldiers grabbed the dog away from Sarah and threw it to the ground, whereupon another soldier ran it through with his bayonet. Yelping in pain, the dog tried to get up but another soldier thrust his bayonet into the animal putting it out of its misery.

Sarah ran to pick up her pet but her mother stopped her. "Leave it there, Honey...he's with God now."

Turning to face the soldiers who ruthlessly killed the little girl's pet, she said, "That must have taken a lot of courage."

The soldiers, not understanding French, knew what she was thinking. The sergeant in the group pointed his bayonet at her, and indicating with his thumb, motioned her to move on. She put her arms around her children and led them down the road leading to Fort Anne. Soldiers lined both sides of the road preventing any possible escape. Some of the soldiers ransacked the house after it was vacated, looking for valuables.

A short distance away, they came to the farm owned by Claude Petipas. Mrs. Petipas, Anne, and her family were next in line to be deported. Living with Anne were her aged in-laws, Jean-Baptiste and Vivienne Petipas. Jean-Baptiste, at eighty-two years of age, was unable to walk so the soldiers forced Anne and her children to haul the aged couple away on a two-wheeled cart. Jeannette Prejean ran to help the Petipas family pull the cart. The weeping Acadians trudged along while the soldiers continued their haranguing yells, "Allez....allez."

Next in line was the residence of Pierre Gaudet where the soldiers had already forced them out. The women and elderly marched out to meet the entourage along the way, joining the throng of despair. This horrendous scene was repeated on the other side of the river where families without husbands, brothers, fathers, were being forced out of their homes.

The Acadians, having received advance notice that the English might remove them from their homes, buried most of their treasures in the belief that they might return. They also knew they would be robbed by the English.

For hundreds of years these hard working, noble, peace loving people had toiled to create one of the most productive lands in the world. Now, their lands and livestock were being taken from them. The English stole an estimated 49,000 sheep, 45,000 cattle, 24,000 hogs, and about 4,000 horses from the

Acadians.

Continuing up the road, this sad procession met their neighbors the Roys being routed from their farm; followed by the Labauves, the Bourgeois, the LeBlancs, and so on.

Looking behind them, the Acadians saw great columns of smoke rising.

"The bastards are burning our homes," said Jeannette Prejean to Anne Petipas, as they pulled the flimsy two-wheeled cart.

Looking across the river, they saw smoke rising over there also. To add to their misery, the thought of knowing their homes were being destroyed brought still more agony. This sad entourage of wailing, praying, and freezing women and children made their way to Annapolis Royal, being goaded all the while by the Catholic hating British and Colonial soldiers. Their only crime was refusing to sign an unconditional oath of allegiance.

It started at first light and lasted all day long. There was mass confusion along the way. The road was dry and dusty. The weather was freezing. Older women fainted only to be goaded by the Colonials with bayonets. The younger women tried to help the aged. Women carried babies in their arms, some seemed to be in a stupor, others cried and moaned, some sang hymns. Children tried to keep up with the group; crying. Dogs ran frantically looking for their masters.

Later that day, this throng of women and children arrived at the home of Jacques and Magdelaine where the English proceeded to evacuate them also. Magdelaine and the children helped eighty-two year old Jeanne Hebert get ready and walked with her. The elderly Jeanne Hebert could not comprehend what was happening. She had not wanted to leave the warmth of the fireplace to walk to the landing sight in mid December.

At the landing, boats were filled with the sorrowful women and children, and rowed to waiting ships. Mothers pleaded with the Colonials to place their children in the same boat, but the soldiers did not understand French so their pleas went on deaf ears. Once aboard the ship, they were escorted into the cargo hold where they met with their loved ones. Luckily, Magdelaine and her children were put aboard the same ship with Jacques. She thanked God for being reunited with her husband, and her son, Joseph.

"Where are they taking us?" asked Magdelaine.

"I don't know," replied Jacques, "maybe to Quebec."

When the ship, a brigantine, was fully loaded, 344 Acadians crammed aboard, she put out to sea. She only had rations for 250. Her destination was New York. The captain's name was Stoddard. There were thirty families in all aboard the ship. This ship was supposed to carry about 150, but the English desirous of using the larger transports to carry away the livestock, overcrowded the smaller ships. Because of the overcrowding, the rations did not last. This was to be one of the most bizarre journeys ever recorded. History records the events.

There was hardly any room to move about inside the cargo hold. The children were placed in the hammocks while the adults arranged themselves as best they could on the hard wooden floor. There was no lantern in the hold for fear of fire breaking out, therefore it was dark and dreary, except for a small port being open.

Their meager rations consisted of a few ounces of salt pork daily and a little flour to make bread. Most of the Acadians were so sick, they cared little to eat. Blankets had been provided in the colonies for the journey, which were contaminated with smallpox.

Three weeks out of Annapolis Royal, nearing their destination, they heard the rumbling of thunder and felt the ship leaning more heavily.

"We must be approaching a storm," said Jacques. He knew the sounds made by masts as they strain at the bottom from the force of the wind. The creaks and moans of twisting timber resonated inside the ship. The hatch covers and port holes were sealed and they prepared to brave the oncoming tempest. The ship now pitched and tossed more and more. In the darkened hole, terror gripped the hapless passengers.

"Jacques," cried Magdelaine. "What is happening?"

The Acadians were being rolled about while the children in the hammocks swung wildly.

"It is only a storm," replied Jacques, "nothing to worry about."

All the Acadians looked to Jacques for comfort. He seemed to be the only elderly person on board who knew anything about sailing. Children wet themselves, while the rest began vomiting. Soon, there was a stench of nauseating smell permeating the cargo hold.

"Don't let this get out of hand," commanded Jacques. "Clean this mess up or we will all die." The women rose and washed the floor and clothing with salt water. Thankfully, this cleared the air a bit. Buckets were passed topside and emptied. The ship's crew did what they could to help.

The storm continued unabated for days. On the fourth day of the storm a loud noise was heard outside, a cracking sound that sent shivers throughout the ship.

"What was that?" asked Magdelaine.

"It sounded like a mast splitting," replied Jacques. "I guess the wind is too much for the timber, or they didn't bring in the sails."

A few seconds later a loud booming thud was heard; something crashed onto the deck above.

"Papa, what do you think is happening?" asked his son, Joseph.

"The only thing I can think off is one of the masts broke and landed on the deck. Now, we are in big trouble."

The hours passed agonizingly slow. They could not get used to the tremendous rolling of the ship, and they were exhausted. Many had not slept for days.

Jacques eventually was finally able to stretch out. In the darkened room, totally fatigued, just before dozing off, he gazed at a tiny ray of light coming from a broken port hole. It seemed to put his mind at ease. As if mesmerized, he stared at the tiny opening for the longest time. It seemed to draw him in...strangely, his mind locked out all the disturbing sobs and wails. He felt at ease...and he let his mind wander.

How had he gotten himself in such a fix, he wondered. How had he ended up in the stinking hold of a ship bound for God only knows? How, he kept asking himself, repeatedly. Exhausted, he fell asleep, but not before his mind raced back to the beginning.

...the day he rode down the street with his parish priest to the orphanage. He remembered enlisting in the army, the trip to Acadie, his old friend, Andre, the battle at the fort in 1710, meeting the Heberts and his dear friend Paul. Then he remembered the dream he had when he spent the winter in the wilderness by himself. The dream about being on an island with many people, and the island drifted far, far away. He remembered the look of the shonan's face when he told her about his dream. He remembered she said, "That is not a good sign."

He felt someone shaking him, and he opened his eyes. "You've been sleeping for almost a whole day," said Magdelaine. "I was worried."

Feeling refreshed from his long sleep, he looked at her and said, "I had a wonderful dream." Then reality set in as he looked about.

"Mrs. Girouard's baby is burning with fever," said Magdelaine. As Jacques looked around, he heard the hacking coughs and cries of the Acadians. The women were doing all they could to clean up the vomit and urine soaked clothing of their children.

This is not good, thought Jacques. He knew disease would spread rapidly. He made his way topside and pleaded with the crew to open the hatch covers to let air in. He made it known that the passengers were very ill. Captain Stoddard allowed an opening in one of the hatches. Fresh air vented into the cargo hold, but it was too late. Smallpox and scurvy was spreading. The captain allowed a few at time topside under the watchful eye of the armed sailors.

The fourth week out, blown way off course, the ship continued southward. The rudder was not responding well, and most of the ship's rigging was destroyed. The rations were reduced still further, and the water became undrinkable.

"How long are they going to keep us in this terrible ship?" asked Magdelaine.

"We should have made land a long time ago. I think they are having problems with the sails," replied Jacques.

"It is getting so hot in here."

"Yes, I noticed that. We must be sailing south where it is warmer. It doesn't normally get this warm in January."

Amidst the wailing of the elderly, and the crying of the young, the shriek of Mrs. Blanchard sent chills into the Acadians. Separated from her husband and all her children, she sat alone, holding her infant child who became ill. She watched him day and night. She had been trying to breast feed her baby, but due to the lack of nourishment for herself, and the spread of sickness, she had been unable to lactate.

"My baby just died," she screamed. The passengers were stunned, it became quiet.

Magdelaine made her way over to help as much as she could. She felt the baby and noticed the fever had gone, and now it felt cold to the touch. The eyes were still open, and it looked as if the baby were just staring peacefully into space. Mrs. Blanchard hugged the lifeless body, not wanting to believe that she had lost the most precious thing in her life. Magdelaine made her way back to Jacques.

"You have to get help for her."

"I'll see what I can do."

Jacques made his way topside again and asked to speak to the captain. His gray hair and imposing physique gave him an air of respect. He was taken to the captain's cabin and admitted.

"Captain, you have to do something about the conditions on this ship."

"There is not much I can do. The storm blew us way off course and wrecked the rigging. Our rations are depleted, and as you know, the water is stale. We should have been in New York by now. We are trying to make for the nearest port which I believe is St. Christopher."

Jacques was aghast when he heard the destination was supposed to be New York.

"We were told that you were taking us to Cape Breton Island, or Quebec!"

"I am only the captain of this ship. I have been hired by the colonial government to transport you and the other Acadians to New York."

"Then they lied to us!"

"I have my orders."

"Mrs. Blanchard's baby just died, and the rest of us are not far behind."

"I will see to Mrs. Blanchard's child."

The captain and the bosun's mate, along with Jacques made their way below to the cargo hold. The captain held a piece of cloth to his mouth to keep the stench and sickness away. The bosun's mate examined the baby and declared it dead. The captain told Mrs. Blanchard that the baby must be thrown overboard. She pleaded with the captain to keep her baby, just a little longer. The bosun's mate tore the little body away from Mrs. Blanchard, and carried it topside. She followed the baby topside, along with Magdelaine, and begged the captain to permit her to say the rosary bead, or at least a short prayer over the body. The captain ignored her plea and ordered the bosun's mate to toss the body over the side. The sight of the baby splashing into the ocean was too much for Mrs. Blanchard, she became hysterical. She watched as the ship sailed away from the little floating bundle. Magdelaine had to hold her up and help her back below deck. Her moans and cries could be heard for hours after. Mercifully, she died a few days later.

The passengers were dying daily from lack of food and water, plus the ever-present smallpox. The crew of the Experiment had taken crates of live chickens before they set sail. They ate sumptuously while the Acadians starved.

Burial at sea became a daily occurrence. History records that about four thousand exiles from different regions of Nova Scotia, on different ships, perished at sea.

After almost six weeks at sea, land was sighted. The crippled ship put into the port of St. Christopher, deep in the Caribbean. This port was unable to repair the ship. After replenishing the ship with much needed supplies, she put out for Antiqua, a British port nearby, capable of completing the repairs.

On January 19, 1756, the Experiment arrived at Antiqua. The Acadians were escorted off the ship under heavy guard and placed in a concentration camp.

When Jacques informed the Acadians that their destination was to be New York, they were devastated. They had been lied to by the British to keep them under control. Of the 344 Acadians crammed into the ship, seventy-two perished.

Antiqua proved to be a most delightful change from the cramped quarters on the ship. The weather was beautiful. It seemed the sun shone every single day and when it rained, it only lasted an hour or so.

The Acadians tasted tropical fruits for the first time in their lives. There was a small waterfall near the camp, where they could go to bathe and refresh themselves. In a few weeks, the Acadians regained their health. The tropical fruits were a welcome change from the horrible diet they endured aboard the ship. They were more or less forced to cut sugar cane, along with the negro slaves, while waiting for the ship to be repaired.

The days became weeks, and the weeks became months, as they languished in the camps. They sat around a fire at night trying to figure out what their next move would be.

"I heard from the local natives that there is a French island south of here," said eighteen-year-old Jean Garceau.

"Maybe we should try to make for the island," said Antoine Aureillon.

"Anything would be better than ending up in New York with the Protestants," said Arthur Devoux.

Five of the Acadian men agreed they would escape, steal a boat and try for the nearest island, which was Guadaloupe, about fifty miles away and indeed a French island. They asked Jacques how they could navigate without a compass so they could find the island.

"During the day, make sure the sun rises on your left. When the sun is directly overhead at noon, head straight for it, then as the sun sets, make sure it is on your right. At night, look behind you and keep the North Star to your backs."

Jacques had showed them how to locate the North Star at night by first locating the big dipper.

"Take as many coconuts as you can load into your boat. This will provide you with food and water. Make a spear out of bamboo to catch fish near the surface. Carry blankets with you for a sail and to provide shade during the day, and to keep you warm at night. You can also use the blankets to carry fruits and coconuts."

Before leaving, the five young men gathered late in the evening with the Acadians. They kissed their mothers and fathers good-bye, said their prayers, and made good their escape. They made it safely to Guadaloupe in a stolen boat, thanks to the instructions provided by Jacques.

In mid April 1756, the Experiment was ready for sea. The Acadians were loaded aboard once more, and she weighed anchor. Escorted by a large British Man-of-War gunship, they made for New York, arriving in May. More unfortunate Acadians died on this crossing due to illness. Of the 344 French that left Annapolis Royal, only 249 survived.

[The following is an excerpt by Dr. Don Landry from Louisiana, and is being used with his permission. I wish to express my gratitude for his generosity.]

THE SHIPS OF THE ACADIAN

EXPULSION

A Compilation Of Information On The Eighteenth Century Transport Vessels, Used By The British To Transport The Acadians, (Neutral French), During The Acadian Expulsion Of 1755

By DR. DON LANDRY, D.D.S. 6512 Schouest Street Metairie, Louisiana 70003 1-504-455-5596 (All Rights Reserved)

INTRODUCTION

In researching for family history and genealogy, the author became curious about the transport vessels that were used to transport his ancestors from Pisiquid, NovaScotia (Acadia) to Maryland on October 28, 1755. Therefore, the following is the result of the research on the Ships of the Acadian Expulsion.

THE EXPULSION

On Friday, September 5, 1755, the French inhabitants of Acadia were taken into custody by the British officer, Lieutenant Colonel John Winslow. Plans were formulated to expel the Acadians from their homeland quickly through mass expulsion relying on a fleet of sailing vessels. It was the British's final solution to what they considered a longtime problem.

THE TRANSPORT SHIPS OF THE EXPULSION

It appears that the ships used for the expulsion of the Acadians from Nova Scotia (Acadia), were a variety of makeshift second hand cargo vessels, making up a fleet of about 24 sailing vessels. Governor Shirley and Colonel Lawrence had contracted, or chartered these vessels, by the month, for a flat fee per head, from Charles Apthorp and Thomas Hancock of the Boston Mercantile firm of Apthrop and Hancock. And, after they were outfitted and converted in Boston to hold 2 persons per ton (in some cases 300 to 500 persons), they were brought over from Boston to Nova Scotia. The transports were ready on the 11th of October. (Maryland Historical Magazine Vol III #1 March 1908 - The Acadians (French Neutrals) Transported to Maryland - Basil Sollers - p. 7) **WHAT WERE THE COLONIAL SAILING VESSELS LIKE?**

According to Howard I. Chapelle in "THE HISTORY OF AMERICAN SAILING SHIPS", the methods employed by the shipbuilding in the early days were crude. The planking was handsawn by two men, one in a pit and one straddling the log. The heavy timber was shaped and fitted by use of an adze, broadaxe and plane. Because of this crude and laborious process, the bulk of the colonial sailing vessels were small.

CLASSIFICATION, TYPE, OR DESCRIPTION OF THE VESSELS USED

It is difficult to find detailed information on all of the types, or classification of ships used during the mid-eighteenth century. The general classifications of type and rig that were popular with the colonists are easily listed, as they are often given in the records. But some allowances must be made for the ignorance of the recorder, for the listing of a single vessel as a "bark", a "ship" and a "brigantine" in a single paper is not at all uncommon. Generally speaking, there were seven classifications of vessels in the colonial records. Ships, Sloops, Pinks, Brigantines, Shallops, Ketches and Barks, and all of them are noted in these records up until 1717 when Schooners were added to the list as a seperate class. The types, or class, of the colonial vessels correspond in design and appearance with their counterparts in England. The most common group on the lists were the Sloops, from twenty five to seventy tons burden. The next in popularity were brigantines, from 30 to 150 tons. The rigging of a brigantine at this time is open to argument, they were sometimes rigged as Brigges, and possibly as Schooners before a destinction was made for the Schooner's rigging.

Following are descriptions and illustrations of the different types of sailing vessels that made up the fleet, or convoy, of ships used for the Acadian expulsion of 1755.

- **BARKS** Barks were square-sterned vessels, usually flush decked, and like the Pinks had no special rig. The name "Bark" was not applied to the rig, but to the hull type. The name was very loosely applied in colonial records, and is often used in place of ship or vessel. Most of the colonial Barks seem to have been Brigantines, although some were rigged as Ships or Ketches. A bark was a three masted vessel square-rigged except for the mizzenmast, which is fore-and-aft rigged. This vessel was also called a Barque.
- **BRIGGE or BRIGANTINE** A brigge or brigantine was a two masted square-rigged vessel that had square sails on the foremast only, and fore-and-aft rigged on the mainmast. The Brig and Snow came into use in the early part of the eighteenth century. Both were two masted, and were square rigged on both masts. There were only minor differences in their rigging, and in time the word Snow went out of use. A brig carried a cross jack yard instead of a main yard, which differentiated it from the snow, which carried a square mainsail in addition to its' fore and aft mainsail that was rigged on a try-sail mast. Brigs were fast and were a favorite of privateering and pirates.
- **CORVETTE** A corvette was a warship equipped with sails and a single tier of guns, and ranking next below a frigate.
- **FRIGATE** A frigate was originally a light and swift vessel of the Mediterranean, propelled by both oars and sails. A frigate was also an old-style war vessel used from 1650 to 1840, a frigate was smaller than a ship of the line, but larger than a corvette. Originally a frigate had a short deck, forward and aft, at about the same level, and a lower long deck amidship. Later they were constructed to have a continuous platform running from end to end of the ship without a break. This type of construction was called "frigate fashion". A frigate was a term used to describe smaller types of warships that had from 24 to 50 cannons that were carried on these flush decks. They were designed for speed and were particularly efficient as commerce destroyers.
- **GOELETTE** It is sometimes difficult to differentiate between closely related types of vessels and perhaps no fine distinction can be made between the the two masted rig the French called a goelette and that which was commonly designated as a schooner. The word Goelette comes from the Breton word for seagull

(gwelon or goelan). Emile Lauvriere, in his "LA TRAGEDIE D'UN PEUPLE" - Histoire du Peuple Acadien - des origines a nos jours - 1923- Editions - Bossard - 43 Rue Madame, 43 - Paris - Tome I - 12th edition Chapter XIV "LE 'GRAND DERANGEMENT'" pp 457-513, in referring to some of the vessels used in the expulsion, refers to the sloop Dove, as ôla goelette Doveö, schooner Racehorse as ôla goelette Race Horseö and and schooner Ranger as ôla goelette Rangerö. And, following a long list of other vessels he refers to one as ôUne Goeletteö. I am not sure if he means that this vessel was named "une Goeletteö, or he is referring to an unknown schooner by the French name goelette, or an unknown sloop.

- **MAN-O-WAR** Any naval vessel armed for active hostilities.
- **SCHOONER** Schooners were small vessels that evolved in New England. Schooners were a constructed with a square stern and fitted with two masts bearing a sloop sail on each, a bowsprit and a jib. These sails were set fore and aft of the masts and parallel to the keel. In later years schooners were designed with as many as seven masts. The schooner was very economical to operate, requiring fewer men to her sail, than any other sailing vessel. Schooners were used in shallow waters and narrow harbors for coastal trade, but could also be used in the open sea.
- **SHIP** Ships were full rigged sailing vessel with three or more masts, with square rigging on all three masts with a spanker on the mizzen as well. A full rigged ship was best for long voyages, where square sails could be set in the trade winds and left untouched for days. Except for the jibs and a little steering sail at the stern, called a spanker, all sails on a ship where square sails and were set afthwartship on three masts. Only a craft so rigged could be properly called a ship.
- **SLOOP** As noted above, according to Howard I. Chapelle in "*THE HISTORY OF AMERICAN SAILING SHIPS*", the majority of the colonial sailing vessels were small. And the largest proportion of vessels in the lists of colonial sailing vessels are sloops, from twenty five to seventy tons burden. Sloop rigging during this time was fore-and-after; one mast, carrying a gaff mainsail, two to three headsails, and a square topsail and "course" (square lower sail). Below the main deck of the sloop were two short decks or "platforms", the forward for the accommodation of the galley fireplace, and in merchant vessels, the crew. Abaft this, in merchantmen, was the cargo hold, but in men-o-war this space had a portable deck for accomodation of the large crews that were required in that class of ship. Aft was the "great cabbin" and after "platform" forming state-rooms or "bedplaces" for the officers. A large hatch was over the hold and a ladderway and sometimes a skylight was over the after platform, which completed the list of deck openings. In the stern there was a short raised quarterdeck, formed by the roof of the "great cabbin." The entrance to the cabin was through a doorway in the bulkhead at the fore end of the quarterdeck, opening on the main deck, and covered by a domed hatch. The floor of the "great cabbin" was sunk below the level of the main deck so that the quarterdeck would not be excessively high. The sloop was steered by a long tiller on the quarterdeck. And the quarter deck had open wooden rails. There was usually a figurehead at the stern or a simple carved billet. The illegal trade business required a sharp and fast vessel. The first mention of sharp and fast vessels appears to be in 1730s, and were probably sloops, but soon schooner rigging was adopted. Colonial shipping vessels were usually small, although, we note that a lot of the transports used in the expulsion, including the

sloops, were closer to 90 tons burden. Naval records are vague at times as to ship descriptions. A Naval-Sloop could be a vessel of almost any rig, as long as it carried her guns on a single deck, or was commanded by an officer one grade below a Captain in rank. It seems that a Naval-Sloop is more a description of rank and battery, than of rig. In old navies, a Sloop-of-War was a vessel rigged either as a ship, brig, or schooner, and mounting between 18 and 32 guns; later any war vessel larger than a gunboat and carrying guns on one deck only. There are no sloop classification in modern navies. The escort ship Baltimore was designated as a Sloop/War vessel. The Royal Navy's brigantine or snow "SWIFT" was called a "sloop" it measured 60 feet long by 19.2 feet in width, and was 90-1/2 tons. In most accounts, sloops are described as a single masted fore-and-aft rigged sailing vessel, having a fixed bowsprit and carrying at least one jib: and is now used principally as a racing vessel. There were a considerable number of sloops used as transport vessels during the expulsion. The Schooners and Sloops used in the expulsion ranged from a low of 69 tons to a high of 91 tons, and as mentioned above, the term sloop and schooner may have been used interchangebly when referring to the type of vessel used in transporting the Acadians.

- **SNOW** A snow was a large two-masted square rigged vessel characterized by having a trysail mast close behind the mainmast. The Snow and the Brig had a common ancestor, and it was difficult to distinguish between the brigs and the snows. The Snow and the Brig came into use in the early part of the eighteenth century. Both were two masted, and were square rigged on both masts. There were only minor differences in their rigging, and in time the word Snow went out of use. A shipping or marine ton is equilivant to 100 cubic feet and the gross tonnage of a vessel refers to the cubic capacity of a vessel, including that of the hull and superstructure, with the exception of certain spaces, such as the pilot house, galleys and companion ways. The net tonnage is the space that remains after the cubic capacity of the engine rooms ballast tanks and crew's quarters are excluded from the gross tonnage, and could be used for either cargo or persons. ("THE YOUNG UNITED STATES" -1783-1830 by Edwin Tunis - "SHIPBUILDING" - pp. 81-87; 134-136)

THE EMBARKMENT

The embarkation began on October 8, 1755 and continued until the 28th of October. In order to hasten the undertaking, the ships used were overloaded and to make room for even more, the Acadians were forced to leave practically all of their goods on shore, where they were found still lying on the shore by the English settlers who came six years later. The crowding of the ships in excess of their complement made conditions aboard the vessels dangerous to health and prevented the Acadians from carrying much of their household goods with them. (page 7 -Maryland Historical Magazine - Vol. III No. 1, March 1908 - "The Acadians (French Neutrals) Transported to Maryland" - Basil Sollers) In an account of the embarkation, manuscripts show that the authorities considered the Acadians being "shipped" with no more concern than they would have in the shipping of cattle. The lack of, or disregard for the ships' manifests, shows that they didn't appear to be concerned with names, only numbers." (N.B.) I have made some blunder by the loss of the principal list of those who embarked - but the number of souls that embarked on board of these transports were 2921 - how many embarked afterwards I know not" -

(ACADIA"-Edourd Richard Vol. 2, Chapter XXXI, pp. 120-121) - (Naomi E.S. Griffiths - "THE ACADIAN DEPORTATION: Deliberate Perfidy or Cruel Necessity" - p. 143 [quoting a manuscript account of Brown compiled in 1760's]) Because of the lack of manifests, or passenger lists, there is no record of those Acadians who died at sea. Only, that they mysteriously disappeared from any record, or census following the expulsion.

DEPORTATION TRANSPORT SHIPS

Following is a list of transports chartered from Apthorp and Hancock of Boston for 40 to 48 pounds per month and used to transport the Acadians out of Acadia in the fall of 1755. The names and the description of the vessels were taken from: Abreviated copies of the accounts transmitted by Apthorp & Hancock of Boston, to Governor Lawrence, that can be found on pages 285-289 of SELECTIONS FROM PUBLIC DOCUMENTS OF THE PROVINCE OF NOVA SCOTIA, Published by resolution of the House of Assembly on March 15, 1865 in 1869; An article on the ("ACADIAN DEPORTATION SHIPS", by Alfred N. LaFreniere - (page 7-9 - Maryland Historical Magazine - Vol. III No. 1, March 1908; "The Acadians [French Neutrals], Transported to Maryland" - Basil Sollers); Canadian Archives, Report [1905], II. Apendix A, Part III, E, p. 81; Photo copy of an article that appeared in the Windsor, N.S. newspaper entitled "EXPULSION OF ACADIANS ORGANIZED AT WINDSOR"); Gregory A. Wood - THE FRENCH PRESENCE IN MARYLAND - 1524-1800 - p. 65-66) - (Nova Scotia Doc., I, 42-4; and, Emile Lauvriere - "LA TRAGEDIE D'UN PEUPLE" - Histoire du Peuple Acadien - des origines a nos jours - 1923- Editions Bossard - 43 Rue Madame, 43 - Paris - Tome I - 12th edition Chapter XIV "LE 'GRAND DERANGEMENT'" pp 457-513.

On August 11, 1755 Col. Charles Lawrence issued instructions to his Field Commanders for the transportation of the Acadians from Pisiquid, Mines, Cannard and Coquebid. He stated that the ships will first be sent from Boston to Col. Moncton, commander of Fort Cumberland (formerly Fort Beausejour) at Chignecto, with orders that those transports that are not needed at Chignecto, will be sent to the Minas Bay area. There they were to join the transports that had been sent to Minas from Boston, to help with the transport of the inhabitants from Minas. Of the ten transports sent to Chignecto, three were not needed, the BOSCOWAN, James Newell, master, the DOVE, Samuel Forbes, master and the RANGER, Nathaniel Munroe, master. These three transports were sent to Minas on October 13, 1755 and joined the fleet in the Bay of Minas. (Albert N. Lafreniere - "ACADIAN DEPORTATION SHIPS" -"Connecticut Maple Leaf", volume 6, published by the French-Canadian Genealogical Society of Connecticut, Inc.) Because Major Handfield had problems in assembling the Acadians in Annapolis Royall, (taking from August until early December), the transports that were sent to him at Annapolis Ro the Acadians in Annapolis Royall, (taking from August until early December), the transports that were sent to him at Annapolis Royall were diverted to Col. Winslow at Minas. Three of these transports were then assigned to Captain Murray at Pisiquid. (The British Empire Before The American Revolution - Vol. VI by Lawrence Henry Gipson - p. 280) After the inhabitants were loaded aboard the ships at Minas, Col Lawrence instructed that the transports that were not needed at Minas, were to be sent to Major Handfield at Annapolis Royall. The Acadians at Annapolis Royal were then shipped off from Goat Island at 5:00 o'clock in the morning on Monday , December 8, 1755. Lawrence specifically instructed that the sloop Dove be sent to Annapolis to take the inhabitants to

Connecticut "to which the vessel belongs". (p. 271 - 273 of SELECTIONS FROM PUBLIC DOCUMENTS OF THE PROVINCE OF NOVA SCOTIA, Published in 1869, by resolution of the House of Assembly on March 15, 1865) "On the 29 Octr 1755 the Fleet saild from the Rendezvous in the Bason of Mines under the Convoy of His Majestys Ships." The transports vessels were as follows :

BOSCOWAN Schooner 95 tons CHIGNECTO TO PENNSYLVANIA

The schooner BOSCOWAN, 95 tons, David Bigham, Captain, sailed to the Minas Basin and joined the fleet that was in the Bay of Minas. The Boscowan departed from Chignecto on October 13, 1755 with 190 exiles, destined for Pennsylvania. The date of arrival in Pennsylvania is unknown. The Schooner Boscowan, like the others, was probably chartered for a monthly fee (per ton), plus a pilot's fee and provisions, by Governor Lawrence, from Charles Apthorp & Thomas Hancock, of the Boston Mercantile Company of Apthorp and Hancock, to be used as a transport for the removal of the Acadian Exiles to the eastern seaboard. The amount of provisions for the transports were included in the sailing orders issued by Lawrence and was to be 5 pounds of flour and one pound of pork (or 1 lb of beef 2 lbs bread and 5 lbs of flour) for (each) 7 days for each person so embarked. (p. 280 of SELECTIONS FROM PUBLIC DOCUMENTS OF THE PROVINCE OF NOVA SCOTIA, Published in 1869, by resolution of the House of Assembly on March 15, 1865) also (Albert N. Lafreniere - "ACADIAN DEPORTATION SHIPS" - "Connecticut Maple Leaf", volume 6, published by the French-Canadian Genealogical Society of Connecticut, Inc.)

BOSCOWAN Schooner 63 tons CHIGNECTO TO MINAS - NOT USED

The schooner BOSCOWAN, 63 tons, James Newell, Captain, was among thetransports that were sent by Col. Charles Lawrence to Chignecto for the use of Col Moncton. When the Boscowan was not needed at Chignecto, Col. Moncton sent the Boscowan to Minas on October 13, 1755. While at Minas, the Boscowan ran aground at Pisiquid, and was not used as a transport. (The British Empire Before The American Revolution - Vol. VI by Lawrence Henry Gipson) also (Albert N. Lafreniere - "ACADIAN DEPORTATION SHIPS" - "Connecticut Maple Leaf", volume 6, published by the French-Canadian Genealogical Society of Connecticut,Inc.) The Schooner Boscowan, like the others, was probably chartered for a monthly fee (per ton), plus a pilot's fee and provisions, by Governor Lawrence, from Charles Apthorp & Thomas Hancock, of the Boston Mercantile Company of Apthorp and Hancock, to be used as a transport for the removal of the Acadian Exiles to the eastern seaboard. The amount of provisions for the transports were included in the sailing orders issued by Lawrence and was to be 5 pounds of flour and one pound of pork (or 1 lb of beef 2 lbs bread and 5 lbs of flour) for (each) 7 days for each person so embarked. (p. 280 of SELECTIONS FROM PUBLIC DOCUMENTS OF THE PROVINCE OF NOVA SCOTIA, published in 1869, by resolution of the House of Assembly on March 15, 1865)

EDWARD CORNWALIS Ship 130 tons CHIGNECTO TO SOUTH CAROLINA

The ship CORNWALIS, 130 tons, Andrew Sinclair, Captain, departed from Chignecto on 13 October, 1755, with 417 exiles under the direction of Col. Moncton. The Cornwalis arrived in South Carolina on 19 November, 1755, with 207 exiles. (The British Empire Before The American Revolution - Vol. VI by Lawrence Henry Gipson) "Half of the people shipped on the Edward Cornwalis, destination South Carolina, died on Routeö. (In Council Records, Columbia, sc, 480 - ôReport of the Edward Cornwalis, by Andrew Sinclair, Master, 17 November, 1755: "210 dead, 207 in healthö,[Naomi E.S. Griffiths - "The Contexts of ACADIAN HISTORY" 1686-1784 p. 93]) The Corwalis was probably chartered for a monthly fee (per ton), plus a pilot's fee and provisions, by Governor Lawrence, from Charles Apthorp & Thomas Hancock, of the Boston Mercantile Company of Apthorp and Hancock, to be used as a transport for the removal of the Acadian Exiles to the eastern seaboard. The amount of provisions for the transports were included in the sailing orders issued by Lawrence and was to be 5 pounds of flour and one pound of pork (or 1 lb of beef 2 lbs bread and 5 lbs of flour) for (each) 7 days for each person so embarked. (p. 280 of SELECTIONS FROM PUBLIC DOCUMENTS OF THE PROVINCE OF NOVA SCOTIA, Published in 1869, by resolution of the House of Assembly on March 15, 1865)

DOLPHIN Sloop 87 tons PISIQUID TO MARYLAND

According to copies of accounts, dated ---, 1756, transmitted by Charles Apthorp & Thomas Hancock, of Boston Mercantile Company Apthorp and Hancock, to Governor Lawrence, the Sloop Dolphin, 87 tons Zebad Forman (Farnam) Master, was chartered from Apthorp & Hancock of Boston ôfrom 25 August to 20th February, 1756 to carry 230 Neutrals, 56 more than his complement of two to a ton, at 9s. per two Hallifax Curry, pr Capt Murray Directions.ö published on pages (p. 285 - 293 of SELECTIONS FROM PUBLIC DOCUMENTS OF THE PROVINCE OF NOVA SCOTIA, published in 1869, by resolution of the House of Assembly on March 15, 1865.)also (The British Empire Before The American Revolution - Vol. VI by Lawrence Henry Gipson, p. 278) Some accounts have 174 men aboard the Dolphin. Sloop Dolphin, 87 tons, Captain Farman arrived in Pisiquid from Port Royal on 12 October, 1755 and embarked on 10-12 October. The Dolphin departed from Pisiquid on 27 October, 1755 and arrived at Annapolis Maryland on 15-30 November, 1755 with 230 (56 surnombres) passengers. (Emile Lauviere - "LaTragTdie d'un peuple , vol 1, Librairie Henry Geulet, Paris, 1924) The monthly charter fee for the Dolphin for 5 months and 26 days was 60 s p. month for hire of a pilott , plus provisions . The amount of provisions for the transports were included in the sailing orders issued by Lawrence and was to be 5 pounds of flour and one pound of pork (or 1 lb of beef 2 lbs bread and 5 lbs of flour) for (each) 7 days for each person so embarked. (p. 280 of SELECTIONS FROM PUBLIC DOCUMENTS OF THE PROVINCE OF NOVA SCOTIA, published in 1869 by resolution of the House of Assembly on March 15, 1865.) On October 14, 1755, Captain Alexander Murray writes: "0n this fateful Oct. 14th: "I am at this moment embarking the people on board the two Sloops: the "Three Friends" and the "Dolphin". The shipping point north end of Pisiquid at the junction of the Avon and St. Croix rivers. (Photo copy of an article that appeared in the Windsor, N.S. newspaper entitled "EXPULSION OF ACADIANS ORGANIZED AT WINDSOR") The Dolphin (87 tons burden, Zebad Farman, master) with 227 (or 230), 56 over her compliment aboard, had embarked from Pisiguit, under the direction of Capt. Alexander Murray on October 27, 1755 and arrived in Maryland on 30 November, 1755. Some accounts have Captain Murray loading the ships on October 27th and the ships leaving the harbour on October 28, 1755 . However, records show that the Sloop Dolphin - Zebad Forman, master - left Pisiquid with 227 aboard. While at sea, The Dolphin, along with 5 other transports, met with a furious gale after their departure from Mines Basin, and entered the harbor of Boston, on November 5, 1755. The fleet of six transports with French Neutrals aboard sought shelter for a number of days, and this delay further depleted their supplies which were low since the begining of the voyage. (Nova Scotia Doc., I, 42-4) - Because of the dreadful overcrowding and the delay in Boston due to the storms, the ships' stores were depleted. While in Boston, the vessels were inspected and it was reported that the passengers aboard the Dolphin were "Sickley, occasioned by being to much crowded, 40 lying on deck;" and their water bad. They want an allow'e of Rum &c." and "The vessels are to much crowded; their allowences of Provisions short ...". Following the inspection at Boston, 47 passengers were removed due to overcrowding and/or health conditions reducing the number of exiles to 2 per ton. Fresh water and minimal supplies and assistance was given to the passengers by the Massachusetts Bay authorities, and the vessels sailed southward. The Dolphin, continuing its voyage, reached Maryland on November 30, 1755 with 180 aboard. (Gregory A. Wood - THE FRENCH PRESENCE IN MARYLAND _ 1524-1800 - p. 65-66) (Basil Sollers - THE ACADIANS (FRENCH NEUTRALS) TRANSPORTED TO MARYLAND, p. 9), (Al Lafreniere - "Acadian Deportation Ships) Edouard Richard refers to the Dolphin as "Corvette Dolphin" 87 tons Captain Zebad Forman, was used to transport 174 Acadian exiles (56 additional). (ACADIA" - Edouard Richard Vol. 2, Chapter XXXI, p. 121) The Dolphin with 230 exiles and the Ranger with 263 exiles followed the arrival of the Elizabeth and Leopard in the Annapolis Harbor. The two vessels carried 493 men, women and children transported from Pisiquid under the directions of Captain Alexandre Murray On the last 2 days of the months, the other 3 sloops were anchored in the Severn, but their captains seemed most anxious about the Maryland council's refusal to permit immediate landing in the absence of Gov. Sharpe, who was attending a conference of colonial executives in New York. (Gregory Wood Acadians in Maryland - A Guide to the Acadians in Maryland in the Eighteenth and Nineteenth Centuries.) In a letter dated 17 February, 1996, Stanley Piet of Bel Air Maryland, writes that the "NOTARY PUBLIC RECORD BOOK 1774-1778 in the Hall of Records for the state of Maryland, located at 350 Rowe Blvd., Annapolis Maryland 21401, show the arrival of the ships in Maryland, but there are no people identified. Information listed on the ships Ranger and Dolphin is as follows: "Ranger - Wm. Burkman, Caines Bay, owner. Francis Peirey, Captain, Order from Alexander Murray, Commander of his Majesty's Troops at Pisgate arrived Severn River, Annapolis 29 November 1755. Sent to Oxford Maryland." "Dolphin - Zebediah Farnman, master, Sent to Lower Marlborough, Patuxent River".

DOLPHIN Sloop 90 tons CHIGNECTO TO SOUTH CAROLINA

The sloop DOLPHIN, 90 tons, William Hancock, Captain, departed from Chignecto with

121 Acadian exiles on 13 October, 1755, destined for South Carolina and arrived in South Carolina on 19 November, 1755. The sloop Dolphin was probably chartered, like the others, for a monthly fee(per ton), plus a pilot's fee and provisions, by Governor Lawrence, from Charles Apthorp & Thomas Hancock, of the Boston Mercantile Company of Apthorpand Hancock, to be used as a transport for the removal of the Acadian Exiles to the eastern seaboard. The amount of provisions for the transports were included in the sailing orders issued by Lawrence was to be 5 pounds of flour and one pound of pork (or 1 lb of beef 2 lbs bread and 5 lbs of flour) for (each) 7 days for each person so embarked. (p. 280 of SELECTIONS FROM PUBLIC DOCUMENTS OF THE PROVINCE OF NOVA SCOTIA, published in 1869 by resolution of the House of Assembly on March 15, 1865)

DOVE Sloop 87 tons GRAND PRE (POINTE DES BOUDRO) TO CONNECTICUT

The sloop DOVE, 87 tons, Samuel Forbes, Captain, departed on 8 (or 13) December, 1755 from Pnte des Boudro (Grand PrT) with 114 exiles, destined for Connecticut and arrived in Connecticut on 30 January, 1756. (The British Empire Before The American Revolution - Vol. VI by Lawrence Henry Gipson, p.280) The sloop DOVE, Forbes, Captain, departed on 18, December, 1755 from Grand PrT with 114 exiles destined for Connecticut. (Emile Lauviere - "La TragTdie d'un peuple, vol 1, Librairie Henry Geulet, Paris, 1924) The sloop Dove was probably chartered, like the others, for a monthly fee (per ton), plus a pilot's fee and provisions, by Governor Lawrence, from Charles Apthorp & Thomas Hancock, of the Boston Mercantile Company of Apthorp and Hancock, to be used as a transport for the removal of the Acadian Exiles to the eastern seaboard. The amount of provisions for the transports were included in the sailing orders issued by Lawrence and was to be 5 pounds of flour and one pound of pork (or 1 lb of beef 2 lbs bread and 5 lbs of flour) for (each) 7 days for each person so embarked. (p. 280 of SELECTIONS FROM PUBLIC DOCUMENTS OF THE PROVINCE OF NOVA SCOTIA, published in 1869 by resolution of the House of Assembly on March 15, 1865) However, in his instructions on 11 August, 1755, Lawrence suggests: "If it is not very inconvenient I would have you send the Sloop Dove to Annapolis to take on board part of the inhabitants there destined for Connecticut to which place that vessel belongs." (p. 273 - SELECTIONS FROM PUBLIC DOCUMENTS OF THE PROVINCE OF NOVA SCOTIA, published in 1869 by resolution of the House of Assembly on March 15, 1865) Emile Lauvriere, in his "LA TRAGEDIE D'UN PEUPLE" - Histoire du Peuple Acadien - des origines a nos jours - 1923- Editions - Bossard - 43 Rue Madame, 43 - Paris - Tome I - 12th edition Chapter XIV "LE 'GRAND DERANGEMENT'" pp 457-513, in listing some of the vessels used in the expulsion on page 500, refers to the Dove, referred to by others as a sloop as ôla goelette Dove, destines for connecticutö, and two other vesselsl, referred to by others as schooners as ôla goelette Race Horse, destines for bostonö and ôla goelette Ranger, destined for virginiaö, probably indicates that some the ships listed as schooners, or sloops were actually goelettes or vice-versa.

EAGLE Sloop Captain McKown Halifax to Boston

According to Al Lafreniere, the Sloop EAGLE, Captain McKown, a commercial vessel, carried some of the stragglers, believed to be the LeBlanc family (4 members and possibily others) from Halifax, leaving on April 1, 1756 andarriving in Boston on May 29, 1756.

EDWARD Snow 139 tons ANNAPOLIS ROYAL TO CONNECTICUT

The snow EDWARD,139 tons, Ephram Cooke, Master, departed from Annapolis Royal with 278 exiles (41 men, 42 women, 86 boys and 109 girls) on 8 December, 1755 destined for Connecticut and was blown off course by violent storms. Itfinally put into Antigua and continued on to Connecticut. It finally arrived in Connecticut on May 22, 1756 with 180 exiles. EDWARDS, 278 persons, for Connecticut. ("Carles Belliveau et les seins durant la Deportation et apres; Prises de batreaux anglais par les Acadiens"by Placide Gaudet, apparently written in 1922 and given near Annapolis Royal. The article appeared in AGE Vols II, 1973 p. 4.) The snow Edward, 139 tons destined for Connecticut, for a 28 day voyage with 41 men 42 women, 86 boys and 109 girls for a total of 278 passengers. (Emile Lauviere - "La TragTdie d'un peuple , vol 1, p. 485, Librairie Henry Geulet, Paris, 1924)

During the voyage, almost 100 had died of malaria and when they arrived in Connecticut their personal items such as blankets, cushions, etc were ordered burned, further adding to their grief. (Albert N. Lafreniere - "ACADIAN DEPORTATION SHIPS" - "Connecticut Maple Leaf", volume 6, published by the French-Canadian Genealogical Society of Connecticut, Inc.). According to copies of accounts transmitted by Charles Apthorp & Thomas Hancock, of Boston Mercantile Company Apthorp and Hancock, to Governor Lawrence published on pages p. 285 - 293 of SELECTIONS FROM PUBLIC DOCUMENTS OF THE PROVINCE OF NOVA SCOTIA, published in 1869 by resolution of the House of Assembly on March 15, 1865 - The "Snow Edward" Ephm. Cook Master was chartered from Apthrop and Hancock from 9th October, 1755 to 29th June, 1756 (Boston Sept 7th, 1756) (New York 22, May 1756). The monthly charter fee for the Edward for 8-2/3 months was 9s sterling per ton per month - plus 60 s p. month for hire of a pilott, plus provisions. The amount of provisions for the transports were included in the sailing orders issued by Lawrence and was to be 5 pounds of flour and one pound of pork (or 1 lb of beef 2 lbs bread and 5 lbs of flour) for (each) 7 days for each person so embarked. (p. 280 of SELECTIONS FROM PUBLIC DOCUMENTS OF THE PROVINCE OF NOVA SCOTIA, published in 1869 by resolution of the House of Assembly on March 15, 1865) The EDWARDS, left Annapolis Royal with 278 persons, bound for Connecticut. The Acadians at Annapolis Royal were shipped off from Goat Island at 5:00 o'clock in the morning on Monday 8 December, 1755.

***** Note: Lucie LeBlanc Consentino writes: "An interesting piece of history..."

The snow, EDWARD, Captain Ephraim Cooke, left Annapolis Royal with 278 exiles and blown off course by violent storms. It finally put into port at Antigua and then continued on to Connecticut, arriving on May 22, 1756 with 180 exiles. Malaria had killed almost 100 exiles. Upon their arrival in New London, Connecticut, their personal items consisting of blankets, cushions and such, were burned causing further dismay and grief to the deported. Among those known to be aboard the EDWARD were Marie BOURG(Bourque), widow of Charles LANDRY with their seven children.

ELIZABETH Ship 166 tons ANNAPOLIS ROYAL TO CONNECTICUT

According to Al Lafreniere, the Ship Elizabeth replaced the TWO SISTERS that never left Annapolis Royal. The TWO SISTERS was supposed to carry 280 French (42 men, 40 women, 95 boys and 103 girls). The ship ELIZABETH, 166 tons, Ebenezer Rockwell, captain, departed from Annapolis Royal on 8 December, 1755 with 280 exiles (42 men, 40 women, 95 boys and 103 girls) destined for Connecticut and arrived in New London Connecticut on 21 January, 1756 with 277 exiles. The Elizabeth left with 280 and three died enroute. Information that supports this can be found in the Connecticut Gazette (copy in the Yale University library).(Albert N. Lafreniere - "ACADIAN DEPORTATION SHIPS" - "Connecticut Maple Leaf", volume 6, published by the French-Canadian Genealogical Society of Connecticut, Inc.). Like all of other transports, the Elizabeth was probably chartered for a monthly fee (per ton), plus a pilot's fee and provisions, by Governor Lawrence, from Charles Apthorp & Thomas Hancock, of the Boston Mercantile Company of Apthorp and Hancock, to be used as a transport for the removal of the Acadian Exiles to the eastern seaboard. The amount of provisions for the transports were included in the sailing orders issued by Lawrence and was to be 5 pounds of flour and one pound of pork (or 1 lb of beef 2 lbs bread and 5 lbs of flour) for (each) 7 days for each person so embarked. (p. 280 of SELECTIONS FROM PUBLIC DOCUMENTS OF THE PROVINCE OF NOVA SCOTIA, Published by resolution of the House of Assembly on March 15, 1865 in 1869) The Acadians at Annapolis Royal were shipped off from Goat Island at 5:00 o'clock in the morning on Monday 8 December, 1755.

ELIZABETH Sloop 97 (93) tons GRAND PRE TO MARYLAND

Sailing orders were given to Captain Milbury of the sloop Elizabeth by Col.Lawrence on October 13, 1755. The sloop ELIZABETH, 97 tons, Nathaniel Millbury, Captain, departed on 27 October, 1755 from Grand PrT with 242 exiles, (52 more that the complement of 2 persons per ton) destined for Maryland and arrived in Maryland on 20 November, 1755 (The British Empire Before The American Revolution - Vol. VI by Lawrence Henry Gipson p. 279 also p. 304) With 186 men aboard. The sloop ELIZABETH, 93 tons, Nathaniel Millbury, Captain, arrived in Grand PrT from Boston on 4 September embarked 186 exiles on October 8 and departed on 8 October, 1755 from Grand PrT with 242 exiles , and arrived in Maryland on 15-30 November, 1755 (Emile Lauviere - "La TragTdie d'un peuple , vol 1, Librairie Henry Geulet, Paris, 1924) On November 20, 1755 - The Maryland Gazette announced the arrival of the Elizabeth (93 tons burden, Nathaniel Milbury, master), with 242 passengers from Grand PrT, an excess of 56 over her complement. (page 7 – Maryland Historical Magazine - Vol. III No. 1, March 1908 - "The Acadians (French Neutrals) Transported to Maryland" - Basil Sollers) Edouard Richard listed a Corvette _____, 93 tons with 186 exiles and with a Captain Milbury listed as master. (Although he does not list the name of the ship, Captain Milbury was the master of of the 97 ton sloop Elizabeth) (ACADIA" - Edouard Richard Vol. 2, Chapter XXXI, p. 121) According to copies of accounts transmitted by Charles Apthorp & Thomas Hancock, of Boston Mercantile Company Apthorp and Hancock , to Governor Lawrence published on pages p. 285 - 293 of SELECTIONS FROM PUBLIC DOCUMENTS OF THE PROVINCE OF NOVA SCOTIA, Published by resolution of the House of Assembly on March 15, 1865 in 1869 - The Sloop Elizabeth, Nathaniel Milberry Master was chartered from Boston Mercantile Co. Apthorp and Hancock to transport the French inhabitants from Nova Scotia to Maryland from 20 august 1755 to 20th March 1756 - 52 persons more than Complement of 2 to a ton, at 5s.4d. (---, 1756). also (The British Empire Before The American Revolution - Vol. VI by Lawrence Henry Gipson p. 278-79) The monthly charter fee for the Elizabeth was 7 months at 49 12 pr month, pounds sterling - plus 60 s p. month for hire of a pilott , plus provisions. The amount of provisions for the transports were included in the sailing orders issued by Lawrence was to be 5 pounds of flour and one pound of pork (or 1 lb of beef 2 lbs bread and 5 lbs of flour) for (each) 7 days for each person so embarked. (p. 280 of SELECTIONS FROM PUBLIC DOCUMENTS OF THE PROVINCE OF NOVA SCOTIA, Published by resolution of the House of Assembly on March 15, 1865 in 1869) Nathanial Milberry, master of the sloop Elizabeth, with its 242 exiles aboard, was the first to file a complaint, arguing that he was unfairly ordered to the Wicomico River area of the Eastern Shore to wait Sharpe's return, but that no provisions were made for any compensation for food and supplies. (Gregory Wood Acadians in Maryland - A Guide to the Acadians in Maryland in the Eighteenth and Nineteenth Centuries.)

ENDEAVOR (ENCHEREE) Ship 83 tons POINTE DES BOUDRO TO VIRGINIA

The Endeavor - Captain John Stone, arrived from Boston on Saturday – August 30, 1755 and anchored at the entrance to the Gaspereau River. The ship ENDEAVOR (ENCHEREE), 83 tons, John Stone Captain departed 27 October, 1755 from Pnte des Boudro (Grand PrT) with 166 exiles for Virginia and arrived in Virginia on 11 (or 13) November, 1755. (The British Empire Before The American Revolution - Vol. VI by Lawrence Henry Gipson p. 300 also p. 277) - Had 166 men aboard. The ship ENDEAVOR , 83 tons, John Stone Captain arrived at Grand Pre (Pnte des Boudro) from Boston on Auigust 30 and embarked on 19 October The Endeavor departed 27 October, 1755 from Pnte des Boudro (Grand PrT) with 166 exiles for Virginia and arrived in Virginia on 15-30 November, 1755. (Emile Lauviere - "La TragTdie d'un peuple , vol 1, Librairie Henry Geulet, Paris, 1924) The Endeavor was one of the six transports that took shelter from a fierce winter storm in the Boston Harbour on November 5, 1755. While at Boston to seek shelter for a number of days, the vessel was inspected and an undisclosed number of Acadians were removed to reduce the numer aboard to 2 persons per ton. The delay in the voyage when they were in the Boston Harbour for a few days further depleted their supplies which were low since the begining of the voyage. So, fresh water and minimal supplies and assistange was given to the passengers on board the Endeavor by the Massachusetts Bay authorities and the vessels sailed southward. (Albert N. Lafreniere - "ACADIAN DEPORTATION SHIPS" - "Connecticut Maple Leaf", volume 6, published by the French-Canadian Genealogical Society of Connecticut, Inc.). Edouard Richard mentions a "Corvette Endeavor", 83 tons with a Captain Stone as master being used to transport 166 exiles. (ACADIA" - Edouard Richard Vol. 2, Chapter XXXI, p. 121) According to copies of accounts transmitted by Charles Apthorp & Thomas Hancock, of Boston Mercantile Company Apthorp and Hancock , to Governor Lawrence published on pages p. 285 - 293 of SELECTIONS FROM PUBLIC DOCUMENTS OF THE PROVINCE OF NOVA SCOTIA, Published by resolution of the House of Assembly on March 15, 1865 in 1869 - the Sloop Endeavor (also known as Encheree), John Stone master was chartered from Boston Mercantile Co. Apthorp and Hancock from hence to Minas & Virginia to carry off French inhabitants from 21 August to 11 December. The monthly charter fee for the Endeavor was 3 months 21 days 44 pounds 54 pr month , pounds sterling - plus 60 s p. month for hire of a pilott , plus provisions. The amount of provisions for the transports were included in the sailing orders issued by Lawrence was to be 5 pounds of flour and one pound of pork (or 1 lb of beef 2 lbs bread and 5 lbs of flour) for (each) 7 days for each person so embarked. (p. 280 of SELECTIONS FROM PUBLIC DOCUMENTS OF THE PROVINCE OF NOVA SCOTIA, Published by resolution of the House of Assembly on March 15, 1865 in 1869) According to the publication "The Acadian Exile in St. Malo", the governor of Virginia refused to accept the acadians that were alloted to Virginia, and the 1,500 Acadians sent to Virginia on October 25, 1755 were in Virginia were not allowed to disembark and more of them diedaboard the crowded ships during the 4 months that the ship were anchored uin the Williamsburg harbor. They were then transported to England and placed in concentration camps in the port cities of their arrival, where they languished until after the Treaty of Paris, in 1763, when they were released and repatriated (sent) to the maritime ports of Normandy and Britanny.

ENDEAVOR Sloop 96 tons CHIGNECTO TO SOUTH CAROLINA

The sloop ENDEAVOR, 96 tons, James Nichols, captain, departed from Chignecto on 13 October, 1755 with 121 exiles destined for South Carolina and arrived in South Carolina on 19 November, 1755. Al Lafreniere lists an ENDEAVOR, James Nichols, master, as arriving at South Carolina with 121 exiles. It is not known how many exiles boarded at Chignecto. (Albert N. Lafreniere - "ACADIAN DEPORTATION SHIPS" - "Connecticut Maple Leaf", volume 6, published by the French-Canadian Genealogical Society of Connecticut, Inc.) The sloop Endeavor was probably chartered for a monthly fee (per ton), plus a pilot's fee and provisions, by Governor Lawrence, from Charles Apthorp & Thomas Hancock, of the Boston Mercantile Company of Apthorp and Hancock, to be used as a transport for the removal of the Acadian Exiles to the eastern seaboard. The amount of provisions for the transports were included in the sailing orders issued by Lawrence was to be 5 pounds of flour and one pound of pork (or 1 lb of beef 2 lbs bread and 5 lbs of flour) for (each) 7 days for each person so embarked. (p. 280 of SELECTIONS FROM PUBLIC DOCUMENTS OF THE PROVINCE OF NOVA SCOTIA, Published by resolution of the House of Assembly on March 15, 1865 in 1869)

ENDEAVOR Sloop 96 tons CHIGNECTO TO SOUTH CAROLINA

The sloop ENDEAVOR, 96 tons, James Nichols, captain, departed from Chignecto on 13 October, 1755 with 121 exiles destined for South Carolina and arrived in South Carolina on 19 November, 1755. Al Lafreniere lists an ENDEAVOR, James Nichols, master, as arriving at South Carolina with 121 exiles. It is not known how many exiles boarded at Chignecto. (Albert N. Lafreniere - "ACADIAN DEPORTATION SHIPS" - "Connecticut Maple Leaf", volume 6, published by the French-Canadian Genealogical Society of Connecticut, Inc.). The sloop Endeavor was probably chartered for a monthly fee (per ton), plus a pilot's fee and provisions, by Governor Lawrence, from Charles Apthorp & Thomas Hancock, of the Boston Mercantile Company of Apthorp and Hancock, to be used as a transport for the removal of the Acadian Exiles to the eastern seaboard. The amount of provisions for the transports were included in the sailing orders issued by Lawrence was to be 5 pounds of flour and one pound of pork (or 1 lb of beef 2 lbs bread and 5 lbs of flour) for (each) 7 days for each person so embarked. (p. 280 of SELECTIONS FROM PUBLIC DOCUMENTS OF THE PROVINCE OF NOVA SCOTIA, Published by resolution of the House of Assembly on March 15, 1865 in 1869)

The British ships Endeavor - Captain John Stone; Industry - Captain George Goodwin and Mary - Captain Andrew Dunning Sunday - August 31, 1755 – arrive and go to Pisiguit. Capt Jonathan Daves of the NEPTUNE was replaced as master OF THE NEPTUNE by the owner William Ford.

EXPERIMENT Brigge 136 tons ANNAPOLIS ROYAL TO NEW YORK

The Brigge EXPERIMENT,136 tons - Benjamin Stoddard, captain departed on December 8, 1755 from Annapolis Royal with 250 exiles (40 men, 45 women, 56 boys and 59 girls) for New York and arrived 30 May, 1756.

[Note: This voyage lasted 5 months! This is the vessel that the author's ancestor was on.]

The Experiment, 136 tons destined for New York ,for a 28 day voyage with 40 men 45 women, 56 boys and 59 girls for a total of 200 passengers. (Emile Lauviere -"La TragTdie d'un peuple , vol 1, p. 485, Librairie Henry Geulet, Paris, 1924) EXPERIMENT, 200 persons, for New York. ("Carles Belliveau et les seins durant la Deportation et apres; Prises de batreaux anglais par les Acadiens" by Placide Gaudet, apparently written in 1922 and given near Annapolis Royal. The article appeared in AGE Vols II, 1973 p. 4.) Al Lafreniere states that the EXPERIMENT, Benjamine Stoddard, master, was blown off course as was the EDWARD and arrived in New York, via Antigua with 200 exiles. The Experiment left Annapolis Royal with 250 exiles. (Albert N. Lafreniere - "ACADIAN DEPORTATION SHIPS" - "Connecticut Maple Leaf", volume 6, published by the French-Canadian Genealogical Society of Connecticut, Inc.) According to copies of accounts transmitted by Charles Apthorp & Thomas Hancock, of Boston Mercantile Company Apthorp and Hancock , to Governor Lawrence published on pages p. 285 - 293 of SELECTIONS FROM PUBLIC DOCUMENTS OF

THE PROVINCE OF NOVA SCOTIA, Published by resolution of the House of Assembly on March 15, 1865 in 1869 - The Brigge Experiment, Benjamin Stoddard Master 136 tons was chartered from Bocton Mercantile Co apthorp and Hancockfrom 10th October 1755 to 27th May 1756. The monthly charter fee for the Experiment was 7 months 16 days at 9s sterling per ton per month , pounds sterling - plus 60 s p. month for hire of a pilott , plus provisions. The amount of provisions for the transports were included in the sailing orders issued by Lawrence was to be 5 pounds of flour and one pound of pork (or 1 lb of beef 2 lbs bread and 5 lbs of flour) for (each) 7 days for each person so embarked. (p. 280 of SELECTIONS FROM PUBLIC DOCUMENTS OF THE PROVINCE OF NOVA SCOTIA, Published by resolution of the House of Assembly on March 15, 1865 in 1869)

HANNAH Sloop 70 tons GRAND PRE AND GASPEREAU TO PENNSYLVANIA

The Sloop HANNAH, 70 tons, Richard Adams, Captain, departed on 27 October, 1755 from Grand PrT and Gaspereau with 140 exiles destined for Pennsylvaniaand arrived in Pennsylvania on19 November, 1755. (The British Empire Before The American Revolution - Vol. VI by Lawrence Henry Gipson p. 277-78) – 140 men aboard. Sloop HANNAH, 70 tons, Adams, Captain, arrived in Grand PrT from Port Royal on 10 October with departed on 27 October, 1755 from Grand PrT and Gaspereau with 140 exiles (2 surnombres) destined for Pennsylvania and arrived in Pennsylvania on115-30 November, 1755 with 137 exiles.(Emile Lauviere - "La TragTdie d'un peuple , vol 1, Librairie Henry Geulet, Paris, 1924) Al Lafreniere states that the HANNAH, Richard Adams, master left Grand PrT with 140 exiles, and arrived in Pennsylvania with 137 exiles. (Albert N. Lafreniere - "ACADIAN DEPORTATION SHIPS" - "Connecticut Maple Leaf", volume 6, published by the French-Canadian Genealogical Society of Connecticut, Inc.). Upon their arrival in Pennsylvania, the colony was in the grips of raging Francophobia, which soon translated into Pennsylvania's governor Robert H. Morris placing the exiles under armed guard aboard the three vessels, the HANNAH, THREE FRIENDS and the SWAN) that brought them from Nova Scotia. Because of this, the acadians on board the three vessels succumbed to epedemic diseases. Because of this, they were quarentined aboard their vessels until legislation on March 5, 1756 provided for their dispersal throughout the easternmost Pennsylvania provinces. (Carl A. Brasseaux - Scattered to the Winds - The Dispersal and Wanderings of the Acadians, p. 19) Edouard Richard mentions a "Corvette Hannah", 70 tons, Captain Adams, was used to transport 140 exiles. (ACADIA" - Edouard Richard Vol. 2, Chapter XXXI, p. 121) According to copies of accounts transmitted by Charles Apthorp & Thomas Hancock, of Boston Mercantile Company Apthorp and Hancock , to Governor Lawrence published on pages p. 285 - 293 of SELECTIONS FROM PUBLIC DOCUMENTS OF THE PROVINCE OF NOVA SCOTIA, Published by resolution of the House of Assembly on March 15, 1865 in 1869 - The Sloop Hannah, Richard Adams, Master was chartered from Boston Mercantile Apthorp and Hancock from hence to Annapolis Royall & Philadelphia, to carry off French inhabitants from 20 August, 1755 to 23 December, 1755. The monthly charter fee for the Hannah was 4 months 3 days at 37 pounds 6s 8d per month, pounds sterling - plus 60 s p. month for hire of a pilott , plus provisions. The amount of provisions for the transports were included in the sailing orders issued by

Lawrence and was to be 5 pounds of flour and one pound of pork (or 1 lb of beef 2 lbs bread and 5 lbs of flour) for (each) 7 days for each person so embarked. (p. 280 of SELECTIONS FROM PUBLIC DOCUMENTS OF THE PROVINCE OF NOVA SCOTIA, Published by resolution of the House of Assembly on March 15, 1865 in 1869) Sloops Hannah, Three Friends and Swan reached the Delaware about 18 November, 1755 with 454 aboard and were sent to province Island and later in ucks, Chester, Lancaster, and Philadelphia Counties. The exiles declared that their plight to be far worse than the old Testament world of Egyptain or Babalonian captivity. (p. 18 - Gregory Wood Acadians in Maryland - A Guide to the Acadians in Maryland in the Eighteenth and Nineteenth Centuries.)

HELENA Ship 166 tons ANNAPOLIS ROYAL TO MASSACHUSETTS

The ship HELENA, 166 tons, Samuel Livingston, Captain, departed from Annapolis Royal on 27 October, 1755 with 323 exiles (52 men, 52 women, 108 boys and 111 girls) destined for Boston Massachusetts and arrived in Boston on 19 November, 1755. HELENA, The other transports were the HELENA, with 323 persons for Boston. ("Carles Belliveau et les seins durant la Deportation et apres; Prises de batreaux anglais par les Acadiens" by Placide Gaudet, apparently written in 1922 and given near Annapolis Royal. The article appeared in AGE Vols II, 1973, p. 4.) The Helena, 166 tons, destined for a 28 day voyage with 52 men, 52 women, 108 boys and 111 girls for a total of 323 passengers. (Emile Lauviere -"La TragTdie d'un peuple, vol 1, p. 485, Librairie Henry Geulet, Paris, 1924) The Helena was probably chartered for a monthly fee (per ton), plus a pilot's fee and provisions, by Governor Lawrence, from Charles Apthorp & Thomas Hancock, of the Boston Mercantile Company of Apthorp and Hancock, to be used as a transport for the removal of the Acadian Exiles to the eastern seaboard. The amount of provisions for the transports were included in the sailing orders issued by Lawrence and was to be 5 pounds of flour and one pound of pork (or 1 lb of beef 2 lbs bread and 5 lbs of flour) for (each) 7 days for each person so embarked. (p. 280 of SELECTIONS FROM PUBLIC DOCUMENTS OF THE PROVINCE OF NOVA SCOTIA, Published by resolution of the House of Assembly on March 15, 1865 in 1869)

HOBSON Ship HALIFAX TO ANNAPOLIS ROYAL TO SOUTH CAROLINA

The ship HOBSON, Edward Whitewood Master departed on 8 December, 1755 from Halifax with 342 exiles (42 men, 46 women, 120 boys and 134 girls) destined for South Carolina and arrived in South Carolina on 15 January, 1756. HOPSON, 342 persons, for South Carolina. ("Carles Belliveau et les seins durant la Deportation et apres; Prises de batreaux anglais par les Acadiens" by Placide Gaudet, apparently written in 1922 and given near Annapolis Royal. The article appeared in AGE Vols II, 1973, p. 4.) The Hopson, 177 tons destined for South Carolina, for a 42 day voyage with 42 men 45 women, 120 boys and 134 girls for a total of 342 passengers. (Emile Lauviere - "La TragTdie d'un peuple, vol 1, p. 485, Librairie Henry Geulet, Paris, 1924) According to copies of accounts transmitted by Charles Apthorp & Thomas Hancock, of Boston

Mercantile Company Apthorp and Hancock, to Governor Lawrence published on pages p. 285 - 293 of SELECTIONS FROM PUBLIC DOCUMENTS OF THE PROVINCE OF NOVA SCOTIA, Published by resolution of the House of Assembly on March 15, 1865 in 1869 - The Ship Hopson, Edward Whitewood Master, was chartered from Bostan Mercantile Co Apthorp and Hancock from Halifax to Annapolis and South Carolina with French infabitants from October 10th, 1755 to 13th April, 1756 (---, 1756). The monthly charter fee for the Hobson was 6 months 4 days at 76 pounds 19s , sterling pr month, pounds sterling - plus 60 s p. month for hire of a pilott , plus provisions. The amount of provisions for the transports were included in the sailing orders issued by Lawrence and was to be 5 pounds of flour and one pound of pork (or 1 lb of beef 2 lbs bread and 5 lbs of flour) for (each) 7 days for each person so embarked. (p. 280 of SELECTIONS FROM PUBLIC DOCUMENTS OF THE PROVINCE OF NOVA SCOTIA, Published by resolution of the House of Assembly on March 15, 1865 in 1869)

INDUSTRY Sloop 86 tons POINTE DES BOUDRO TO VIRGINIA

On Saturday - August 30, 1755 Sloop INDUSTRY, 86 tons- Captain George Goodwin, Captain arrives from Boston and anchors at the entrance to the Gaspereau River, and on 27 October, 1755 she departed from Pnte des Boudro with 177 exiles arriving in Virginia on13 November, 1755. (Some records list 172 men as passengers) Sloop INDUSTRY, 86 tons- Captain George Goodwin, Captain arrives from Boston and anchors at the entrance to the Gaspereau River, Pointe-aux- Boudreaux on 30 October, 1755 embarked 19 October with 177 exiles and she departed from Pnte des Boudro destined for Williamsburg Virginia. (Emile Lauviere - "La TragTdie d'un peuple , vol 1, Librairie Henry Geulet, Paris, 1924) The sloop Industry was one of 5 transports that departed from Grand PrT and Gaspereau to Pennsylvania (The British Empire Before The American Revolution - Vol. VI by Lawrence Henry Gipson p. 277 and also on p. 300) Edouard Richard mentions a "Corvette Industry", 86 tons, Captain Goodwin, being used to transport 172 exiles. (ACADIA" - Edouard Richard Vol. 2, Chapter XXXI, p. 121) According to copies of accounts transmitted by Charles Apthorp & Thomas Hancock, of Boston Mercantile Company Apthorp and Hancock, to Governor Lawrence published on pages p. 285 - 293 of SELECTIONS FROM PUBLIC DOCUMENTS OF THE PROVINCE OF NOVA SCOTIA, Published by resolution of the House of Assembly on March 15, 1865 in 1869 - The Sloop Industry, George Goodwan, Master was chartered from the Boston Mercantile Co Apthorp and Hancock from the 20th August to 26th December, 1755 to carry French inhabitants from Minas to Virginia. (---, 1755). - (pages 285-293 of SELECTIONS FROM PUBLIC DOCUMENTS OF THE PROVINCE OF NOVA SCOTIA, Published by resolution of the House of Assembly on March 15, 1865 in 1869) The monthly charter fee for the Industry was 4 months 6 days 45 17 4 pr month , pounds sterling - plus 60 s p. month for hire of a pilott, plus provisions. The amount of provisions for the transports were included in the sailing orders issued by Lawrence was to be 5 pounds of flour and one pound of pork (or 1 lb of beef 2 lbs bread and 5 lbs of flour) for (each) 7 days for each person so embarked. (p. 280 of SELECTIONS FROM PUBLIC DOCUMENTS OF THE PROVINCE OF NOVA SCOTIA, Published by resolution of the House of Assembly on March 15, 1865 in 1869) According to the publication "The Acadian Exile in St. Malo", the governor of Virginia refused to accept the acadians that were alloted to Virginia, and the 1,500 Acadians sent to Virginia on October 25, 1755 were in Virginia were not allowed to disembark and more of them diedaboard the crowded ships during the 4 months that the ship were anchored uin the Williamsburg harbor. They were then transported to England and placed in concentration camps in the port cities of their arrival, where they languished until after the Treaty of Paris, in 1763, when they were released and repatriated (sent) to the maritime ports of Normandy and Britanny.

JOLLY PHILLIP Schooner 94 tons CHIGNECTO TO GEORGIA

The schooner JOLLY PHILLIP, 94 tons- Jonathan Waite, Captain, departed from Chignecto on 13 October, 1755 with 129 exiles destined for Georgia and arrived in Georgia with approximately 120 exiles on 30 December, 1755. This Schooner was from Falmouth (now Portland) Maine.(Albert N. Lafreniere - "ACADIAN DEPORTATION SHIPS" - "Connecticut Maple Leaf", volume 6, published by the French-Canadian Genealogical Society of Connecticut, Inc.). The Jolly Philip was probably chartered for a monthly fee (per ton), plus a pilot's fee and provisions, by Governor Lawrence, from Charles Apthorp & Thomas Hancock, of the Boston Mercantile Company of Apthorp and Hancock, to beused as a transport for the removal of the Acadian Exiles to the eastern seaboard. The amount of provisions for the transports were included in the sailing orders issued by Lawrence was to be 5 pounds of flour and one pound of pork (or 1 lb of beef 2 lbs bread and 5 lbs of flour) for (each) 7 days for each person so embarked. (p. 280 of SELECTIONS FROM PUBLIC DOCUMENTS OF THE PROVINCE OF NOVA SCOTIA, Published by resolution of the House of Assembly on March 15, 1865 in 1869)

LEOPARD Schooner 87 tons GRAND PRE TO MARYLAND

The schooner LEOPARD (Leonard, Leynard), 87 tons, Thomas Church Master, departed from Grand PrT on 27 October, 1755 with 178 exiles (an excess of 4 over her complement) destined for Maryland and arrived in Maryland on 30 December, 1755. With 174 men aboard. The schooner LEOPARD (Leonard, Leynard), 87 tons, Thomas Church Master, arrived in Grand PrT from Boston on 6 September and embarked 178 exiles on 8 October. She departed from Grand PrT on 27 October, 1755 with 178 exiles (an excess of 4 over her complement) destined for Annapolis Maryland and arrived in Maryland on 30 December, 1755. With 174 exiles aboard. (Emile Lauviere - "La TragTdie d'un peuple , vol 1, Librairie Henry Geulet, Paris, 1924) The LEOPARD (also known as Leonard or Leynard)- Captain Thomas Church arrived at Minas Basin on Saturday - September 6, 1755. Edouard Richard mentions a Schooner Leopard, Captain Church, 87 tons being used to transport 174 exiles. (ACADIA" - Edouard Richard Vol. 2, Chapter XXXI, p. 121) According to copies of accounts transmitted by Charles Apthorp & Thomas Hancock, of Boston Mercantile Company Apthorp and Hancock , to Governor Lawrence published on pages p. 285 - 293 of SELECTIONS FROM PUBLIC DOCUMENTS OF THE PROVINCE OF NOVA SCOTIA, Published by resolution of the House of Assembly on March 15, 1865 in 1869 - The Schooner LEYNORD,

THOMAS CHURCH MASTER was chartered from 20th Auigust 1755 to 10th February 1756, is 5 months 21 days at 46 pounds 8 lawful money pr. month., etc.. The monthly charter fee for the Leynord was 5 months 21 days at 46 pounds 8s lawful money per month, pounds sterling - plus 60 s p. month for hire of a pilott , plus provisions. The amount of provisions for the transports were included in the sailing orders issued by Lawrence and was to be 5 pounds of flour and one pound of pork (or 1 lb of beef 2 lbs bread and 5 lbs of flour) for (each) 7 days for each person so embarked. (p. 280 of SELECTIONS FROM PUBLIC DOCUMENTS OF THE PROVINCE OF NOVA SCOTIA, Published by resolution of the House of Assembly on March 15, 1865 in 1869) Thomas Church, Master of the Scooner Leopard, 87 tons burden, was given sailing orders for the Leopold by John Winslow on October 13, 1755 and the Leopard left Grand PrT on October 28, 1755 with 178 passengers aboard , an excess of 4 over her complement. She arrived in Annapolis harbor on November 20, 1755. The ship had carried the Acadians from Grand PrT. The arrival was announced on November 20, 1755 by the Maryland Gazette (page 7 – Maryland Historical Magazine - Vol. III No. 1, March 1908 - "The Acadians (French Neutrals) Transported to Maryland - Basil Sollers) Later when the Leopard was transporting troops under the command of General Preble from Halifax to Boston, they picked up 70 exiles at Pubnico that were destined for North Carolina. When the Leopard landed at Boston , the Acadian exiles disembarked. Captain Church reported: " They arose a great dissention among the French and they all rose, forced their way on shore with their baggage and it was not in my power to proceed . . . " (p. 7 Basil Sollers) also (The British Empire Before The American Revolution - Vol. VI by Lawrence Henry Gipson p. 277 and also p. 298) Nathanial Milberry, master of the sloop Elizabeth, with its 242 exiles aboard, was the first to file a complaint, arguing that he was unfairly ordered to the Wicomico River area of the Eastern Shore to wait Sharpe's return, but that no provisions were made for any compensation for food and supplies.

The Leopard, with 178 passengers aboard, was the first to anchor in Annapolis Harbor, on November 24, 1755. The Leopard was newly constructed in New England and registered on April 10, 1755 at Cambridge. The schooner was owned and captained by Thomas Church, who alone of the four seemed adequately prepared to wait in Severn for Maryland officials to decide the proper disembarkation of a group practicaly equal to the population of Annapolis. The Passengers of the Leopard wound up in Baltimore and Annapolis, Maryland. On the last 2 days of the months, the other 3 sloops were anchored in the Severn , but their captains seemed most anxious about the Maryland council's refusal to permit immediate landing in the absence of Gov. Sharpe, who was attending a conference of colonial executives in New York. (Gregory Wood Acadians in Maryland - A Guide to the Acadians in Maryland in the Eighteenth and Nineteenth Centuries.)

MARY Sloop 90-1/2 tons POINTE DES BOUDRO TO VIRGINIA

On Saturday - August 30, 1755 Sloop MARY, sloop, 90 tons - Andrew Dunning, captain arrived from Boston and anchored at the entrance to the Gaspereau River, and on 27 October, 1755 departed from Pnte des Boudro (Grand PrT) with 182 exiles arriving in Virginia on13 November, 1755. (The British Empire Before The American Revolution - Vol. VI by Lawrence Henry Gipson p. 277 also p. 300) 181 men aboard Sloop MARY, sloop, 90-1/2 tons - Andrew Dunning, captain arrivedfrom Boston on 30 August and anchored at the entrance to the Gaspereau River (pointe-aux- Boudreaux) , she embarked 182 exiles on 10 October and on 27 October, 1755 departed from Pnte des Boudro (Grand PrT) destined for Williamsburg Virginia. (Emile Lauvriere - La TragTdie d'un peuple, vol I, librairie Henry Geulet, Paris, 1924)Edouard Richard mentions a "Corvette Mary", 90-1/2 tons, Captain Denny, being used to transport 181 exiles (ACADIA" - Edouard Richard Vol. 2,Chapter XXXI, p. 121) According to copies of accounts transmitted by Charles Apthorp & Thomas Hancock, of Boston Mercantile Company Apthorp and Hancock , to Governor Lawrence published on pages p. 285 - 293 of SELECTIONS FROM PUBLIC DOCUMENTS OF THE PROVINCE OF NOVA SCOTIA, Published by resolution of the House of Assembly on March 15, 1865 in 1869 - Sloop Mary, Andrew Dunning master was chartered from Boston Mercantile Co Apthorp and Hancock from hence to Minas &Virginia , to carry off French inhabitants from 20th August to 12 December, 1755 (---,1755). The monthly charter fee for the Mary, was 3 months and 23 days at 48 pounds 5 4d pr mth. pounds sterling - for a total (including p[ilot at 60s pr month) of 139 pounds 166 pounds sterling, plus provisions. The amount of provisions for the transports were included in the sailing orders issued by Lawrence was to be 5 pounds of flour and one pound of pork (or 1 lb of beef 2 lbs bread and 5 lbs of flour) for (each) 7 days for each person so embarked. (p. 280 of SELECTIONS FROM PUBLIC DOCUMENTS OF THE PROVINCE OF NOVA SCOTIA, Published by resolution of the House of Assembly on March 15, 1865 in 1869) According to the publication "The Acadian Exile in St. Malo", the governor of Virginia refused to accept the acadians that were alloted to Virginia, and the 1,500 Acadians sent to Virginia on October 25, 1755 were in Virginia were not allowed to disembark and more of them diedaboard the crowded ships during the 4 months that the ship were anchored uin the Williamsburg harbor. They were then transported to England and placed in concentration camps in the port cities of their arrival, where they languished until after the Treaty of Paris, in 1763, when they were released and repatriated (sent) to the maritime ports of Normandy and Britanny.

MARY Schooner CAPE SABLE TO NEW YORK

(The Schooner Mary was listed as an unknown Schooner, but probably was Capt. Durning's 2nd voyage) The Schooner, (name and tonnage unknown), Andrew Durning, Captain departed from Cape Sable with 94 exiles destined for New York. The date of departure is unknown, but the schooner arrived at New York on 28 April, 1756. Captain Andrew Dunning, must have returned to Nova Scotia after his voyage on the Mary to Virginia, as he is reported to have shipped about 100 exiles (94 arrived), in a schooner from Cape Sable to New York. His schooner arrived in New York on April 28, 1756.(Albert N. Lafreniere - "ACADIAN DEPORTATION SHIPS"-"Connecticut Maple Leaf", volume 6, published by the French-Canadian Genealogical Society of Connecticut, Inc.). This schooner was probably chartered for a monthly fee (per ton), plus a pilot's fee and provisions, by Governor Lawrence, from Charles Apthorp & Thomas Hancock, of the Boston Mercantile Company of Apthorp and Hancock, to be used as a transport for the removal of the Acadian Exiles to the eastern seaboard. The amount of provisions for the transports were included in the sailing orders issued by Lawrence and was to be 5 pounds of flour and one pound of pork (or 1 lb of beef 2 lbs bread and 5 lbs of flour) for (each) 7 days for each person so embarked. (p. 280 of SELECTIONS FROM PUBLIC DOCUMENTS OF THE PROVINCE OF NOVA SCOTIA, Published by resolution of the House of Assembly on March 15, 1865 in 1869)

NEPTUNE Schooner 90 tons PISIQUID TO VIRGINIA

On Saturday - August 30, 1755 the Schooner NEPTUNE, 90 tons – Jonathan Davis, captain - arrives from Boston and anchors at the entrance to the Gaspereau River. Some reports have the Neptune arriving on Sunday - August 31, 1755.With 180 Men aboard. Schooner NEPTUNE, 90 tons - Jonathan Davis, (Ford) captain - arrives in Pisiquid from Boston on 31 August and anchors at the entrance to the Gaspereau River She embarques 206 exiles (27 surnombres) on October 10-12 and departs on 27 November destined for Williamsburg, arriving on 15-30 November. (Emile Lauvriere - La TragTdie d'un peuple, vol I, librairie Henry Geulet, Paris, 1924) On October 14, 1755 , Jonathan Davis was Captain of the "Neptune" 156 tons and he was replaced by the owner William Ford as Master." (Photo copy of an article that appeared in the Windsor, N.S. newspaper entitled "EXPULSION OF ACADIANS ORGANIZED AT WINDSOR"). The Schooner NEPTUNE, 90 tons with owner William Ford as Master.- 1755 departed from Pisiquid with 207 exiles 27 more than the complement on 27 October, 1755 and arrived in Virginia on13 November, 1755.(The British Empire Before The American Revolution - Vol. VI by Lawrence Henry Gipson p. 278-279 also p. 300) The Neptune was one of the six transports that took shelter from a fierce winter storm in the Boston Harbour on November 5, 1755. While at Boston to seek shelter for a number of days, the vessel was inspected and said to be "healthy tho 40 lie on the deck". 29 Acadians were removed by the horbor authorities to reduce the numer aboard to 2 persons per ton. (Maryland Historical Magazine - Vol. III No. 1, March 1908 - "The Acadians (French Neutrals) Transported to Maryland" - Basil Sollers p. 7) The delay in the voyage when they were in the Boston Harbour for a few days further depleted their supplies which were low since the begining of the voyage. So, fresh water, minimal supplies and assistange was given to the passengers on board the Neptune by the Massachusetts Bay authorities and the vessels then sailed southward. Edouard RICHARD mentions a Schooner Neptune, 90 tons, Captain Davis, being used to transport 180 exiles - (27 additional). (ACADIA" - Edouard Richard Vol. 2, Chapter XXXI, p. 121) According to copies of accounts transmitted by Charles Apthorp & Thomas Hancock, of Boston Mercantile Company Apthorp and Hancock , to Governor Lawrence published on pages p. 285 - 293 of SELECTIONS FROM PUBLIC DOCUMENTS OF THE PROVINCE OF NOVA SCOTIA, Published by resolution of the House of Assembly on March 15, 1865 in 1869 - The Schooner Neptune, William Ford master was chartered from the Boston Mercantile Co. Apthorp and Hancock from hence to Virginia to carry off the French inhabitants. The Neptune was chartered from 20th August to 17th December, and carried 27 Neutrals more than Compliment at 5s. 43/4d. and supplies for 207. The monthly charter fee for the Neptune was 3 months 28 days at 48 pounds pr mth., pounds sterling - plus 60 s p. month for hire of a pilott , plus provisions. The amount of provisions for the transports were included in the sailing orders issued by Lawrence was to be 5 pounds of flour and one pound of pork (or 1 lb of beef 2 lbs bread and 5 lbs of flour) for (each) 7 days for each person so embarked. (p. 280 of SELECTIONS FROM PUBLIC DOCUMENTS OF THE PROVINCE OF NOVA SCOTIA, Published by resolution of the House of Assembly on March 15, 1865 in 1869) According to the publication "The Acadian Exile in St. Malo", the governor of Virginia refused to accept the acadians that were alloted to Virginia, and the 1,500 Acadians sent to Virginia on October 25, 1755 were in Virginia were not allowed to disembark and more of them diedaboard the crowded ships during the 4 months that the ship were anchored uin the Williamsburg harbor. They were then transported to England and placed in concentration camps in the port cities of their arrival, where they languished until after the Treaty of Paris, in 1763, when they were released and repatriated (sent) to the maritime ports of Normandy and Britanny.

PEMBROKE Snow 139 tons ANNAPOLIS ROYAL TAKEN OVER AND DIVERTED TO ST. JOHN RIVER

The Snow PEMBROKE, 139 tons, Milton __?__ , Captain, departed in January from Annapolis Royal,under the direction of Major Handfield, with 232 exiles destined for North Carolina . The Pembroke was taken over by the Acadians and sailed to St. Mary's Bay in Newfoundland and then across the Bay of Fundy to the St. John River. - (The British Empire Before The American Revolution - Vol. VI by Lawrence Henry Gipson 281) Pembrook ôThe Pembrook was of 42 tons, victualized for 139 days; she had on board 33 men. 37 women, 70 sons, and 92 daughters forming a total of 232 persons. She sailed from Goat Island on December 8, 1755, bound for North Carolina. The Pembrook was taken over by the Acadians aboard and sailed to St. John River and landed the Acadians at the port on February 8, 1756. ("Carles Belliveau et les seins durant la Deportation et apres; Prises de batreaux anglais par les Acadiens" by Placide Gaudet, apparently written in 1922 and given near Annapolis Royal. The article appeared in AGE Vols II, 1973, p.4.) The Pembroke, 139 tons destined for North Carolina , for a 42 day voyage with 33 men, 37 women, 70 boys and 92 girls for a total of 232 passengers. (Emile Lauviere -"La TragTdie d'un peuple, vol 1, p. 485, Librairie Henry Geulet, Paris, 1924) The Snow Pembroke was probably chartered for a monthly fee (per ton), plus a pilot's fee and provisions, by Governor Lawrence, from Charles Apthorp & Thomas Hancock, of the Boston Mercantile Company of Apthorp and Hancock, to be used as a transport for the removal of the Acadian Exiles to the eastern seaboard. The amount of provisions for the transports were included in the sailing orders issued by Lawrence and was to be 5 pounds of flour and one pound of pork (or 1 lb of beef 2 lbs bread and 5 lbs of flour) for (each) 7 days for each person so embarked. (p. 280 of SELECTIONS FROM PUBLIC DOCUMENTS OF THE PROVINCE OF NOVA SCOTIA, Published by resolution of the House of Assembly on March 15, 1865 in 1869) Some reports say that the crew of the Pembroke was turned over to the Amerindians, and that the Acadian exiles joined Boishebert in his fight against the British. Another report says that the PEMBROKE was captured by privateers and that the Acadian exiles were returned to Annapolis Royal, (Perhaps to be exiled again on the ELIZABETH?).(Albert N. Lafreniere - "ACADIAN DEPORTATION SHIPS" - "Connecticut Maple Leaf", volume 6, published by the French-Canadian Genealogical Society of Connecticut, Inc.). The Pembrook was of 42 tons, victualized for 139 days; she had on board 33 men. 37 women, 70 sons, and 92 daughters forming a total of 232 persons. She sailed from Goat Island on

December 8, 1755, bound for North Carolina. The Pembrook was taken over by the Acadians aboard and sailed to St. John River and landed the Acadians at the port on February 8, 1756 The Acadians at Annap[olis Royal were shipped off from Goat Island at 5:00 o'clock in the morning on Monday 8 December, 1755.

PRINCE FREDRICK Ship 170 tons CHIGNECTO TO GEORGIA

The ship PRINCE FREDRICK, 170 tons, William Trattles Captain, escorted by H.M.S. Syren, departed 13 October, 1755 from Chignecto under the direction ofCol. Moncton, with 280 exiles (mostly men who had born arms at Fort Beausejour) destined for to Georgia). The Prince Fredrick arrived in Georgia on 30 December, 1755. The governor of Georgia ordered the ship away, but the captain refused and was allowed to land on December 14, 1755. (The British Empire Before The American Revolution - Vol. VI by Lawrence Henry Gipson 288) The PRINCE FREDRICK, William Trattles, Master, arrived in Georgia with approximately 280 exiles about the end of Deccember, 1755. (Albert N. Lafreniere - "ACADIAN DEPORTATION SHIPS" - "Connecticut Maple Leaf", volume 6, published by the French-Canadian Genealogical Society of Connecticut, Inc.). The Ship Prince Fredrick was probably chartered for a monthly fee (per ton), plus a pilot's fee and provisions, by Governor Lawrence, from Charles Apthorp & Thomas Hancock, of the Boston Mercantile Company of Apthorp and Hancock, to be used as a transport for the removal of the Acadian Exiles to the eastern seaboard. The amount of provisions for the transports were included in the sailing orders issued by Lawrence and was to be 5 pounds of flour and one pound of pork (or 1 lb of beef 2 lbs bread and 5 lbs of flour) for (each) 7 days for each person so embarked. (p. 280 of SELECTIONS FROM PUBLIC DOCUMENTS OF THE PROVINCE OF NOVA SCOTIA, Published by resolution of the House of Assembly on March 15, 1865 in 1869)

PROSPEROUS Sloop 75 tons POINTE DES BOUDRO TO VIRGINIA

The sloop PROSPEROUS, 75 tons, Daniel Bragdon, Captain, was one of 5 transports that departed from Pnte des Boudro (Grand PrT) on 27 October, 1755. The Prosperous transported 152 exiles to Virginia arriving in Virginia on 13 November, 1755. (The British Empire Before The American Revolution - Vol. VI by Lawrence Henry Gipson 300) With 150 Men aboard. The sloop PROSPEROUS, 75 tons, Daniel Bragdon, Captain, arrived at Pnte des Boudro (Grand PrT) from Port Royal on 10 October departed from Pnte des Boudro (Grand PrT) . She embarked 152 exiles on 19 October and departed on 27 October, 1755destined for Williamsburg Virginia arriving on 15-30 November, 1755. (Emile Lauvriere - La TragTdie d'un peuple, vol I, librairie Henry Geulet, Paris, 1924) Edouard Richard mentions a "Corvette Prosperous", 75 tons, Captain Bragdon, being used to transport 150 exiles. (ACADIA" - Edouard Richard Vol. 2, Chapter XXXI, p. 121) According to copies of accounts transmitted by Charles Apthorp & Thomas Hancock, of Boston Mercantile Company Apthorp and Hancock, to Governor Lawrence published on pages p. 285 - 293 of SELECTIONS FROM PUBLIC DOCUMENTS OF THE PROVINCE OF NOVA SCOTIA, Published by resolution of the House of Assembly on March 15, 1865 in 1869 - The Sloop Prosperous - Daniel Bragdon, Master was chartered from the Boston Mercantile Co. Apthorp and Hancock from 20th August, 1755 to 21 January, 1756 (---, 1756). - The monthly charter fee for the Prosperous was 5 months 1 day at 40 pr month - lawful money - plus 60 s p. month for hire of a pilott, plus provisions. The amount of provisions for the transports were included in the sailing orders issued by Lawrence and was to be 5 pounds of flour and one pound of pork (or 1 lb of beef 2 lbs bread and 5 lbs of flour) for (each) 7 days for each person so embarked. (p. 280 of SELECTIONS FROM PUBLIC DOCUMENTS OF THE PROVINCE OF NOVA SCOTIA, Published by resolution of the House of Assembly on March 15, 1865 in 1869) According to the publication "The Acadian Exile in St. Malo", the governor of Virginia refused to accept the acadians that were alloted to Virginia, and the 1,500 Acadians sent to Virginia on October 25, 1755 were in Virginia were not allowed to disembark and more of them diedaboard the crowded ships during the 4 months that the ship were anchored uin the Williamsburg harbor. They were then transported to England and placed in concentration camps in the port cities of their arrival, where they languished until after the Treaty of Paris, in 1763, when they were released and repatriated (sent) to the maritime ports of Normandy and Britanny.

PROVIDENCE Sloop HALIFAX TO NORTH CAROLINA

According to copies of accounts transmitted by Charles Apthorp & Thomas Hancock, of Boston Mercantile Company Apthorp and Hancock , to Governor Lawrence dated January 13, 1756 and published on pages p. 285 - 293 of SELECTIONS FROM PUBLIC DOCUMENTS OF THE PROVINCE OF NOVA SCOTIA, Published by resolution of the House of Assembly on March 15, 1865 in 1869. The PROVIDENCE, Sloop, ? tons - Samuel Barron, Captain (John Campbell Master)- carried some 50 of the exiles from Halifax to North Carolina - ThePROVIDENCE departed from Halifax on 30 December, 1755 and arrived in North Carolina on ?? . The monthly charter fee for the Providence per certificate was 12s 6 d , pounds sterling - plus 60 s p. month for hire of a pilott , plus provisions. The amount of provisions for the transports were included in the sailing orders issued by Lawrence and was to be 5 pounds of flour and one pound of pork (or 1 lb of beef 2 lbs bread and 5 lbs of flour) for (each) 7 days for each person so embarked. (p. 280 of SELECTIONS FROM PUBLIC DOCUMENTS OF THE PROVINCE OF NOVA SCOTIA, Published by resolution of the House of Assembly on March 15, 1865 in 1869) Among the financial record of the dispersion is the following: "To John Campbell to freight of fifty French people brought from Halifax to N.C. in sloop Providence, per certif. at 12s 6d...(The British Empire Before The American Revolution - Vol. VI by Lawrence Henry Gipson 300)

RACEHORSE Schooner POINTE DES BOUDRO TO MASSACHUSETTS

The schooner RACEHORSE, ? tons - John Banks, Captain, departed on 20 December, 1755 from Pnte des Boudro (Grand PrT) with 120 exiles destined for Massachusetts and arrived in Boston on 26 December, 1755. (The British Empire Before The American

Revolution - Vol. VI by Lawrence Henry Gipson 280) The schooner RACEHORSE, ? tons - John Banks, Captain, departed on 20 December, 1755 from Pnte des Boudro (Grand PrT) with 120 exiles destined for Boston Massachusetts. (Emile Lauviere - "La TragTdie d'un peuple, vol 1, Librairie Henry Geulet, Paris, 1924) The Racehorse was probably chartered for a monthly fee (per ton), plus a pilot's fee and provisions, by Governor Lawrence, from Charles Apthorp & Thomas Hancock, of the Boston Mercantile Company of Apthorp and Hancock, to be used as a transport for the removal of the Acadian Exiles to the eastern seaboard. The amount of provisions for the transports were included in the sailing orders issued by Lawrence and was to be 5 pounds of flour and one pound of pork (or 1 lb of beef 2 lbs bread and 5 lbs of flour) for (each) 7 days for each person so embarked. (p. 280 of SELECTIONS FROM PUBLIC DOCUMENTS OF THE PROVINCE OF NOVA SCOTIA, Published by resolution of the House of Assembly on March 15, 1865 in 1869) Emile Lauvriere, in his "LA TRAGEDIE D'UN PEUPLE" - Histoire du Peuple Acadien - des origines a nos jours - 1923- Editions - Bossard - 43 Rue Madame, 43 - Paris - Tome I - 12th edition Chapter XIV "LE 'GRAND DERANGEMENT'" pp 457-513, in listing some of the vessels used in the expulsion on page 500, refers to the Dove, referred to by others as a sloop as ôla goelette Dove, destines for connecticutö, and two other vessesl, referred to by others as schooners as ôla goelette Race Horse, destines for bostonö and ôla goelette Ranger, destined for virginiaö, probably indicates that some the ships listed as schooners, or sloops were actually goelettes or vice-versa.

RANGER Sloop 90 (91) tons PISIQUID TO MARYLAND

According to copies of accounts transmitted by Charles Apthorp & Thomas Hancock, of Boston Mercantile Company Apthorp and Hancock , to Governor Lawrence published on pages p. 285 - 293 of SELECTIONS FROM PUBLIC DOCUMENTS OF THE PROVINCE OF NOVA SCOTIA, Published by resolution of the House of Assembly on March 15, 1865 in 1869 - The Sloop RANGER, 90 tons burden - Frances Piery (Piercy) Master was chartered from the Boston Mercantile Co. of Apthorp and Hancock from 20th August 1755 to 30th January, 1756 to carry 208 French persons 81 persons more than the complement of 2 to ton at 4s. 6d. With 182 Men aboard. The Sloop RANGER, 91 tons burden - Frances Piery (Piercy) Master arrived in Pisiquid from Port Royal on 16 October and embarked on 10-12 October, She departed on 27 October destined for Annapolis Maryland and arrived on 15-30 November with 263 exiles (81 surnombres). (Emile Lauviere - "La TragTdie d'un peuple , vol 1, Librairie Henry Geulet, Paris, 1924) The monthly charter fee for the Ranger was 5 months 10 days at 48 pounds 10 8 pr. month , pounds sterling - plus 60 s p. month for hire of a pilott , plus provisions. The amount of provisions for the transports were included in the sailing orders issued by Lawrence was to be 5 pounds of flour and one pound of pork (or 1 lb of beef 2 lbs bread and 5 lbs of flour) for (each) 7 days for each person so embarked. (p. 280 of SELECTIONS FROM PUBLIC DOCUMENTS OF THE PROVINCE OF NOVA SCOTIA, Published by resolution of the House of Assembly on March 15, 1865 in 1869) "The sloop Ranger 90 tons burden, Nathaniel Monroe, Master had originally been sent to Chignecto, but was not needed and on October 13, 1755 was sent to Minas to join the fleet assembled in the Grand PrT and Pisiquid area. The Sloop Ranger arrived in Pisiquid October 16, 1755

("EXPULSION OF ACADIANS ORGANIZED AT WINDSOR"). On October 14, 1755 , Captain Alexander Murray writes: "0n this fateful Oct.14th: " I am at this moment embarking the people on board the two Sloops: the "Three Friends" and the "Dolphin" . He also mentions his waiting for another transport vessel that later turns out to be the Ranger and he uses the Ranger to load the remainder of the inhabitants of Pisiquid. The shipping point of the transports from Pisiquid was the north end of Pisiquid at the junction of the Avon and St. Croix rivers. (Photo copy of an article that appeared in the Windsor, N.S. newspaper entitled "EXPULSION OF ACADIANS ORGANIZED AT WINDSOR") The Sloop Ranger, 90 tons - Francis Piecrey, master - was loaded with the Acadians from Pisiquid with about 323 (or 263), 83 over her compliment (it is believed that Firmin Landry and his family were included) and departed for Maryland, under the direction of Capt. Alexander Murray, on 28, October, 1755 and arrived in Annapolis Maryland on November 30, 1755. (Albert N. Lafreniere - "ACADIAN DEPORTATION SHIPS" - "Connecticut Maple Leaf", volume 6, published by the French-Canadian Genealogical Society of Connecticut, Inc.). RANGER, Sloop, 90 tons - Frances Piery, captain - departed 27 October, 1755 from Piziquid (Minas Basin) with 263 exiles (83 in excess of her complement) and arrived in Maryland on 30 November, 1755 (Maryland Historical Magazine - Vol. III No. 1, March 1908 - "The Acadians (French Neutrals) Transported to Maryland" - Basil Sollers p. 7) Sloop Ranger, Captain Peiry, 91 tons arrived at Pisiquid from Port Royal on 16 October and embarked from Pisiquid on October 10-12 and departed on 27 October arriving at Annapolis Maryland between November 15-30 November 1755 with 263 passengers. (Emile Lauvriere - La TragTdie d'un peuple, 1924, vol I) On November 5, 1755 - Six transports with French Neutrals aboard that having met with a furious gale after their departure from Mines Basin, had entered the harbor of Boston, to seek shelter for a number of days. Among these five ships was the Ranger. The had also sought shelter in Boston Harbour for a few days and the delay further further depleted their supplies which were low since the begining of the voyage. (Maryland Historical Magazine - Vol. III No. 1, March 1908 - "The Acadians (French Neutrals) Transported to Maryland" - Basil Sollers p. 7) While at Boston, the vessel was inspected and it was reported that the passengers aboard the Ranger were "Sickley and their water very bad. They want an allow'e of Rum &c." " Their provisions were reported as short, being 1 lb. of beef, 5 lb. Flour and 2 lb. Bread per man per week and too small a quantity to that allowance to carry them to the Parts they are bound to especially at this season of the year; and their water is very bad. (page 7-9 – Maryland Historical Magazine - Vol. III No. 1, March 1908 - "The Acadians (French Neutrals) Transported to Maryland" - Basil Sollers) - (Canadian Archives, Report (1905), II. Apendix A, Part III, E, p. 81) . Also 25 passengers were removed from the Ranger by the Massachusetts Bay authorities to bring the ship's passenger load to the complement of 2 persdons per ton. Fresh water and minimal supplies and assistange was given to the passengers on board the Ranger by the Massachusetts Bay authorities and the vessels sailed southward. After unloading its passengers in Maryland, the Scooner Ranger returned to Nova Scotia and on December 20. 1755 deported 112 French inhabitants from Grand PrT. (Gregory A. Wood - THE FRENCH PRESENCE IN MARYLAND _ 1524-1800 - p. 65-66) (Basil Sollers - THE ACADIANS (FRENCH NEUTRALS) TRANSPORTED TO MARYLAND , p 9), (Al Lafreniere - "Acadian Deportation Ships The Ranger, Captain Piery, evidently a smaller vessel than either of the other two, arrived with 208, an excess of 81 persons beyond the proper compliment (Nova Scotia Doc., I, 42-4) Edouard Richard mentions a "Corvette Ranger", 91 tons, Capt. Piercy, being used to transport 182 exiles - (81 additional). (ACADIA" - Edouard Richard Vol. 2, Chapter XXXI, p. 121) The Dolphin with 230 exiles and the Ranger with 263 exiles followed the arrival of the Elizabeth and Leopard in the Abnnapolis Harbor. The two vessels carried 493 men, women and children from evacuated from Pisiquid under the directions of Captain Alexandre Murray On the last 2 days of the months, the other 3 sloops were anchored in the Severn , but their captains seemed most anxious about the Maryland council's refusal to permit immediate landing in the absence of Gov. Sharpe, who was attending a conference of colonial executives in New York. In a like manner, Francis Piercey, master of the Ranger, apparently the second boat in harbor, presented the same argument, for he and his sikly 263 exiles from Pisiquid would be required to cross the Bay and sit in port in Oxford, inTalbot County. The Choptank contingent of 208 Acadians reached Oxford on 8 December, 1755, and was placed under the supervision of Henry Callister. (Gregory Wood Acadians in Maryland - A Guide to the Acadians in Maryland in the Eighteenth and Nineteenth Centuries.) In a letter dated 17 February, 1996, Stanley Piet of Bel Air Maryland, writes that the "NOTARY PUBLIC RECORD BOOK 1774-1778 in the Hall of Records for the state of Maryland located in the, located at 350 Rowe Blvd., Annapolis Maryland 21401, show the arrival of the ships in Maryland, but there are no people identified. Information listed on the ships Ranger and Dolphin is as follows: "Ranger - Wm. Burkman, Caines Bay, owner. Francis Peirey, Captain, Order from Alexander Murray, Commander of his Majesty's Troops at Pisgate arried Severn River, Annapolis 29 November 1755. Sent to Oxford Maryland." "Dolphin - Zebediah Farnman, master, Sent to Lower Marlborough, Patuxent River".

RANGER Schooner 57 tons POINTE DES BOUDRO TO VIRGINIA

The schooner RANGER, 57 tons - Nathan Monroe Captain - departed from Pnte des Boudro (Grand PrT) on 20 December, 1755 with 112 exiles, 81 more that the complement, and was the 6th transport to arrive in Virginia on 20 January, 1756 with with 208 exiles. (The British Empire Before The American Revolution - Vol. VI by Lawrence Henry Gipson p. 279 -80 and also p.304) The schooner RANGER, Monroe Captain - embarked 112 exiles on 20 December departed from Grand PrT on 20 December, 1755 destined for Williamsburg Virginia. (Emile Lauviere - "La TragTdie d'un peuple , vol 1, Librairie Henry Geulet, Paris, 1924) The Ranger was probably chartered for a monthly fee (per ton), plus a pilot's fee and provisions, by Governor Lawrence, from Charles Apthorp & Thomas Hancock, of the Boston Mercantile Company of Apthorp and Hancock, to be used as a transport for the removal of the Acadian Exiles to the eastern seaboard. The amount of provisions for the transports were included in the sailing orders issued by Lawrence and was to be 5 pounds of flour and one pound of pork (or 1 lb of beef 2 lbs bread and 5 lbs of flour) for (each) 7 days for each person so embarked. (p. 280 of SELECTIONS FROM PUBLIC DOCUMENTS OF THE PROVINCE OF NOVA SCOTIA, Published by resolution of the House of Assembly on March 15, 1865 in 1869) According to the publication "The Acadian Exile in St. Malo", the governor of Virginia refused to accept the acadians that were alloted to Virginia, and the 1,500 Acadians sent to Virginia on October 25, 1755 were in Virginia were not allowed to disembark and more of them diedaboard the crowded ships during the 4 months that the ship were anchored in the Williamsburg harbor. They were then transported to England and placed in concentration camps in the port cities of their arrival, where they languished until after the Treaty of Paris, in 1763, when they were released and repatriated (sent) to the maritime ports of Normandy and Britanny. Emile Lauvriere, in his "LA TRAGEDIE D'UN PEUPLE" - Histoire du Peuple Acadien - des origines a nos jours - 1923- Editions - Bossard - 43 Rue Madame, 43 - Paris - Tome I - 12th edition Chapter XIV "LE 'GRAND DERANGEMENT'" pp 457-513, in listing some of the vessels used in the expulsion on page 500, refers to the Dove, referred to by others as a sloop as "la goelette Dove, destines for connecticut", and two other vessesl, referred to by others as schooners as ôla goelette Race Horse, destined for bostonö and "la goelette Ranger, destined for virginia", probably indicates that some the ships listed as schooners, or sloops were actually goelettes or vice-versa

---

SARAH AND MOLLY or MOLLY (Mully) AND SARAH Corvette (Sloop), 70 tons
Captain Haslum

Edouard Richard mentions a "Corvette Molly and Sarah", 70 tons, Captain Haslum, master being used to transport140 exiles. (ACADIA" - Edouard Richard Vol. 2, Chapter XXXI, p. 121) With 140 men aboard.

SALLY AND MOLLY SOMETIMES CALLED SARAH AND MOLLY Sloop 70 (80)
tons GRAND PRE TO VIRGINIA

SARAH AND MOLLY, Sloop , 70 tons - James Purrington, captain - was one of 5 transports that departed from Grand PrT and Gaspereau on 27 October, 1755 with 154 exiles for Virginia and arrived 13 November, 1755. Sloop Sarah & Molly was also known as the Sarah and Molly. (The British Empire Before The American Revolution - Vol. VI by Lawrence Henry Gipson p. 277 also p. 300) With 160 men aboard. The sloop, SARAH AND MOLLY, 70 tons - James Purrington, captain – arrived in Grand PrT from Port Royal on 10 October and embarked 154 exiles on 19 October. She departed from Grand PrT on 27 October, 1755 destined for Williamsburg Virginia. (Emile Lauviere - "La TragTdie d'un peuple , vol 1, Librairie Henry Geulet, Paris, 1924) According to copies of accounts transmitted by Charles Apthorp & Thomas Hancock, of Boston Mercantile Company Apthorp and Hancock , to Governor Lawrence published on pages p. 285 - 293 of SELECTIONS FROM PUBLIC DOCUMENTS OF THE PROVINCE OF NOVA SCOTIA, Published by resolution of the House of Assembly on March 15, 1865 in 1869 - - The monthly charter fee for the Sarah and Molly was 3 months 13 days at 60s pr month , pounds sterling - plus 60 s p. month for hire of a pilott , plus provisions. The amount of provisions for the transports were included in the sailing orders issued by Lawrence and was to be 5 pounds of flour and one pound of pork (or 1 lb of beef 2 lbs bread and 5 lbs of flour) for (each) 7 days for each person so embarked. (p. 280 of SELECTIONS FROM PUBLIC DOCUMENTS OF THE PROVINCE OF NOVA SCOTIA, Published by resolution of the House of Assembly on March 15, 1865 in 1869) The Sloop SARAH AND MOLLY, 70 tons, Jamess Purrenton (Purrington) master from 29 August to 12 December to carry off the French inhabitants from Annapolis Royal to

Virginia. The Sarah and Molly was one of the six transports that took shelter from a fierce winter storm in the Boston Harbour on November 5, 1755. While at Boston to seek shelter for a number of days, the vessel was inspected and an 11Acadians were removed to reduce the numer aboard to 2 persons per ton. The delay in the voyage when they were in the Boston Harbour for a few days further depleted their supplies which were low since the begining of the voyage. Fresh water and minimal supplies and assistange was given to the passengers on board the Sarah and Molly by the Massachusetts Bay authorities and the vessels sailed southward. Edouard Richard mentions a "Corvette _____", Captain Puddington, (could this be James Purrington, if so, then the unnamed transport is the Sarah and Molly repeated by Edouard Richard) 80 tons - 160 exiles (ACADIA" – Edourd Richard Vol. 2, Chapter XXXI, p. 121) According to the publication "The Acadian Exile in St. Malo", the governor of Virginia refused to accept the acadians that were alloted to Virginia, and the 1,500 Acadians sent to Virginia on October 25, 1755 were in Virginia were not allowed to disembark and more of them died aboard the crowded ships during the 4 months that the ship were anchored in the Williamsburg harbor. They were then transported to England and placed in concentration camps in the port cities of their arrival, where they languished until after the Treaty of Paris, in 1763, when they were released and repatriated (sent) to the maritime ports of Normandy and Britanny.

SEAFLOWER Sloop 81 tons PISIQUID TO MASSACHUSETTS

The sloop SEAFLOWER, 81 tons - Samuel Harris, Captain, departed from Pisiquid with 206 exiles on 27 October, 1755 destined for Massachusetts, and arrived on 15 November, 1755. The sloop SEAFLOWER, 81 tons - Donnel (Harris), Captain, arrived in Grand Pre from Kitterney Point, Maine in September and embarked 206 exiles (18 surnombres) on 22 October and departed on 27 October, 1755 destined for Boston, Massachusetts, and arrived on 15-30 November, 1755. (Emile Lauviere - "La TragTdie d'un peuple, vol 1, Librairie Henry Geulet, Paris, 1924) According to copies of accounts transmitted by Charles Apthorp & Thomas Hancock, of Boston Mercantile Company Apthorp and Hancock, to Governor Lawrence published on pages p. 285 - 293 of SELECTIONS FROM PUBLIC DOCUMENTS OF THE PROVINCE OF NOVA SCOTIA, Published by resolution of the House of Assembly on March 15, 1865 in 1869 - the Sloop Seaflower, 81 tons, Samuel Harris master, Chartered by Captain Alexander Murray from the Boston Mercantile Co. Apthorp and Hancock to bring off the French inhabitants from Minas to the Province of Massachusets from 29 Sept to 1 Dec.,1755. (---, 1755). The monthly charter fee for the Seaflower was 2 months 82 days 43 pounds 4 pr month , pounds sterling - plus 60 s p. month for hire of a pilott, plus provisions. The amount of provisions for the transports were included in the sailing orders issued by Lawrence and was to be 5 pounds of flour and one pound of pork (or 1 lb of beef 2 lbs bread and 5 lbs of flour) for (each) 7 days for each person so embarked. (p. 280 of SELECTIONS FROM PUBLIC DOCUMENTS OF THE PROVINCE OF NOVA SCOTIA, Published by resolution of the House of Assembly on March 15, 1865 in 1869)

The SEAFLOWER left Kittering Point Maine for Grand PrT in the beginning of September and used a few weeks to transport 206 Acadians from Grand Pre to Boston.

Sunflower (Seaflower) Corvette (Sloop), 81 tons Captain Donnell

According to Al Lafreniere the SEAFLOWER and the SUNFLOWER are most likely one and the same. However, Edouard Richard mentions a "Corvette Sunflower", 81 tons, with Captain Donnell as master, being used to transport 180 exiles.(ACADIA" - Edouard Richard Vol. 2, Chapter XXXI, p. 121) With 180 men aboard. And, Emile Lauviere lists the names Donnell and (Harris) as captains of the Sealower (see details of the Seaflower above)(Emile Lauviere - "La TragTdie d'un peuple , vol 1, Librairie Henry Geulet, Paris, 1924)

SWALLOW Brigge 102 tons POINTE DES BOUDRO TO MASSACHUSETTS

The brigge SWALLOW, 102 tons - William Hayes, Captain, departed on 13 December, 1755 from Pointe des Boudro (Grand PrT) with 236 exiles destined for Massachusetts, and arrived in Boston on 30 January, 1756.(The British Empire Before The American Revolution - Vol. VI by Lawrence Henry Gipson p. 279 -80 and also p. 277) The brigge SWALLOW, - Hayes, Captain, embarked 236 Acadians in Grand PrT on 18 December destined for Boston Massachusetts. (Emile Lauviere - "La TragTdie d'un peuple , vol 1, Librairie Henry Geulet, Paris, 1924) The Brigantine Swallow was probably chartered for a monthly fee (per ton), plus a pilot's fee and provisions, by Governor Lawrence, from Charles Apthorp & Thomas Hancock, of the Boston Mercantile Company of Apthorp and Hancock, to be used as a transport for the removal of the Acadian Exiles to the eastern seaboard. The amount of provisions for the transports were included in the sailing orders issued by Lawrence and was to be 5 pounds of flour and one pound of pork (or 1 lb of beef 2 lbs bread and 5 lbs of flour) for (each) 7 days for each person so embarked. (p. 280 of SELECTIONS FROM PUBLIC DOCUMENTS OF THE PROVINCE OF NOVA SCOTIA, published in 1869 by resolution of the House of Assembly on March 15, 1865)

SWAN Sloop 80 tons GRAND PRE TO PENNSYLVANIA

The sloop SWAN, 80 tons - Jonathan Loviette, Captain, departed from Grand PrT and Gaspereau on 27 October, 1755 with 168 exiles destined for Pennyslvania - The Swan departed with the sloop Hannah and they arrived on 19 November, 1755.(The British Empire Before The American Revolution - Vol. VI by Lawrence Henry Gipson p. 279 - 80 and also p.277) The sloop SWAN, 80 tons - Loviett, Captain, arrived in Grand PrT from Port Royal on 10 October. She embarked 168 Acadials and departed from Grand PrT and Gaspereau destined for Philadelphia Pennyslvania - The Swan arrived with 161 Acadians. (Emile Lauviere - "La TragTdie d'un peuple , vol 1, Librairie Henry Geulet, Paris, 1924) According to copies of accounts transmitted by Charles Apthorp & Thomas Hancock, of Boston Mercantile Company Apthorp and Hancock , to Governor Lawrence published on pages p. 285 - 293 of SELECTIONS FROM PUBLIC DOCUMENTS OF THE PROVINCE OF NOVA SCOTIA, Published by resolution of the House of Assembly on March 15, 1865 in 1869 - The Sloop Swan, Jona. Loviett, Master was chartered from Boston Mercantile Co. Apthorp and Hancock from the 27th Aug to 23 Dec, 1755 to carry off French inhabitants from Annapolis Royall to Philidelphia. (---, 1755) - The monthly charter fee for the Swan was 3 months 26 days at 44 16 per month , pounds sterling - plus 60 s p. month for hire of a pilott, plus provisions. The amount of provisions for the transports were included in the sailing orders issued by Lawrence and was to be 5 pounds of flour and one pound of pork (or 1 lb of beef 2 lbs bread and 5 lbs of flour) for (each) 7 days for each person so embarked. (p. 280 of SELECTIONS FROM PUBLIC DOCUMENTS OF THE PROVINCE OF NOVA SCOTIA, Published by resolution of the House of Assembly on March 15, 1865 in 1869) Upon their arrival in Pennsylvania, the colony was in the grips of raging Francophobia, which soon translated into Pensylvania's governor Robert H. Morris' placing the exiles under armed guard aboard the three vessels, the HANNAH, THREE FRIENDS and the SWAN) that brought them from Nova Scotia. Because of this, the Acadians aboard these vessels succumbed to epedemic diseases. They were then quarentined aboard their vessels until legislation on March 5, 1756 provided for their dispersal throughout the easternmost Pennsylvania provinces. (Carl A. Brasseaux - Scattered to the Winds – The Dispersal and Wanderings of the Acadians, p. 19) According to Al Lafreniere the SWAN, Jonathan Loviett, Master, left Grand PrT with 168 exiles, and arrived in Pennsylvania with 161 exiles. (Albert N. Lafreniere - "ACADIAN DEPORTATION SHIPS" - "Connecticut Maple Leaf", volume 6, published by the French-Canadian Genealogical Society of Connecticut, Inc.). Sloops Hannah, Three Friends and Swan reached the Delaware about 18 November, 1755 with 454 aboard and were sent to province Island and later in ucks, Chester, Lancaster, and Philadelphia Counties. The exiles declared that their plight to be far worse than the old Testament world of Egyptian or Babalonian captivity. (p. 18 - Gregory Wood Acadians in Maryland - A Guide to the Acadians in Maryland in the Eighteenth and Nineteenth Centuries.)

SYREN Sloop 30 tons Escort Vessel and Transport GRAND PRE TO S. CAROLINA

The sloop SYREN, 30 tons - Charles Proby Captain, served as both transport and escort vessel. The Syren departed from Grand PrT on 13 October, 1755 with 21 exiles and arrived in South Carolina on 19 November, 1755. The SYREN, Charles Proby, master, was an escort ship, but also carried 21 French prisoners to South Carolina. Nine of these prisoners were considered to be too dangerous to remain in the colonies, and were shipped to England almost immediately. The SYREN continued escorting the other transports to Georgia. (Albert N. Lafreniere - "ACADIAN DEPORTATION SHIPS" - "Connecticut Maple Leaf", volume 6, published by the French-Canadian Genealogical Society of Connecticut, Inc.).

THREE FRIENDS Sloop 69 tons PISIQUID TO PENNSYLVANIA

167

The sloop THREE FRIENDS, 69 tons - Thomas Curtis, Captain (Capt. Carlile) - departed from Pisiquid on 27 October, 1755 with 156 exiles 18 more that the complement destined for Pennsylvania. The transport arrived in Pennsylvania on 21 November, 1755 (The British Empire Before The American Revolution - Vol. VI by Lawrence Henry Gipson p. 279 -80 and also p.279) The sloop THREE FRIENDS, 69 tons - Capt. Carlile - arrived in Pisiquid from Port Royal on 12 October. She departed from Pisiquid on 27 October, 1755 with destined for Philidelphia Pennsylvania. The transport arrived in Philidelphia on 15-30 November with 156 Acadians.. (Emile Lauviere - "La TragTdie d'un peuple , vol 1, Librairie Henry Geulet, Paris, 1924) According to copies of accounts transmitted by Charles Apthorp & Thomas Hancock, of Boston Mercantile Company Apthorp and Hancock , to Governor Lawrence published on pages p. 285 - 293 of SELECTIONS FROM PUBLIC DOCUMENTS OF THE PROVINCE OF NOVA SCOTIA, Published by resolution of the House of Assembly on March 15, 1865 in 1869 - The Sloop "Three Friends" Jas Carlile master was chartered from the Boston Mercantile Co. Apthorp and Hancock from hence to Annapolis Royal & Philadelphia to carry off French Inhabitants from August 20th to 23 December, 1755 - 18 Neutrals more than Compliment. The monthly charter fee for the Three Friends was 4 months 3 days at 36 16s pr mth , pounds sterling - plus 60 s p. month for hire of a pilott, plus provisions. The amount of provisions for the transports were included in the sailing orders issued by Lawrence and was to be 5 pounds of flour and one pound of pork (or 1 lb of beef 2 lbs bread and 5 lbs of flour) for (each) 7 days for each person so embarked. (p. 280 of SELECTIONS FROM PUBLIC DOCUMENTS OF THE PROVINCE OF NOVA SCOTIA, Published by resolution of the House of Assembly on March 15, 1865 in 1869) On October 14, 1755 , Captain Alexander Murray writes: "0n this fateful Oct. 14th: " I am at this moment embarking the people on board the two Sloops: the "Three Friends" and the "Dolphin". The shipping point north end of Pisiquid at the junction of the Avon and St. Croix rivers. (Photo copy of an article that appeared in the Windsor, N.S. newspaper entitled "EXPULSION OF ACADIANS ORGANIZED AT WINDSOR") Upon their arrival in Pennsylvania, the colony was in the grips of raging francophobia, which soon translated into Pensylvania's governor Robert H. Morris placing the exiles under armed guard aboard the three vessels, the HANNAH, THREE FRIENDS and the SWAN that had transported them from Nova Scotia. Because of this, the Acadians aboard these three vessels succumbed to epedemic diseases. They were then quarentined aboard their vessels until legislation on March 5, 1756 provided for their dispersal throughout the easternmost Pennsylvania provinces. (Carl A. Brasseaux - Scattered to the Winds – The Dispersal and Wanderings of the Acadians, p. 19) Edouard Richard mentions a Schooner Three Friends, 69 tons, Captain Carlisle being used to transport 138 exiles - (18 additional) (ACADIA" – Edouard Richard Vol. 2, Chapter XXXI, p. 121) Sloops Hannah, Three Friends and Swan reached the Delaware about 18 November, 1755 with 454 aboard and were sent to province Island and later in ucks, Chester, Lancaster, and Philadelphia Counties. The exiles declared that their plight to be far worse than the old Testament world of Egyptain or Babalonian captivity. (p. 18 - Gregory Wood Acadians in Maryland - A Guide to the Acadians in Maryland in the Eighteenth and Nineteenth Centuries.)

TWO BROTHERS Brigge 161 tons CHIGNECTO TO SOUTH CAROLINA

The brigge TWO BROTHERS, 161 tons - James Best, Captain, departed from Chignecto with 132 exiles on 13 October, 1755 and arrived in S. Carolina on 11 November, 1755. The exiles tried a takeover of the Bragintine TWO BROTHERS, but failed. (Albert N. Lafreniere - "ACADIAN DEPORTATION SHIPS" - "Connecticut Maple Leaf", volume 6, published by the French Canadian Genealogical Society ofConnecticut, Inc.). The Brigantine Two Brothers was probably chartered for a monthly fee (per ton), plus a pilot's fee and provisions, by Governor Lawrence, from Charles Apthorp & Thomas Hancock, of the Boston Mercantile Company of Apthorp and Hancock, to be used as a transport for the removal of the Acadian Exiles to the eastern seaboard. The amount of provisions for the transports were included in the sailing orders issued by Lawrence and was to be 5 pounds of flour and one pound of pork (or 1 lb of beef 2 lbs bread and 5 lbs of flour) for (each) 7 days for each person so embarked. (p. 280 of SELECTIONS FROM PUBLIC DOCUMENTS OF THE PROVINCE OF NOVA SCOTIA, Published by resolution of the House of Assembly on March 15, 1865 in 1869)

TWO SISTERS Snow 140 tons ANNAPOLIS ROYAL TO CONNECTICUT

According to Al Lafreniere, the TWO SISTERS never left Annapolis Royal. It was replaced with the ship ELIZABETH. The TWO SISTERS was supposed to carry 280 French. This is what the Ship ELIZABETH carried (42 men, 40 women 95 boys and 103 girls for a total of 280 exiles). The Two Sisters, 140 tons, with a total of 280 Acadians, 42 men, 40 women, 95 boys and 103 girls destined for Connecticut on a voyage of 28 days (Emile Lauviere -"La TragTdie d'un peuple , vol 1, p. 485, Librairie Henry Geulet, Paris, 1924)Two Sisters, 280, for Connecticut. ("Carles Belliveau et les seins durant la Deportation et apres; Prises de batreaux anglais par les Acadiens" by Placide Gaudet, apparently written in 1922 and given near Annapolis Royal. The article appeared in AGE Vols II, 1973, p. 4.) The snow TWO SISTERS, 140 tons - (T. Ingram ?) Captain, departed on 13 October, 1755 from Annapolis Royal with 280 exiles and arrived in Connecticut on ?? The TWO SISTERS, Captain's name unknown, (perhaps T. Ingram, who was master of this snow in 1757, The Two Sisters is not shown arriving in Connecticut. It is possible that this is the ship reported in the newspapers of the day as putting in at Rhode Island. The ship was bound for New London, Connecticut with approximately 250 exiles. It is also possible that it could have sunk. (Albert N. Lafreniere - "ACADIAN DEPORTATION SHIPS" - "Connecticut Maple Leaf", volume 6, published by the French-Canadian Genealogical Society of Connecticut, Inc.). The Snow Two Sisters was probably chartered for a monthly fee (per ton), plus a pilot's fee and provisions, by Governor Lawrence, from Charles Apthorp & Thomas Hancock, of the Boston Mercantile Company of Apthorp and Hancock, to be used as a transport for the removal of the Acadian Exiles to the eastern seaboard. The amount of provisions for the transports were included in the sailing orders issued by Lawrence and was to be 5 pounds of flour and one pound of pork (or 1 lb of beef 2 lbs bread and 5 lbs of flour) for (each) 7 days for each person so embarked. (p. 280 of SELECTIONS FROM PUBLIC DOCUMENTS OF THE PROVINCE OF NOVA SCOTIA, published 1865 in 1869by resolution of the House of Assembly on March 15,)

UNION Ship 196 tons CHIGNECTO TO PENNSYLVANIA

The ship UNION, 196 tons, Jonathon Crathorne, Captain, departed from Chignecto on 13 October, 1755 with 392 exiles and was to arrive in Pennsylvania on ?? According to Al Lafreniere, the UNION probably sunk off the coast of Maryland or Pennsylvania. Several of the newspapers of the day reported two ships carrying French sinking in the area. The UNION, Jonathan Crathorn, Captain, probably sunk off the coast of Pennsylvania, or may have gone to Boston. There is no record of its arrival in Pennsylvania. (Albert N. Lafreniere - "ACADIAN DEPORTATION SHIPS" - "Connecticut Maple Leaf", volume 6, published by the French-Canadian Genealogical Society of Connecticut, Inc.). The Ship Union was probably chartered for a monthly fee (per ton), plus a pilot's fee and provisions, by Governor Lawrence, from Charles Apthorp & Thomas Hancock, of the Boston Mercantile Company of Apthorp and Hancock, to be used as a transport for the removal of the Acadian Exiles to the eastern seaboard. The amount of provisions for the transports were included in the sailing orders issued by Lawrence and was to be 5 pounds of flour and one pound of pork (or 1 lb of beef 2 lbs bread and 5 lbs of flour) for (each) 7 days for each person so embarked. (p. 280 of SELECTIONS FROM PUBLIC DOCUMENTS OF THE PROVINCE OF NOVA SCOTIA, Published in 1869 by resolution of the House of Assembly on March 15, 1865)

UNKNOWN GOELETTE 30 tons destined for South Carolina

30 tons destined for South Carolina, for a 42 day voyage with 1 man, 1 woman, 4 boys and 3 girls for a total of 9 passengers. (Emile Lauviere -"La TragTdie d'un peuple, vol 1, p. 485, Librairie Henry Geulet, Paris, 1924). Emile Lauvriere, in his "LA TRAGEDIE D'UN PEUPLE" - Histoire du Peuple Acadien - des origines a nos jours - 1923- Editions - Bossard - 43 Rue Madame, 43 - Paris - Tome I - 12th edition Chapter XIV "LE 'GRAND DERANGEMENT'" pp 457-513, refers to this vessel as "une Goelette". However, in listing some of the other vessels used in the expulsion, he refers to the sloop Dove, as la goelette Dove, schooner Racehorse as la goelette Race Horse and and schooner Ranger as la goelette Ranger. And, following a long list of other vessels he refers to one as Une Goelette. I am not sure if he means that the vessel was named "une Goelette, or he is referring to an unknown schooner by the French name goelette. This is possible, because as noted above, he refers to other vessels, described by others as being, schooners or sloops, as la goelete, probably indicating the vessel was an unknown goelette. A schooner, for South Carolina, with 9 persons. ("Carles Belliveau et les seins durant la Deportation et apres; Prises de batreaux anglais par les Acadiens" by Placide Gaudet, apparently written in 1922 and given near Annapolis Royal. The article appeared in AGE Vols II, 1973, p. 4.) (See description of vessels)

UNKNOWN Sloop MINAS BAY TO CONNECTICUT

According to Al Lafreniere, the Connecticut Gazette (copy in the Yale University library) mentions the sloop (name and tonnage unknown(John?) Worster, Captain - departed from

Minas Bay with 173 exiles on 30 November, 1755 and arrived in Connecticut on 22 January, 1756. (I corrected a typographical error on the list of ships in the LaFreniere article) The Sloop (NAME UNKNOWN), Captain Worster, master, arrived in Connecticut with 173 exiles from Minas Bay on January 22, 1756. This may be Captain John Worster of Stanford, Connecticut, who died March, 1775. He had lived the last 12 years of his life in Barbados. Captain Worster is mentioned in Col. Winslow's Journal. On October 27. 1755, he left Fort Cumberland with two letters for Col. Winslow. From this we know that he did not depart with the main body of the fleet, but departed later. Since there are exiles in Connecticut from Cape Sable, Beaubassin, Piziquid and Grand PrT. It is possible that he was assigned to pick up stragglers, and finally fill out at Grand PrT before departing Minas Bay. Winslow shows 732 exiles shipped by Osgood, but only 600 are accounted for. The remainder could have been shipped earlier on Captain Worster's sloop. This sloop was probably chartered for a monthly fee (per ton), plus a pilot's fee and provisions, by Governor Lawrence, from Charles Apthorp & Thomas Hancock, of the Boston Mercantile Company of Apthorp and Hancock, to be used as a transport for the removal of the Acadian Exiles to the eastern seaboard. The amount of provisions for the transports were included in the sailing orders issued by Lawrence and was to be 5 pounds of flour and one pound of pork (or 1 lb of beef 2 lbs bread and 5 lbs of flour) for (each) 7 days for each person so embarked. (p. 280 of SELECTIONS FROM PUBLIC DOCUMENTS OF THE PROVINCE OF NOVA SCOTIA, Published in 1869 by resolution of the House ofAssembly on March 15, 1865).

VULTURE Sloop PORT LATURE TO MASSACHUSETTS

The sloop VULTURE, ? tons, Johnston Scaife, Captain, departed from Port Lature on ?? with 70 exiles and arrived in Massachusetts on 10 May, 1756. The Vulture was probably chartered for a monthly fee (per ton), plus a pilot's fee and provisions, by Governor Lawrence, from Charles Apthorp & Thomas Hancock, of the Boston Mercantile Company of Apthorp and Hancock, to be used as a transport for the removal of the Acadian Exiles to the eastern seaboard. The amount of provisions for the transports were included in the sailing orders issued by Lawrence and was to be 5 pounds of flour and one pound of pork (or 1 lb of beef 2 lbs bread and 5 lbs of flour) for (each) 7 days for each person so embarked. (p. 280 of SELECTIONS FROM PUBLIC DOCUMENTS OF THE PROVINCE OF NOVA SCOTIA, Published in 1869 by resolution of the House of Assembly on March 15, 1865)

The newspapers of the time also reported three other vessels with exiles that were sent to Boston, or just passing through. They were:

- December 26, 1755 -- a vessel with a considerable number of French exiles.
- January 5, 1756 -- A ship from Halifax.
- January ?, 1756 -- A snow with the largest number of French exiles yet, from Malagash.(Albert N. Lafreniere - "ACADIAN DEPORTATION SHIPS" - "Connecticut Maple Leaf", volume 6, published by the French-Canadian Genealogical Society of Connecticut, Inc.)

ESCORT SHIPS OF THE EXPULSION

"On the 29 Oct. 1755 the Fleet sailed from the Rendezvous in the Bason of Mines under the Convoy of His Majesty's Ships": These ships were charged with escorting the ships being used in the deportation of the Acadians. **BALTIMORE** SLOOP/WAR FROM GOAT ISLAND AT ANNAPOLIS ROYALL TO SOUTH CAROLINA

The war/sloop Baltimore, T. Owen, Captain, escorted a convoy of 2 ships, 3 snows and one brigantine from Goat Island, at Annapolis Royal, to South Carolina. The Baltimore departed from Goat Island on 8 December, 1755 arrived in South Carolina on ??. The 6 transports that the Baltimore escorted in December, 1755, carried an average of 278 Acadian exiles each. This is in contrast to the average of 167 per transport that was carried off in October, 1755. (The British Empire Before The American Revolution - Vol. VI by Lawrence Henry Gipson p. 269) Vice Admiral Edward Boscawen, informed John Cleveland, Esq., Secretary to the Admiralty, that he included the Baltimore, Captain Owen, as one of the ships to convoy the transports that were to carry the Acadians from Annapolis Royal to New York; ("Charles Belliveau et les seins durant la Deportationet apres; Prises de batreaux anglais par les Acadiens" by Placide Gaudet, apparently written in 1922 and given near Annapolis Royal. The article appeared in AGE Vols II, 1973, p. 4)

CAROLINA (2 SHIPS NAMED CAROLINA)FROM MINAS BAY TO VIRGINIA

Vice Admiral Edward Boscawen, informed John Cleveland, Esq., Secretary to the Admiralty, that he included the two Carolinas as two of the ships to convoy the transports that were to carry the Acadians from Mines to Virginia, and Maryland ("Charles Belliveau et les seins durant la Deportationet apres; Prises de batreaux anglais par les Acadiens" by Placide Gaudet, apparently written in 1922 and given near Annapolis Royal. The article appeared in AGE Vols II, 1973, p. 4)

HALIFAX SNOW FROM MINAS BAY TO VIRGINIA

The snow Halifax, John Taggart Captain, departed from Minas Bay to Virginia. The dates of her departure and arrival is unknown. However, the Snow (Halifax), Captain Taggert, was listed by Edouard Richard as an escort for the transports that departed in October, 1755. (ACADIA" - Edouard Richard Vol. 2, Chapter XXXI, p. 121)

HORNET SHIP ANNAPOLIS ROYALL TO MASSACHUSETTS

The ship Hornet, Captain __?__ Salt, Master departed from Annapolis Royal on 28

October, 1755 and arrived in Massachusetts on 17 November, 1755. The Hornet was to proceed to Boston and then on to Spithead. - (Albert N. Lafreniere - "ACADIAN DEPORTATION SHIPS" - "Connecticut Maple Leaf", volume 6, published by the French-Canadian Genealogical Society of Connecticut, Inc.). Vice Admiral Edward Boscawen, informed John Cleveland, Esq., Secretary to the Admiralty, that he included the Hornet, Captain Salt, as one of the ships to convoy the transports that were to carry the Acadians from Annapolis Royal to Boston, and then to Spithead; ("Charles Belliveau et les seins durant la Deportationet apres; Prises de batreaux anglais par les Acadiens" by Placide Gaudet, apparently written in 1922 and given near Annapolis Royal. The article appeared in AGE Vols II, 1973, p. 4)

MERMAID SHIP FROM ANNAPOLIS ROYAL TO MASSACHUSETTS

The ship Mermaid, Captain Wash. Shirley, departed from Annapolis Royal on 13 October, 1755 and arrived at Massachusetts on 17 November, 1755. Vice Admiral Edward Boscawen, informed John Cleveland, Esq., Secretary to the Admiralty, that he included the Mermaid, captain SHIRLEY, as one of the ships to convoy the transports that were to carry the Acadians to Connecticut.("Charles Belliveau et les seins durant la Deportationet apres; Prises de batreaux anglais par les Acadiens" by Placide Gaudet, apparently written in 1922 and given near Annapolis Royal. The article appeared in AGE Vols II, 197, p. 4)

NIGHTINGALE SHIP MINAS BAY TO MARYLAND

The ship Nightingale, Dudley Diggs Captain, was part of the 3 warship escort to the 24 transports that sailed from Minas Bay on October 28, 1755 (some sayOctober 13th). The Nightingale was destined for Maryland and the date of arrival is unknown. (probably didn't arrive at all). The Nightingale was seperated from the rest of the convoy of transports and escort vessels during a violent storm (Severe Storms and a massive earthquake occured at the time of the deportation) and landed at New York. (The British Empire Before The American Revolution - Vol. VI by Lawrence Henry Gipson p. 287) - also (Albert N. Lafreniere - "ACADIAN DEPORTATION SHIPS" - "Connecticut Maple Leaf", volume 6, published by the French-Canadian Genealogical Society of Connecticut, Inc.).(ACADIA" - Edouard Richard Vol. 2, Chapter XXXI, p. 121) Vice Admiral Edward Boscawen, informed John Cleveland, Esq., Secretary to the Admiralty, that he included the Nightingale, Captain DIGGS, to convoy the transports that were to carry the Acadians from Mines to Pennsylvania, then proceed to his station at New York. ("Charles Belliveau et les seins durant la Deportationet apres; Prises de batreaux anglais par les Acadiens" by Placide Gaudet, apparently written in 1922 and given near Annapolis Royal. The article appeared in AGE Vols II, 1973, p. 4)

SUCCESS SHIP FROM CHIGNECTO TO SOUTH CAROLINA

The ship Success, John Rouse, Captain, departed from Chignecto on 13 October, 1755 and was to proceed with the fleet to South Carolina. Her arrival date is unknown. (Albert N. Lafreniere - "ACADIAN DEPORTATION SHIPS" - "Connecticut Maple Leaf", volume 6, published by the French-Canadian Genealogical Society of Connecticut, Inc.) Vice Admiral Edward Boscawen, informed John Cleveland, Esq., Secretary to the Admiralty, that he included the Success, Captain ROUS, as one of the ships to convoy the transports that were to carry the Acadians ,to assist in embarking them and to look into the St. John River. ("Charles Belliveau et les seins durant la Deportationet apres; Prises de batreaux anglais par les Acadiens", by Placide Gaudet, apparently written in 1922 and given near Annapolis Royal. The article appeared in AGE Vols II, 1973, p. 4)

H.M.S. SYREN FROM CHIGNECTO (FORT BEAUSEJOUR) TO GEORGIA

H.M.S. Syren, Charles Proby, Esq. Commander, escorted 2 transports that were sent from Chignecto (Fort Beausejour) and destined for Georgia. The Syren arrived at Tybee island at the mouth of the Savanah River with 120 exiles , mostly women and children. (The British Empire Before The American Revolution - Vol. VI by Lawrence Henry Gipson p. 287) They passed the bar on Novenber 27th (reported in the N.Y. newspaper N.Y. Mercury). They were prevented from landing so they departed for Agusta. An account of the arrival of 3 ships escorted by H.M.S. Syren: "on Saturday arrived here, under convoy of H.M.S. Syren, Charles Proby, Esq., Commander, from the Bay of Fundy in Nova Scotia, a ship, a Brigantyine and a sloop, having on board 471 of French Neutrals (ship 210, bragintine 137, and sloop 124, and we hear that several children have been born in passage.ö. And the next day: "The same day (yesterday) arrived here another sloop with 127 French from Nova Scotia, but last from Boston. (The British Empire Before The American Revolution - Vol. VI by Lawrence Henry Gipson, p. 291) Vice Admiral Edward Boscawen, informed John Cleveland, Esq., Secretary to the Admiralty, that he included the SYREN, Captain PROBY, as one of the ships to convoy the transports that were to carry the Acadians from Chignecto to Georgia.("Charles Belliveau et les seins durant la Deportationet apres; Prises de batreaux anglais par les Acadiens", by Placide Gaudet, apparently written in 1922 and given near Annapolis Royal. The article appeared in AGE Vols II, 1973, p. 4)

WARREN SCHOONER FROM MINAS BAY TO SOUTH CAROLINA

The armed schooner, Warren, Captain Adams, was an escort for the transports. (ACADIA" - Edouard Richard Vol. 2, Chapter XXXI, p. 121) The schooner Warren, Abraham Adams, Captain, departed from Minas Bay on 13 October, 1755, destined for South Carolina. The date of arrival in South Carolina is unknown.

YORK SHIP FROM ANNAPOLIS ROYALL TO BOSTON

The ship York, Sylvanns Cobb, Captain, departed from Annapolis Royal on 13 October, 1755 and arrived at Boston on 17 November, 1755.

THE EXILE EXTENDS TO EUROPE AS THE TRAGEDY CONTINUES IN THE STORMY NORTH ATLANTIC

The ships that are reported to have transported the Acadians from the Bay of Canso to St. Malo France were:

ANTELOPE Tonnage and Captain unknown. Ile Royale (Cape Breton), Ile St-Jean (Prince Edward Island) and then to ST MALO, France.

The ANTELOPE, disembarked at St. Malo on November 1, 1758. No additional information about the ANTELOPE is known to the writer at this time.

DUKE WILLIAM Tonnage and Captain unknown. Ile Royale (Cape Breton), Ile St-Jean (Prince Edward Island) and then to France.

The Duke William was among the transports used in November, 1758 to transport the Acadians of Ile Royale (now Cape Breton), Ile St-Jean (Prince Edward Island) to France. The Duke William was delayed with the other vessels, shortly after their departure in the Gut of Canso until November 25, 1758 when they finally set sail for France. After three days at sea a storm blew at night with rough and high seas and sleet and rain. The storm lasted a couple of days. After a couple of weeks, the Duke William, with 300 Exiles aboard, and the Violet, with 400 Acadian Exiles aboard, joined together, but the Violet was taking on water and was in danger of sinking, and on about December 10th or,15th, (some say December 13th), following a squall in the early morning, the Violet had sunk to the bottom and all 400 Acadians board perished. After working frantically for 4 days, trying to bale out the water, they gave up and the captain and the crew of the Duke William abandoned the ship in the lifeboats (twenty seven in one and nine in the other, including captain Nicols) four Acadians threw over a small jolly boat and miraculously reached England with the two life boats. It is believed that some 300 + Acadians perished aboard the Duke William, while the captain and crew saved themselves with the lifeboats. However, it was reported that the DUKE WILLIAM, that had embarked with 346, had disembarked, in St. Malo on November 1, 1758, and 147 had died during the voyage. (The Duke William was also reported to have sunk with the Violet in a storm on December 13, 1758. This is an error, or there may have been two vessels named Duke Williams, used.)

HIND Tonnage and Captain unknown. Ile Royale (Cape Breton), Ile St-Jean (Prince Edward Island) and then to ST MALO, France

No additional information about the HIND is known to the writer at this time.

JOHN SAMUELS Tonnage and Captain unknown Ile Royale (Cape Breton), Ile St-Jean (Prince Edward Island) and then to ST MALO, France

The JOHN SAMUEL, disembarked at St. Malo on January 23, 1759. No additional information about the JOHN SAMUEL is known to the writer at this time.

MATHIAS Tonnage and Captain unknown Ile Royale (Cape Breton), Ile St-Jean (Prince Edward Island) and then to ST MALO, France

The MATHIAS, disembarked at St. Malo on January 23, 1759. No additional information about the MATHIAS is known to the writer at this time.

NAUTILES Tonnage and Captain unknown Ile Royale (Cape Breton), Ile St-Jean (Prince Edward Island) and then to ST MALO, France

No additional information about the NAUTILES is known to the writer at this time.

NARCISSUS Tonnage and Captain unknown Ile Royale (Cape Breton), Ile St-Jean (Prince Edward Island) and then to ST MALO, France

No additional information about the NARCISSUS is known to the writer at this time.

PATIENCE Tonnage and Captain unknown Ile Royale (Cape Breton), Ile St-Jean (Prince Edward Island) and then to ST MALO, France

The PATIENCE, disembarked at St. Malo on January 23, 1759. No additional information about the PATIENCE is known to the writer at this time.

QUEEN OF SPAIN Tonnage and Captain unknown Ile Royale (Cape Breton), Ile St-Jean (Prince Edward Island) and then to ST MALO, France

The QUEEN OF SPAIN embarked with 108 aboard , and disembarked at St. Malo on November 17, 1758 with only 50 Acadians. It was reported that 58 died during the voyage.

RESTORATION Tonnage and Captain unknown Ile Royale (Cape Breton), Ile St-Jean (Prince Edward Island) and then to ST MALO, France

The RESTORATION, disembarked at St. Malo on January 23, 1759. No additional information about the RESTORATION is known to the writer at this time.

SUPPLY Tonnage and Captain unknown Ile Royale (Cape Breton), Ile St-Jean (Prince Edward Island) and then to ST MALO, France

The SUPPLY embarked with 163, disembarked at St. Malo on 9 March, 1759 –25 died. No additional information about the SUPPLY is known to the writer at this time.

TAMBERLAN Tonnage unknown, Captain unknown Ile Royale (Cape Breton), Ile St-Jean (Prince Edward Island) destination St. Malo France

The TAMERLAN, disembarked at St. Malo on January 16, 1759. No additional information about the TAMERLAN is known to the writer at this time.

VIOLET Tonnage unknown, Captain Nichols ?? Ile Royale (Cape Breton), Ile St-Jean (Prince Edward Island) destination, St. Malo, France

After the fall of Louisbourg in July of 1758, the Violet was among the transports that were assembled in November, 1758 to transport the Acadians of Ile Royale (now Cape Breton), Ile St-Jean (Prince Edward Island) to France. However, soon after their departure, the transports were delayed in the Gut of Canso until November 25, 1758 when they finally set sail for France. After three days at sea a storm blew at night with rough and high seas and sleet and rain. The storm lasted a couple of days. After a couple of weeks, the Violet, with 400 Acadian Exiles aboard, and the Duke William, with 300 Exiles aboard, joined together, but the Violet was taking on water and was in danger of sinking and had to seperate. After a squall in the early morning, on about December 10th, or 15th, (some say December 13th), the Violet sank to the bottom with all 400 Acadians board.

YARMOUTH Tonnage and Captain unknown Ile Royale (Cape Breton), Ile St-Jean

(Prince Edward Island) and then to ST MALO, France

The YARMOUTH, disembarked at St. Malo on January 23, 1759. No additiona
information about the YARMOUTH is known to the writer at this time.

Name of Ship? Tonnage and Captain unknown Ile Royale (Cape Breton), Ile St-Jean
(Prince Edward Island) and then to St Malo, France

The "FIVE SHIPS " embarked from of Ile Royale (now Cape Breton), Ile St-Jean (Prince
Edward Island) with 992, and disembarked at St. Malo on January 23, 1759. It was
reported that 340 died during the voyage. The vessels referred to as the "five ships" could
have included the: YARMOUTH, MATHIAS, RESTORATION, PATIENCE and JOHN
SAMUEL.

Name Unknown Tonnage and Captain unknown Ile Royale (Cape Breton), Ile St-Jean
(Prince Edward Island) and then to France

After the fall of Louisbourg in July of 1758, this unknown vessel was among the
transports that were assembled in November, 1758 to transport the Acadians of Ile
Royale (now Cape Breton), Ile St-Jean (Prince Edward Island) to France. This vessel and
all of the Acadians aboard met with a similar fate as those mentioned above.

After the fall of Louisbourg in July of 1758, It was decided that the Acadians of Ile
Royale (now Cape Breton), Ile St-Jean (Prince Edward Island) transport to France and the
transports were assembled in November, 1758. However, soon after their departure, the
transports were delayed in the Gut of Canso until November 25, 1758 when they finally
set sail for France. After three days at sea a storm blew at night with rough and high seas
and sleet and rain, and these stormy conditions seperated the ships. The storm lasted a
couple of days, and it is believed that at least three of the transports with all of the
Acadians aboard perished It is estimated that some 1300 Acadians were lost at sea during
the voyage to France in the winter of 1758. Between September 8, 1758 and November 5,
1758 it was believed that 2,200 Acadians were embarked on 16 ships destined for France.
Although these transports embarked from Acadia some 3 years after the massive
expulsion of the fall of 1755, some of the transports that were known to be used for this
expulsion are listed above. An account of the three ships that are believed to have sunk
with all of the Acadians aboard, can be found in the Acadian Genealogy Exchange, Vol
XIX # 3 p. 75 and again In the AGE, Vol XIX # 2 1990 p. 38-40 and in the publication,
"The Acadian Exile in St. Malo". Steven White and Father d'Entremont discuss the
sinking of the Duke William and the Violet. The Acadians that were shipped directly to
France, disembarked at St. Malo on January 23, 1759 from the "five ships", later

identified as the YARMOUTH, MATHIAS, RESTORATION, PATIENCE and JOHN SAMUEL. After the loss of the DUKE WILLIAM and VIOLET, 9 ships were reported to be in the convoy.

Very stormy conditions seperated the ships and on December 10, 1758, the DUKE WILLIAM came upon the VIOLET that was listing and in danger of sinking. While assisting the Violet, there was a violent explosion aboard the DUKE WILLIAM. The Violet sank on December 12, 1758 and the DUKE WILLIAM sank on December 13, 1758. Some survivors from the DUKE WILLIAM reached the seaport of Penzanet England in a life boat. Of the 346 aboard the Duke William, only 4 Acadians and a priest survived. It was reported that 199 Acadians disembarked from the DUKE WILLIAM at St. Malo on November, 1758. This caused some confusion, unless there were two ships named DUKE WILLIAM.

LIVING CONDITIONS ON THE DEPORTATION SHIPS

Before leaving Boston the ships had been renovated by removing the balast stones and the bulk heads of the holds. This created a large area in the hold of the vessel measuring approximately 24 feet wide by 60 feet long and 15 feet high. This space was then divided into three levels, and allowing for the thickness of the two floors that seperated the space the three levels were just slightly over 4 feet high. 300 people, some times more, were crowded into this space for up to 3 months. During this time, only half of the passengers could lie down shoulder to shoulder, the rest would have to sit or stoop shoulder to shoulder, since a grown person could not stand erect in the hold of the ship. Most of the other deportation vessels had cargo holds were much smaller that the space on the schooner described above, yet they were filled with over 5,000 prisoners during the fall months of 1755. In each case, there were no sanitary facilities available, which resulted in outbreaks of small pox, and their rations consisted mainly of bread, water and flour and they lacked sufficient clothing for an Atlantic voyage in the middle of the winter.

THE INHUMANITY OF THE EXPULSION TAKES A TRAGIC TOLL LOST AT SEA

Four ships left from the Minas Bay for Pennsylvania, but only three ships arrived in Pennsylvania on November 21 and 22, 1755. When the fourth vessel failed to arrive at its destination in Pennsylvania, it was reported to have been lost during a hurricane, disappearing with all on board. (THE BRITISH EMPIRE BEFORE THE AMERICAN REVOLUTION - Gipson - p. 308) The sloop Three Friends, sloop Swan, sloop Hannah are reported to have left from the Minas Basin on October 27, and arrived in Pennyslvania on November 21-22, 1755, while the schooner Boscowans and the Ship Union, are reported to have sailed from Chignecto on October 13th and joined the fleet in the Minas Basin and probably set sail with the rest of the fleet on Oct 27-28, 1755, there is no record of their arrival in Pennysylvannia. One of these vessels, or both may have sunk. A "Memoire sur les Acadiens" (1763) has the following comment: "The Acadians on the fourth transport destined for Pennsylvania suffered less than those of whom we have spoken; a hurricane, having engulfed their ship, suddenly put an end to the miseries that awaited them" (Canadian Archives, Report (1905), II, Appendix G, 151). Governor Morris also was notified of the coming of a fourth vessel. Writing to the proprietors on November 22, 1755, he stated: "Yesterday and today three vessels are arrived from Nova

Scotia, and a fourth is coming with Neutral French that Governor Lawrence has sent to remain in this province". (Pennsylvania Archives, fourth series, II, 554) ("The British Empire before the American Revolution" - p. 308)

CHAPTER FOURTEEN

Indentured

Ship's log: May 15, 1756.
The Experiment
Captain Stoddard
Ship's manifest: 249 Neutral French Acadians.
Arrived New York five months out of Annapolis Royal, Nova Scotia, Canada.

- - - - - - - - - - - - - - - -

One of the most bizarre voyages ever recorded ended when the Experiment arrived in New York in May of 1756. Only 249 Acadians survived the journey. The Acadians, or Neutrals as they would be classified later, were detained aboard the Experiment for a few weeks more, while the authorities determined what to do with them. There had been another ship carrying Neutrals that stopped at the port of New York earlier. This ship had been originally ordered to take the Neutrals to Georgia, but the Southerners did not wish to receive them so the ship made its way North and docked in New York. Those Neutrals were farmed out to different villages as indentured servants.

The population in New York at this time, 18,000, was actually smaller than Philadelphia, at 23,000. The 1750s in New York was a time of intellectual revival. The arts were just being introduced and people became interested in educating their children. Up until that time, it was said that having the best education in the world would not help in the least, in one's ability to chop wood, or plow the fields.

Diseases were widespread, especially smallpox which took a huge number of victims. It was at this time that experiments were carried out to inoculate against smallpox.

Health officials became alarmed at the quality of meats sold. In some cases even carrion was passed off to the public. There were more Negro slaves in New York than in the south. Those unfortunates were harshly dealt with.

After much complaining by Captain Stoddard to the New York authorities, he was paid his promised fee for delivering his 'cargo' and the Neutrals were taken ashore. They were held in a large warehouse until the constables could come for them. They waited --- and wondered what would become of them.

After being confined for hours upon landing, the doors of the warehouse were flung open and they were allowed outside to a waiting cart where a large kettle of soup was prepared for them. Armed soldiers surrounded the hapless victims.

A French Huguenot, Jean Depuis, stood on a wagon nearby, and addressed the Neutrals.

"Welcome to New York," he began, facetiously. "You will be divided up and taken to area farms where, hopefully, you will find meaningful employment. Those of you who are too old or too ill, will be placed in the town poor-house where you will be taken care of. The state of New York has been empowered to provide for you while you are here. There are strict laws in this state and anyone breaking these laws will be severely punished. You are forbidden to travel about on your own. Anyone caught without a proper pass will be jailed. The sheriff will transport you to farms that need help. Do what you are told and there will be no problems. Catholic priests are not allowed in this state, thank God, so you will have to attend to religious services yourself. You will do well to learn the English language as quickly as you can. That is all for now."

The local constables and their deputies arrived in horse-drawn wagons. Some of the Neutrals were ordered to get on the wagons, and were driven away, the rest were ordered back into the warehouse.

"Where are they taking them?" asked Magdelaine.

"I don't know," replied Jacques.

The following day, the constables arrived again and took more Acadians to nearby farms. On the third day, Jacques and his family were taken by the constables to Long Island. By late afternoon they arrived.

"This is the Taylor farm," said the officer, as he pulled into the driveway.

Eric and Rhonda Taylor met the Neutrals as they arrived.

"Good afternoon, Eric," said the constable. "I've brought some laborers for you."

The Taylors looked over the new arrivals.

"My god," exclaimed Rhonda, "they are filthy!"

"Yup," replied the sheriff, "looks like they haven't had a bath in months."

"Where do they come from?"

"These are some of the newly arrived Neutrals from Nova Scotia. We have hundreds of them to relocate, and more coming later."

Jacques helped his family disembark. They gathered around him for support, not knowing what to expect. Rhonda just kept staring at the group in disbelief.

"What are your names?" asked Eric. Jacques knew enough English to communicate a little.

"My name, Jacques. This my wife, Magdelaine. This my daughter, Ange. This my daughter, Louise."

Ange was fourteen years of age, and Louise was thirteen. They were indeed a sorry looking lot. Eric thanked the sheriff, and slipped him a little reward for bringing laborers to him.

"Follow me," said Eric, as he led the way to the worker's cottages. "This one is yours."

There were five cottages behind the main house; each used to house his employees, most of whom were indentured servants. Eric gave the last shack to Jacques and his family.

"It's kind of messy right now, but you can clean it up," said Eric. "You can eat with the other workers in the main cabin, in the middle here." Eric turned and left the Neutrals to their own devices. They entered the dusty building and looked about.

"This is like some kind of bad dream," said Magdelaine. "I am waiting to wake up any minute now."

"I'm afraid this is for real. I don't know what we have done to deserve this," said Jacques.

The two young daughters had tears in their eyes. "We can clean this up, Mama," said Ange.

As they busied themselves, they heard a knock at the door. Jacques opened the creaky door and saw a shabbily dressed individual standing there. He doffed his hat, bowed and said, "Master sent me to have you come and join us for supper." They followed the man to the largest of the buildings where they were fed. They met the indentured servants; men, women, and children who came to the colonies by having Eric Taylor pay their fare in return for seven years labor. Many had been there over their allotted seven years due to not having the resources to buy their own farms.

Jacques heard horrible stories of some indentured servants who came over and fled at the first chance they had, only to be captured and returned, bound in chains. Their terms extended an extra ten years.

"Its not so bad here," said Tom MacFarland, "you'll get used to it."

They were served a delicious meal of rice and beans, corn bread and tea.

The following morning, Eric, the landowner, knocked at their door and was amazed to see that they had all taken baths, washed their clothes, and looked like decent human beings. Eric took them to the main house where Rhonda was waiting. Magdelaine and the girls were put to work as housekeepers and cooks for the Taylors. Jacques was taken to the barn where the animals were kept.

"Let me see you harness the horse for plowing," said Eric. Jacques expertly harnessed the animal and prepared it for pulling the plow. He handled the horse so well, it took Eric by surprise. "She's all yours," said Eric, smiling. He pointed out what he wanted done.

And so, they settled into their daily routine. They became good friends with their English and Scottish indentured servants. In the evenings, Magdelaine would tell Jacques how the Taylors lived in their big house.

"She sits by the fire with a blanket wrapped around her. We have to warm some stones by the fire, and place the warmed stones under the blanket by her feet. She sits there and smokes a pipe!"

In order to get his produce to market it was necessary for the Taylors to construct a road. Each landowner was responsible for building and maintaining roads along their properties. Eric Taylor used his servants to build and keep the road in good order.

Jacques would spend hours talking with other indentured servants about escaping. He wanted to go back to Canada. It would have been a simple matter for him to make his way back to Nova Scotia by himself, he knew survival tactics better than anyone did, but he had his family to consider.

There was a law in New York regarding vagrants. Any householder that observed a stranger was to report the same to the constable or the justice-of-the-peace. This law made it very difficult for runaways to make it through the state. Many of the Neutrals in New York did attempt to escape, but most were captured and returned, some to jails.

In the fall of 1756, Jacques accompanied Eric to the city to sell his produce. At the market square, Jacques saw Negroes doing heavy work. The Negroes loaded and unloaded the wagons as they lined up at the square. Jacques could not take his eyes off the darkies. He had seen some of them in the Caribbean cutting sugar cane; they were well fed and seemed be happy, but these poor unfortunates toiled hard at the tasks of unloading the wagons. Eric noticed Jacques's curiosity.

"Those are slaves," said Eric. Jacques was taken back, but not overly surprised; wasn't he in fact some kind of slave himself.

"How long they work before freedom?" asked Jacques. Eric laughed and said, "They are not indentured like my workers. They are slaves for life."

Slaves for life, thought Jacques, that makes them no better than a horse. He wondered how long he himself would be a slave. He longed for his home in Nova Scotia. He dearly missed the hunting, fishing, and the fruits of his own land.

Jacques had many stories to tell when he arrived back at the farm.

"I saw dark skinned people working like horses. I saw huge buildings, and a large sprawling village, the likes of which I have never seen before."

"My God," said Magdelaine. The children listened intensely.

"I saw ships of every description in the harbor," he went on.

In the state of New York, a law was enacted on July 9, 1756 stating that all Acadians under 21 years of age were to be made slaves! These slaves were to be distributed among the inhabitants of the different colonies of that commonwealth. The law read:

"Whereas it has been judged necessary for his Majesties service to remove his subjects of Nova Scotia, commonly called Neutral French, to some other of his Majesties colony's, and in consequence thereof a certain number has been received into his colony poor, naked and destitute of every convenience and support of life to the end that they not continue, as they now really are, useless to his majesty themselves and a burden to this colony.

"Be it enacted by His Excellency the Governor, the Council and the General Assembly, and it is hereby enacted by the authority of the same – that his Majesty's Justices of the peace of the raid several and respective County's, or any two of them the whereof to be of the Quorum, shall be and hereby are empowered and required to bind with reputable families such of them as are not arrived to the age of twenty-one years for such space of time as the said justices shall judge proper, not exceeding the time they shall respectively attain the age of twenty-one years. During which time they shall be obliged faithfully and industriously to discharge their service as other indented persons within this colony are."

In New York, the Acadians had their French names changed into English versions. LeBlanc became White, Foret became Foray, Maillet became Mayet, etc.

In the summer of 1756, the colonies were embroiled in a battle with the French and Indians. The French controlled all areas west of the Ohio River. It was mainly a struggle for the lucrative fur trade with the Indians of the Ohio valley. Up to this time, all the colonies were more or less self sufficient, depending on England to settle all their problems. There were no united colonies.

The stalwart Benjamin Franklin, from Pennsylvania, well known and respected throughout all the colonies managed to get the governors of the colonies to send representatives to Albany, New York, for a plan to combat the French and Indians.

They were: Benjamin Tasker from Maryland, Thomas Hutchinson from Massachusetts, William Pitkin from Connecticut, Theodore Atkinson from New Hampshire, Stephen Hopkins from Rhode Island, William Smith from New York, and Benjamin Franklin himself.

Franklin said, "A voluntary union entered into by the colonies themselves, would be preferable to one imposed by Parliament; for it would be perhaps not much more difficult to procure, and more easy to alter and improve as circumstances should require and experience direct."

This was a profound statement! The United States of America can thank Benjamin Franklin for laying the cornerstone for uniting the colonies, which later became the United States.

Franklin went on to state, regarding the struggle with the French and Indians, "The confidence of the French in this undertaking seems well grounded in the present disunited state of the British colonies, and the extreme difficulty of bringing so many different governments and assemblies to agree to any speedy and effectual measure for our common defence and security; while our enemies have the great advantage of being under one direction, with one council, and one purse."

Franklin had a woodcut made depicting a snake separated into different parts, which represented the divided colonies. The caption for the woodcut read, "Join or Die." This motto was stamped on a copy of his speech to the representatives, to take back home with them.

This motto was adopted at the beginning of the Revolutionary War! It became a rallying cry to energize the defenders of the American Colonies.

In Nova Scotia at this time, the English were still pursuing Acadians to deport them. The English hunted the Acadians for seven years after the initial deportation began. Some of the Acadians had escaped into the wilderness and eluded capture. All the unfortunate Acadians caught were imprisoned and waited their turn to be transported to the colonies. Some of the Acadians were incarcerated in Halifax. When this number had increased enough, ships were called for and the Acadians shipped off to England to a concentration camp. Many of these never arrived. Storms took their toll on English as well as Acadians.

In New Brunswick, the English sought out any French settlers they could find. Those were forcibly removed and sent back to France, or taken to England. In their quest to oust the French farmers, the English systematically burned all the farms they came across. The English had not been successful in obtaining the rifles and ammunition from those colonists, so they had a struggle to capture the French.

Beausoliel and his group kept the English engaged during this struggle. Many British soldiers were ambushed and killed. A steep price was placed on all the resistance fighters.

Colonel Monckton, stationed at Fort Cumberland (Old Fort Beausejour), sent his rangers across the Bay of Fundy by ship, to New Brunswick to round up the French settlers. Major Anderson was in charge of this expedition.

On one of their advances through the interior, the rangers could hear the animals scurrying to safety. They heard the crows in the distance --- or were they crows! Suddenly, shots rang out and some of the redcoats dropped. The British took off after the partisans, firing as they went. The French took off in all directions, trying to reload as they ran.

Jacques's son, Charles, was chased to a stream, bullets flying all around him. As he tried to run through the water, it slowed him down enough for a redcoat to take aim and fire at him, hitting him in the leg. Unable to run any further, the English captured him and dragged him back to their ship.

Aboard the ship, badly bleeding, Charles was interrogated by Major Anderson. Weakened by the loss of blood, Charles cared not what happened to him, he knew he was done. Two British soldiers held him up. He refused to answer any of the Major's questions until the Major blared at him, "Who is your leader!"

"The Lord, God Almighty, is my leader!" replied Charles.

"You insolent pig," retorted Major Anderson, as he drew his sword and ran him through, killing him instantly.

Some of the English soldiers observing this related later how they had been moved by the courage of the Acadian, willing to die for a cause he believed in; defending his homeland. They would probably have done the same.

Major Anderson had Charles's body tossed overboard. They weighed anchor and left. Micmac Indians, who had witnessed the whole thing from ashore, recovered his body. They carried his body back to Beausoleil.

When the news reached Charles's wife, Marie, she was devastated. She was carrying their unborn child. A few months later, she gave birth to a son. She named him Charles, in honor of his father.

"Never forget what your father did for his country," said Marie to her children as they matured. His name would long be remembered, along with Joseph Broussard, better known as, Beausoleil; the leader of the resistance movement in New Brunswick.

The following year, 1757, Marie, her children, and her parents were rounded up, along with hundreds of French settlers in New Brunswick and deported to Massachusetts.

Life in the colonies for the French settlers was extremely unpleasant. They were forced to live in a country that did not want them, with people that hated them, and with an alien government. They were not allowed to practice their religion since Catholic priests were banned from the colonies. The Holy Sacraments were denied them.

In Massachusetts the state assembly wrote the following:

In council, March 6, 1756. Read & Concurred.

J Willard, Sec.

An act to prevent any mischief that may arise to this government by the late inhabitants of Nova Scotia traveling from town to town or being employed in the fishing or coasting vessels.

"Whereas many inconveniences and mischief may arise to this government by the liberty at present given to the late inhabitants of Nova Scotia and their being employed in the fishery or coasting vessels of this province.

"Wherefore be it enacted by the Governor, Council and House of Representatives that from and after the first day of may 1757, all the late inhabitants of Nova Scotia shall confine themselves within the bounds of the town where this government have placed them unless they shall have liberty further given them under the hand of one at least of the selectmen of the town who has the care of them, or under the hand of the Master unto whom such person or persons are or shall be bound and whenever such inhabitants as aforesaid shall be found out of the bounds of such towns, he, she or they shall be liable immediately to be taken up and carried before one of His Majesty's Justices of the Peace who on conviction of such offense shall commit such person or persons until they can be sent to the town where they were first ordered and the charge arising by such commitments and return shall be borne by the province and charged by the selectmen who had the care of such persons the other accounts relating to them and whenever such inhabitants shall offend the second time he or she or they shall forfeit and pay a fine not exceeding ten shillings or be publicly whipped not exceeding ten stripes.

"If the justice sees fit and so as often as he or she or they shall offend against this act and be convicted thereof and all tithing men constables and other officers of the Government are hereby required directed and empowered to arrest such persons and restrain them from traveling the country by carrying them before one of his Majesty's justices of the peace in the same county where such persons shall be found contrary to this act.

"And be it further enacted that no person within this province shall ship any of the late inhabitants of Nova Scotia on board any fishing or coasting vessels whatever and if any person shall be convicted thereof, he shall forfeit and pay the sum of ten pounds and half to go for the use of the Province and the other half to him or them that shall inform and sue for the same which sum shall be recovered in any of his Majesty's Courts proper to try the same."

In 1764, France and England signed a peace treaty. They had been at war for years. With the signing of this peace treaty, France ceded all of Canada to England in return for land elsewhere that the British held. This treaty meant that the French Neutrals now living in the colonies were free to go where they pleased.

After nine years of servitude in New York, Jacques opted to leave and relocate to Martinique, where the French government offered free land and assistance.

Charles's wife, Marie, and her children left Massachusetts and returned to New Brunswick. The only land they could obtain was in the North East portion of the province. Marie followed the coast until they came to an Indian village called Richibuctou where she was able to obtain some land. Her eldest son, Jean-Baptiste, at twelve years of age, became the principal breadwinner, fishing and hunting to feed the family.

Soon, other refugees joined them and in a few years, the village prospered. A Catholic church was built, and the first recorded names in its records are those of Jean-Baptiste Maillet, and his brother, Charles. Almost all the Maillets of New Brunswick can trace their lineage back to the two brothers, Jean-Baptiste and Charles.

Jacques and Magdelaine relocated to the beautiful Caribbean island of Martinique where they were joined by their sons, Louis-Cyrille, Joseph, and Etienne, and their daughter Marie-Elizabeth. They were free, at last.

With the assistance of their parish priest, they were able through years of communication to locate their grandchildren living in Richibuctou, New Brunswick, Canada.

Many of the refugees living in Martinique had left the island for the cooler region of Louisiana. The oppressive heat in the summer was unbearable for most of the Canadians. Besides the heat, Jacques could not bear to live in a country that condoned slavery. Unless you were a slave yourself, you could not appreciate what those poor people were going through.

At seventy-two years of age, Jacques still longed for his beloved Canada. In the cool of the evening, as they enjoyed the beauty of the sunset, he looked at his lovely wife and reminisced.

"I'd give anything to be in the wilderness again," said Jacques. "To hear the crows in the distance, to hunt, to cook my food over an open fire, to smell the fragrance of the wild flowers, to see the geese flying in formation, to just feel the exhilaration of being one with the universe."

Magdelaine, who understood how hard it was to confine a free spirit looked lovingly at her husband and said, "Why don't we go home?"

For the first time in twelve years, Jacques felt his heart beat in excitement. He could not believe what he was hearing…home!

They booked passage on the next ship sailing for New Brunswick arriving in the summer of 1768. They lived with their grandchildren in Richibuctou where Jacques was able to once more enjoy what he had loved in Nova Scotia.

Seventy-three year old Jacques (white haired, a little stooped, much slower, eyes failing and with aching legs) entered the nearby wilderness. He carried a little leather pouch of dried tobacco leaves. He took in the beauty of the big timbers, the smell of the boughs, the sights of small animals scurrying about, with tears in his eyes he removed a bit of tobacco and sprinkled it to the wind and said, "Migamawesu, It is I, Jacques. I have returned."

The leaves rustled a bit and he took that to mean that the spirit of the forest was welcoming him back. He smiled and looked about, remembering the beautiful moments he enjoyed with his Micmac friend, Paul. The chipmunks scurried about, deer peered from the thickets and birds flew overhead. He was indeed home.

"Migamawesu," said Jacques. "I have arrived in the direction of the North. Soon, I will be joining my grandfathers. I hear the white wolves in the distance."

He took great satisfaction in knowing that during his lifetime, the British soldier who fought against the French in Pittsburgh, none other than George Washington, was now being considered for the presidency of the new Republic, thanks to the assistance given the colonist by the very people they fought against --- the French.

Through Benjamin Franklin's diplomacy, France sent its naval fleet to assist the colonists in the fight for freedom. Bombarding Yorktown, the British stronghold, they were instrumental in forcing the British to surrender. George Washington, who was once a British officer, resigned his commission, joined the freedom fighters and led the nation to victory against British tyranny.

At the start of the Revolution, any of the colonists who did not side with the movement for freedom were forced to leave the colonies. In a strange twist of fate, the very same colonist from Massachusetts who earlier eagerly went to Nova Scotia to remove the Acadians, were themselves removed from their homes, and settled --- in Nova Scotia!

Had the British left the Acadians alone to live in peace in Nova Scotia, the world would certainly be a different place today. The British Empire would have encompassed most of the world, as we know it. They would have reigned supreme.

Because a few freedom-loving farmers refused to sign an oath of allegiance, the British Government took great pains to remove them. The cost of this endeavor cost the British huge sums of money. In order to recover some of this money, it was decided to tax the British subjects living in the colonies. This taxation was the catalyst that started the American Revolution.

Years later, after the American Revolution, George Washington, President of the United States of America, paid homage to the French for their assistance. This included Count de Rochambeau, who marched with Washington to Chesapeake Bay; Lafayette, who fought with the Americans between the James and York rivers; DeGrasse, whose fleet bombarded Yorktown culminating in the final victory for the Americans. And finally Major Pierre Charles L'Enfant, who was selected by Washington to plan and lay out the streets of the new nation's capitol, later to be known as Washington, District of Columbia.

In 1782, the United States of America became the home of the free and the brave. It was also the same year that Jacques life entered the direction of the North, the direction of his ancestors. He died at the ripe old age of eighty-seven.

In later years, France sent a token of its friendship to America --- the Statue of Liberty. The lady stands in majestic splendor overlooking the harbor of New York, the same harbor that saw the arrival of the Neutrals from Nova Scotia.

The expulsion of the Acadians was one of the most despicable acts ever perpetrated on a group of innocent people. The poet Longfellow made the world aware of this British atrocity when he wrote his poem titled, Evangeline.

The deportation of the Acadian people, commonly known as The Great Upheaval, began on September 5, 1755 and continued until 1763. This period tragically affected thousands of Acadians. The Government of Canada recognized the historic importance of The Great Upheaval through a Royal Proclamation and has designated July 28 as "A Day of Commemoration of the Great Upheaval".

The world should long remember the brave souls who fought for their beloved Canada, some of whom paid the ultimate sacrifice. One in particular was Charles Maillet, son of Jacques and Magdelaine, who was killed by British soldiers in 1756. Among the other heroes were: Joseph Broussard, known as Beausoleil; Jean LeBlanc, better known as Bonnand; Joseph Leblanc, better known as Maigre; and Jacques Hebert, claimed to be the bravest of all, and his faithful Micmac companion Nagontaga.

EPILOQUE

Return of the Exiles

They came back...the Acadians trickled back to their beloved Acadie, some by themselves, others in groups. The land beckoned them all back, as if some strong magnetic force drew them home again. All longed to be back where the soil had a deep calling to their souls. They longed to feel the freshness of the seasons, to inhale deeply of the invigorating Canadian air, to feel the rich soil once more, to plant their crops and live in harmony.

Acadie, now called Nova Scotia, was no longer theirs. The whole of Canada now belonged to the British Empire. It was still necessary to pledge an oath of allegiance to the English Crown to obtain land from the British. Weary after years of depravation in the colonies, the returning Acadians willingly acquiesced to the will of the Empire in order to obtain land.

As they returned in sailing vessels along the coast of New Brunswick, where land was plentiful, they made stops at places such as Shediac, Cocogne, Buctouche, Richibucto, Chatham, Caraquet, Bathurst, and Campelton, to name a few.

Records of the early settlers following the deportation can still be found in the many parishes along the coast.

Many of the Acadians deported to France opted to return following the signing of the peace treaty in 1763. Some settled in Chiticamp in Cape Breton, Nova Scotia, where even to this day the French language in prominent. Some went to Louisiana, some to Quebec, and many to New Brunswick.

As time went on, the descendants of the French Canadians, as they are called now, resettled all along the coast of North America, and eventually throughout the world. Wherever they have scattered, the Grandparents have always instilled in their grandchildren that they come from the hardy souls that first settled in Canada.

Following the signing of the peace treaty between France and England, the Neutrals, now in the colonies, were free to leave. Jacques's daughter-in-law, Marie (the wife of the slain Charles) along with her three children settled in Peticodiac, New Brunswick, Canada. She later married Germain Thibodeau in 1765. We later find church records in Richibuctou Village, New Brunswick, Canada, showing Jean-Baptiste and his brother, Charles living there. The Maillet clan eminiated from Richibuctou and spread throughout North America.

By 1770, England almost bankrupt from the war with France, tried to collect as much money as possible from its subjects living in the colonies. Of course, this led to the great revolution.

We now meet the famous Col. Jonathan Eddy.

When the American Revolutionary War began in Massachusetts in 1775 Col. Jonathan Eddy openly supported the rebellion. Following Governor Francis Legge's crackdown on seditious persons and seeing an opportunity, Jonathan Eddy fled to his riding in Cumberland. He made frequent excursions to see Samuel Adams and the General Court of Massachusetts as well as to General George Washington. Here he was met with varying degrees of support for his proposed rebellion. Adams pledged full support, troops, weapons, ammunition, and more, while Washington basically said not to expect any support at all.   He was eventually able to convince the Massachusetts legislature to provide logistical support in the form of small arms (muskets) and other military supplies.

In the summer of 1776, Mariot Arbuthnot, the new governor of Nova Scotia, ordered Colonel Joseph Goreham's Royal Fencible Americans to secure Fort Cumberland and keep watch for any signs of an American invasion of the province. Eddy, knowing he was being monitored by authorities loyal to the King, fled to Massachusetts where he was made a full colonel in the Continental Army and given authority to raise a regiment of his own with the sole purpose of invading Nova Scotia through Cumberland and Truro and then east into Halifax.

Attempt on Fort Cumberland

Main article: Battle of Fort Cumberland

Shortly after General William Howe's army departed Nova Scotia to attack New York in 1776, Eddy made his move. His force of 180 American militiamen, Natives, and Nova Scotians marched on Fort Cumberland. They attempted to storm the fort on November 13, 1776 and were repulsed. Two more attempts were made on the 22nd and 23rd of November, but on the 28th the HMS *Vulture* arrived at the head of the Bay of Fundy with British regulars aboard and relieved the fort. Eddy and his militia force were scattered, eventually regrouping near the Saint John River. Eddy and many of his supporters who had lived near the fort had their properties destroyed in retaliation.

Eddy spent the remainder of the war managing the defense of Machias in the District of Maine (then a part of Massachusetts), and was awarded a tract of land in the Ohio Country in 1801 for his role in the war. He moved to Stoughtonham after the war, where he served in the Massachusetts legislature. In 1784 he established a settlement on the eastern shore of Penobscot Bay that grew to become Eddington, Maine, where he died in 1804.

Jean-Baptiste, and his brother, Charles, grandsons of Jacques, joined forces with Col. Eddy and took part in the battle of Fort Cumberland.   There is a wonderful book titled "The Siege Of Fort Cumberland" by Ernest Clarke printed in 1939 by McGill-Queens University Press, Montreal & Kinsgston * London * Ithaca. All the patriots are listed in appendix one.

Prof. Stephen White from the University of Moncton in New Brunswick, Canada writes:The Companyof Frenchmen in the County of Cumberland, Province of Nova Scotia

Many people may qualify for membership in patriotic organizations such as the Daughters of the American Revolution or the Sons of the American Revolution without realizing that they so qualify. What is required is descent from one or more of the men who served in the various military units who contributed to the winning of American independence from Great Britain. The contribution of the particular unit must have been recognized, and the applicant for admission to the patriotic organization must be able to provide satisfactory proof of his or her descent from someone who served in such unit.

Many of the military groups who fought in the thirteen colonies themselves are quite famous, from the Minutemen of Lexington and Concord to Francis Marion's brigade in South Carolina. But there are others who served outside the present territory of the United States whose service nonetheless entitles their descendants to eligibility. One such group is the company of "Frenchmen" raised by Captain Isaïe Boudrot in 1776 in Cumberland County, Nova Scotia, for the brief campaign under the command of Lieutenant Colonel Jonathan Eddy.

The existence of this company was brought to the general attention of the genealogical community as long ago as 1955, when Atty. Laurie Ebacher caused a list of its members to be published in the Mémoires de la Société généalogique **canadienne-française (vol. VI, pp. 317-318). Mr. Ebacher mentioned that some descendants of the soldiers in the unit had by that time already been admitted to membership in the Daughters of the American Revolution (ibid., p 317).**

At the time of the bicentennial of American independence in 1976, Father Clarence d'Entremont described in some detail the activities of this company in his article "La participation acadienne à l'indépendance américaine," which was published in the Cahiers de la Société historique acadienne (vol. VII, No. 1, Mar. 1976, pp. 5-13). A plan for the conquest of Nova Scotia had been developed by one John Allan, a resident of Cumberland County (ibid., p. 7). Allan recruited the support of Jonathan Eddy, and early in the summer of 1776 Eddy went to Boston to submit Allan's plan to the Massachusetts General Court. The latter approved it and appointed Eddy a lieutenant colonel, authorizing him to secure eight schooners and sloops for transportation and to raise a force of 3000 men. Unfortunately, Eddy only managed to recruit about 200 volunteers, at Machias and Passamaquoddy in what is now Maine and at Maugerville in what is now New Brunswick. Twenty Indians also joined the force (ibid., p. 8). Eddy then shipped his soldiers from the Saint John River to Chipoudy, on the Cumberland Basin, where they seized a detachment of troops from Fort Cumberland. Encouraged by this success, they immediately launched an unsuccessful attack on the fort itself during the night of Nov. 14,

When I received notification from Prof. Stephen White that I was elegible for membership in the Sons Of The American Revolution, I immediately applied and was accepted. I am very grateful for the privilage of belonging to such an esteemed organization. At all our family reunions, I eagerly inform all my Maillet cousins that they are missing out on a great opportunity.

Never forget your heritage.

O Canada
Our home and native land
True patriot love in all they sons command.

Genealogy

Husband	DOB	DOD	Wife	DOB	DOD
Antoine Maillet	1670		Francoise Choppart	1680	
Jacques	1695		Magdelaine Hebert	1699	
Charles	1726	1756	Marie Baineau	1731	
Jean Baptiste	1753	1837	Marguerite Richard	1762	1856
Olivier	1795	1861	Marie Richard	1796	1864
Aime	1815	1904	Marguerite Maillet	1824	1904
Francois X	1863	1905	Caroline Leger	1874	1948
Andre	1904	1956	Rose Gallant	1904	1977
Joseph A.	1930		Theresa Inferrera	1934	
Joseph M.	1966		Darlene Minerva		
Joseph D.	2002				

The Story Of The Great Upheaval

Joseph A. Maillet

Author Bio

Joseph A. Maillet was born in Fitchburg, MA in 1930. He attended parochial grade and high schools in Fitchburg. He enlisted in the U. S. Navy when he was seventeen years old and served seven years. Following his tour of duty, he enrolled at DeVry Technical Institute in Chicago, Illinois, graduating in 1956.

Married to Theresa Inferrera and father of four children, he retired from Shore Memorial Hospital in Somers Point, New Jersey as a Biomedical Engineer. He was also certified as a Radiological Equipment Specialist. His hobbies were in photography and amateur radio operation. He held several patents in musical instruments, namely the piano and organ. He is a member of the Masonic Fraternity and of the Sons Of The American Revolution.

The story of the Great Uheaval is a true account of a brave young orpha from Paris, France. At the age of thirteen, he enlisted in the French Army fo duty in the wilderness outpost of Nova Scotia. He, along with 100 other young o phans, was stationed at Port Royal, now called Annapolis Royal. Soon after the arrival, the fort was attacked by English and Colonial soldiers and fell into the hands. He escaped being deported back to France and lived with the Hebert Famil

He befriended a local Micmac Indian boy about his own age and to gether they learned the secrets of the wilderness and survival. With hi skills in the wilderness he was able to amass a small fortune collecting pelt

He won the heart of beautiful Magdelaine and thought his world could no get any better, but friction between the two super powers of the world at that tim caught himin the middle. What followed was the darkest period in Canadian histor

He was forced to leave his beloved Acadie with his family, along with a the Acadian Roman Catholics, to a life of servitude in the American Colonie After nine years of depravation in the colony of New York he was fre to leave. He opted to relocate to the beautiful island of Martinique

His heart ached for his homeland. He prayed to the Great Spirit of th wilderness, Migamawesu, who directed him back to his beloved Canada

This book also describes the forced relocation (The Great Up heaval) of all the Catholic French Canadians to all parts of the worl

www.ingramcontent.com/pod-product-compliance
Lightning Source LLC
LaVergne TN
LVHW011226080426
835509LV00005B/337